ELIZABETHAN AND JACOBEAN
JOURNALS 1591–1610

ELIZABETHAN AND JACOBEAN JOURNALS 1591–1610

G. B. Harrison

VOLUME I
An Elizabethan Journal
being a record of those things most talked of during the years 1591–1594

VOLUME II
A Second Elizabethan Journal
being a record of those things most talked of during the years 1595–1598

VOLUME III
A Last Elizabethan Journal
being a record of those things most talked of during the years 1599–1603

VOLUME IV
A Jacobean Journal
being a record of those things most talked of during the years 1603–1606

VOLUME V
A Second Jacobean Journal
being a record of those things most talked of during the years 1607–1610

ELIZABETHAN AND JACOBEAN JOURNALS 1591–1610

Volume V

A Second Jacobean Journal

G. B. Harrison

London and New York

First published 1958 by Constable & Co. Ltd

Reprinted by Routledge 1999, 2002
2 Park Square, Milton Park,
Abingdon, Oxon, OX14 4RN

Simultaneously published in the USA and Canada
by Routledge
270 Madison Ave, New York NY 10016

First issued in paperback 2010

Routledge is an imprint of the Taylor & Francis Group

© 1958 G. B. Harrison

British Library Cataloguing in Publication Data
A CIP record of this set is available from the British Library

Library of Congress Cataloging in Publication Data
A catalogue record for this book has been requested

ISBN 978-0-415-22148-1 (hbk) (Volume 5)
ISBN 978-0-415-60599-1 (pbk) (Volume 5)
5 Volumes: ISBN 978-0-415-22143-6 (Set)

A SECOND JACOBEAN JOURNAL

A SECOND
JACOBEAN
JOURNAL

Being a Record
of Those Things Most Talked of
during the Years 1607 to 1610

by

G. B. HARRISON

Routledge
Taylor & Francis Group

LONDON AND NEW YORK

First published 1958
by Routledge
2 Park Square, Milton Park,
Abingdon, Oxon, OX14 4RN

CONTENTS

INTRODUCTION

The Second Jacobean Journal is the fifth volume in a series begun in 1928 with the publication of *An Elizabethan Journal* [1] for the years 1591-4. Method and intention are the same: to see life as the contemporaries of Shakespeare, Donne and Ben Jonson saw it, and to record it, day by day, in their own words, or—to use the more grandiloquent and modern phrase—to recreate the Shakespearean World Picture, not intellectually, impressionistically or symbolically, but as it was. In this volume the setting and format have been somewhat changed to meet the high costs of printing.

As eighteen years have gone by since the first *Jacobean Journal* appeared, it will be relevant to recall the origin of the work in the realization that Elizabethan and Jacobean literature cannot be fully understood without some knowledge of those matters and persons which were exciting to the original reader or playgoer; even Shakespeare's plays were written to give immediate pleasure to his contemporaries—a fact usually overlooked by modern critics. This knowledge is not to be found in the works of professional historians, for their values differ from those of the common man, who is less interested in movements and cycles, economic and climatic fluctuations, Kings, Presidents, Dictators and Prime Ministers, senates, parliaments and conferences at a high level, treaties and enactments, than in scandal, crime, plays and the weather.

The common man's frivolous sense of values may be regrettable, but it is for him that dramatists and novelists write and not for academic persons and professional critics, of whose ancestors Thomas Heywood complained feelingly in *Troia Britannica* (see p. 116)—'The favourable and gracious Reader, I salute with a submiss congé, both of heart and knee. To the scornful I owe not so much hypocritical intreat or dissembled courtesy. I am not so inexperienced in the envy of this Age but that I know I shall encounter most sharp and severe censurers, such as continually carp at other men's labours, and superficially perusing them with a kind of negligence and scorn, quote them by the way thus: "This is an error. That was too much stretched. This is too slightly neglected. Here many things might have been added. There it might have been better followed. This is

[1] The three *Elizabethan Journals* were reprinted in one volume in 1955 (London and Ann Arbor).

superfluous; that ridiculous." These indeed knowing no other means to have themselves opinioned in the rank of understanders but by calumniating other men's industries.'

Those matters which most interested the common man are not wholly lost, but they are widely scattered and not easily accessible. The aim of the *Elizabethan* and *Jacobean Journals* is to bring together a record of those things most talked of during the working years of Shakespeare's life.

It has become a custom with some writers—in Sir John Neale's memorable phrase—to remove 'the elaborate scaffolding of documentary authority used in the construction of the book' lest the delicate reader be disturbed by a display of erudition. I have, however, suffered so much inconvenience from those who thus cover their tracks (and deficiencies), that I have risked the irritation of the reader and the condemnation of the historian by recording in the Notes the source of every entry in the *Journal*. With few exceptions these sources are contemporary, many of them coming from letters or pamphlets. The date of the entry is, as near as may be, that on which the event is likely to have been known in London by one with good access to general information. When it was not possible to give an exact or close date, I have given that which seemed reasonably likely.

As for the style: I have used my sources freely, borrowing sometimes whole pages, sometimes phrases, at other times condensing or using my own words as seemed best. If it is not easy to separate the Jacobean from the modern, that was my intention; for the *Journal* endeavours to convey mood as well as fact; it is (I hope) as much a work of art as of scholarship.

The Second Jacobean Journal covers the years 1607 to 1610. Although no single event in these years was quite so dramatic as the Gunpowder Plot of 1605, or Essex's tragedy in 1601, yet there were abundant troubles to entertain the cynical observer. King James had now been wedded to his kingdom of England for four years, and the honeymoon was over. Friction between King and Commons was growing apace as each party became more irritatingly aware of the other's shortcomings. King James continues to be the most important item of news. His naïve and genuine belief that as God's vicegerent on earth he was not as other men; his vanity in controversy; his slavering fondness for his favourites; his cruelty to those whom he feared or disliked—Arbella Stuart, Northumberland or Ralegh; his inability to say no, especially to a handsome Scot; his crude sense of humour; his neglect of state business while he retired to Newmarket or Royston to chase the deer in all weathers; these traits were notorious to the onlooker. In a Journal of 'those things most talked of' it is less easy to illustrate the King's intelligent grasp of affairs or the shrewd judgements delivered in private conference. But he was a sore trial to his servants, and not least because of his everlasting restlessness. In each of the four years covered in this book, the King changed his nightly lodging more than *forty* times.

Many other matters occupied the gossips: extravagant Court entertainments; the love affairs of the unfortunate Arbella; the Great Frost; the Shirley brothers; controversies between the King and his theologians and Cardinal Bellarmine; religious persecutions as cruel and bitter as ever; the maturing of the young Prince Henry; the impudence of the pirates; the many fatal duels; the first settlement of Ulster; the rise of the favourite Robert Carr; the search for the Northwest Passage; the building of great ships; troubles in Parliament; the murder of Henri Quatre; the capture of Juliers which at the time seemed so unimportant. In retrospect these four years were certainly a seed time of enormous troubles.

Few important books were published, but in drama these were great months, during which first appeared on the stage or in print *Antony and Cleopatra*, *Coriolanus*, *The Tragedy of King Lear*, *Volpone*, *Troylus and Cressida*, *Bussy D'Ambois*, *The Woman Killed with Kindness*, *The Faithful Shepherdess*, *Philaster*, *Epicoene* and *The Alchemist*.

Considerable space has been given to events in Virginia, for indeed the misfortunes of the first colonists aroused great interest, and not only among those who had invested their money in the hope of a quick return. An impartial reader who goes back to *The Tempest* straight from a reading of the events of 1609 and 1610 will surely be surprised to find how topically significant the play must have been to its first spectators, phrase after phrase echoing their own sentiments.

It has long been noted that the shipwreck in the first scene was founded on the wreck of Sir Thomas Gates and his company in the Bermudas (pp. 217–20), and Rudyard Kipling persuasively claimed that the immediate source of the play was the conversation of a drunken sailor from the *Sea Adventure*.[1] There are many other echoes scattered throughout. The dislike of the passengers for the sailors from whom they suffered so much was well founded. The ideals of plantation, as expounded by Gonzalo, were everywhere being discussed, but the general opinion of the Jamestown colonists

[1] In a letter to *The Spectator* of 2nd July 1898.

ix

was that they were—in Antonio's words—'all idle: whores and knaves'. Antonio and Sebastian plotting to murder their leader, or Stephano supplying his 'salvage' with liquor and planning with him to murder Prospero—these but mirrored in poetic surroundings the treachery and venality of those who plotted against Gates or Smith, or intrigued with Powhatan. Caliban's complaint—

> This Island's mine by Sycorax my mother,
> Which thou tak'st from me—

had been more prosaically countered in sermons and pamphlets (see pp. 181, 231), which justified the appropriation on the ground that the settlers were bringing civilization and religion to the benighted or, as Prospero expressed it—

> I pitied thee,
> Took pains to make thee speak, taught thee each hour
> One thing or other.

The Tempest is in some ways Shakespeare's most philosophic and contemplative play; but it was woven of contemporary material.

Of the many friends and colleagues who have given me much help, I would especially mention the late R. L. Atkinson, formerly Secretary to the Historical Manuscripts Commission (a friend since 1914), Miss Mary Flower, Mr. H. Pearson Gundy, Librarian of Queen's University Canada, and his assistants, Professor Warner G. Rice, and last, but perhaps most gratefully, Miss Lidie McKinney, who assisted me in the later stage of these researches and—a thirteenth labour—typed my manuscript.

G. B. HARRISON

University of Michigan,
Ann Arbor, Michigan
27th December 1957

1607

1st January. His Majesty King James is now in the 43rd year of his age, and the 4th of his reign in England. He is by nature placid, averse from cruelty, and a lover of justice. He goeth to Chapel on Sundays, and on Tuesdays, on which day he escaped from the conspiracy of Gowry in 1600. He loves quiet and repose, and hath no inclination to war whereat his subjects are little pleased, and less that he leaveth all government to the Council while he followeth nothing but the chase. He showeth no liking for the people, nor maketh them that good cheer whereby our late Queen won their loves, for our English worship their Sovereigns in so much that if the King were to pass through the same street a hundred times a day, they would still run out to see him. But the King shows no taste for them but rather contempt and dislike, for which he is despised and almost hated; for of a truth he is more disposed to live retired with eight or ten of his favourites than openly.

The Queen, by birth a Dane and sister of the Danish King (whom he married in 1589), is in her 35th year, very gracious and moderately good looking. She is a Lutheran. The King tried to make her of his own religion, and others a Catholic, to which she is much inclined, and so rumoured to be one. She is very fond of pleasure and dancing and masques, but withal intelligent and prudent, knowing the disorders of government but taking no part therein, for she is averse to trouble, and knows well that those who govern desire most to be left alone. She therefore professeth indifference, except to beg favours for her friends, for whom she is full of tenderness, but terrible and proud to her enemies.

Of their four children two are boys and two girls, Prince Henry the eldest being 12 years old. Next unto these is the Lady Arbella, descended from Margaret, daughter of King Henry VII. She was born *anno* 1575, of no great beauty but highly accomplished, for besides most courtly manners she speaketh well Latin, Italian, French, and Spanish, readeth Greek and Hebrew and is for ever studying. She is not passing rich, for Queen Elizabeth (who was ever jealous and especially of all that were near to her throne) took away most of her income. The King declareth his love for her, and she frequents the Court. The King promised he would restore her inheritance, but she has it not as yet, nor will have till her marriage,

1

but so far no husband has been found for her, so she remaineth single and without estate.

The King is so devoted to the chase that he leaves all to his Councillors, who follow him unless he goes privately, and then they stay at the Court in London. The power of the Council was never greater than now, by reason of the King's carelessness of rule. The Council dealeth with all things, not only affairs of State, but money also and justice, so that whoso would attain anything he must be protected by one of the Lords of the Council, and that by means of presents and gifts. These gifts they take not only from the subject but as well from strangers and Ambassadors of Princes, which breeds a great hatred of these Lords.

Of the Lords of the Council, the greatest is Sir Robert Cecil, Earl of Salisbury, Secretary of State, whose authority is so absolute that he may be called King indeed. He is a man of some 44 years, little and crookbacked, but with a noble countenance, an admirable speaker, and well skilled in the French tongue. In all matters of State, he is of greatest weight, a bitter foe to his enemies, but a friend to his friends, though more prone to revenge than to affection. He is haughty and terrible, using violent language to people of all sorts, and an extreme enemy to the Catholics. He is closely allied to the House of Howard, of whom there are three or four in the Council by whose aid he sways the rest. He in truth is the Prince of this kingdom.

The young Prince Henry is much noted for noble wit, his every action marked by a gravity beyond his years; but he has little delight in study for which his father often rebukes him. Of late the King, after admonishing him thereon, said that if he did not attend more diligently to his books the crown would be left to his brother the Duke of York, who is far quicker in learning and a more eager student. The Prince made no answer out of respect to his Majesty, but when he went to his own chamber and his tutor began to rebuke him in like terms he replied, 'I know what becomes a Prince. There is no need for me to be a scholar, but a soldier and a man of the world. If my brother is as learned as they say, we will make him Archbishop of Canterbury.' The King took this answer in ill part, nor is he pleased to see his son so much beloved and of such promise that the subjects set all their hopes in him.

3rd. M. Simon Harward hath written a *Discourse* of the several kinds and causes of lightnings, on the occasion of the fearful lightning at Bletchingley in Surrey in November last, whereby the spire of the church was consumed with fire in three hours' space, and the bells

2

also melted into fragments. This grievous loss was by some inter-preted as a particular judgement of God against the sins of the towns-men, but M. Harward would not have it so, because the iniquities of the towns near adjoining are nothing inferior; and besides, the people of the town were miraculously preserved from the fire which con-sumed the steeple. Concludeth the cause of this lightning to be the good pleasure of God, and citeth many instances of destruction by the same cause. Noteth that philosophers and astronomers declare the natural causes of thunders and lightnings to be: first, a viscous vapour with a hot exhalation is lifted up to the highest part of the middle region of the air by virtue of the planets. Then the watery vapour by the coldness both of the place and matter is thickened into a cloud, and the exhalation (which is drawn up with it) is shut within the cloud and driven into straits. This hot exhalation courseth up and down in the cloud seeking some passage out, which when it can-not find, maketh a way out by force. If the sides of the cloud be thick and the exhalation dry and copious, there is both thunder and lightning; but if the cloud be thin and the exhalation also thin and rare, then lightning without thunder.

6th. Today being Twelfth Night, the L. James Hay was married to the Lady Anne, daughter of my L. Denny at the Court at Whitehall, the sermon being preached by M. Robert Wilkinson on the text, 'She is like the merchant's ships; she bringeth her food from afar.' At night in the Great Hall there was a masque written by Campion, with stages set up before the screen for the musicians and the dancers. The scene was the bower of Flora on the one side and on the other the house of Night, the principal speakers being Flora, Zephyrus, Night and Hesperus, and the maskers 9 in number, young gentlemen of the Court.

7th. There is come forth a book concerning the late excommunica-tion of the Venetians, containing a discourse against Cardinal Caesar Baronius by Nicholas Vignier; a copy of the Bull of Pope Paulus V; also an Apology of Friar Paul Sarpi of the Order of the Servites, protesting the condemnation of his books and declaring that he cannot obey the citation to appear in Rome by reason of the late edict in Venice forbidding ecclesiastical persons to depart out of the kingdom.

8th. A new breve is recently come from the Pope to our English Catholics, which greatly moves the King, in so much that he sent a copy of it by a gentleman to the Venetian Ambassador. The King finds much in the breve that impeaches his authority and that perfect

3

liberty which every Prince is bound to sustain, and besides sundry doctrines which feed the spirit of rebellion. He is especially offended at the prohibition to take the Oath of Allegiance, as if the Pope holdeth him not for a legitimate Sovereign and claimeth superiority even in matters temporal, and moreover seems to approve the late Powder Plot.

10th. In his breve Pope Paulus V admonisheth all English Catholics that by no means they come into the churches of the heretics, nor hear their sermons, nor communicate with them in their rites lest they incur the wrath of God, for these things they cannot do without endamaging the worship of God and their own salvation; nor can they, without most evident and grievous wronging of God's Honour, bind themselves by the Oath seeing it contains many things contrary to Faith and Salvation. Exhorteth them therefore to hold fast to the Faith and to have mutual charity.

Nevertheless Blackwell the Archpriest, alleging that the breve is lacking in particularity concerning the Oath, has neither made it generally known nor refrained from commending the Oath.

The words of the Oath of Allegiance, set forth by the last Parliament, are these:

'I A.B. do truly and sincerely acknowledge, profess, testify and declare in my conscience before God and the World, that our Sovereign Lord King JAMES, is lawful King of this Realm, and of all other his Majesty's Dominions and Countries. And that the Pope neither of himself, nor by any authority of the Church or See of Rome, or by any means with any other, hath any power or authority to depose the King, or to dispose of any of his Majesty's Kingdoms or Dominions, or to authorize any Foreign Prince to invade or annoy him or his Countries, or to discharge any of his subjects of their allegiance and obedience to his Majesty, or to give licence or leave to any of them to bear arms, raise tumults, or to offer any violence or hurt to his Majesty's Royal Person, State or Government, or to any of his Majesty's subjects within his Majesty's Dominions. Also I do swear from my heart that notwithstanding any declaration or sentence of excommunication or deprivation made or granted, or to be made or granted, by the Pope or his successors, or by any Authority derived or pretended to be derived from him or his See, against the said King, his heirs or successors, or any absolution of his said subjects from their obedience; I will bear faith and true allegiance to his Majesty, his heirs and successors, and him and them will defend to the uttermost of my power, against all conspiracies and attempts whatsoever, which shall be made against his

4

or their Persons, their Crown and dignity, by reason or colour of any such sentence, or declaration, or otherwise, and will do my best endeavours to disclose and make known unto his Majesty, his heirs and successors, all treason and traitorous conspiracies, which I shall know or hear of to be against him or any of them. And I do further swear, that I do from my heart abhor, detest and abjure as impious and heretical, this damnable doctrine and position, that Princes which be excommunicated or deprived by the Pope, may be deposed or murthered by their subjects, or any other whatsoever. And I do believe, and in conscience am resolved, that neither the Pope nor any person whatsoever hath power to absolve me of this Oath, or any part thereof; which I acknowledge by good and full authority to be lawfully ministered unto me, and do renounce all pardons and dispensations to the contrary. And all these things I do plainly and sincerely acknowledge and swear according to these express words by me spoken, and according to the plain and common sense of the same words, without any equivocation, or mental evasion, or secret reservation whatsoever. And I do make this recognition and acknowledgment heartily, willingly, and truly, upon the true faith of a Christian. So help me GOD.'

12th. Sir Thomas Shirley, the youngest of those three famous brothers, since his return to England in October last year hath written an account of the Turks, and of all places and kingdoms which he saw on his journeyings from Constantinople. Noteth that there are two sorts of Turks, the natural Turks and the renegadoes. Their manner of living in private and in general is most uncivil and vicious, for in their vices they are all pagans and infidels, sodomites, liars and drunkards, and for their sodomy they use it so publicly and impudently as an honest Christian would shame to accompany his wife as they do with their buggering boys. Their pride cannot be described with tongue nor pen, for they scorn all men and that in the most base, vile and contemptible manner as appeareth by the entertainment they give to all Christian Ambassadors sent by any Christian Prince, for he may not be admitted to the Great Turk's presence without kissing the hem of his vesture, and to this he must add the giving of a present in the name of the King his master who sent him, which the Turk esteemeth a tribute and homage of superiority. Moreover all negotiations with him must be by petitions written, which are to be delivered to him as he rideth by the way as though a beggar were to beg an alms from him. The French and the Venetians do much scorn of this usage but are forced to bear it for reason of state.

Their King is young, a rash, drunken, bloody, headstrong boy, who did so violently and cruelly punish all such bashaws as dared advise him to any course misliked or seek to dissuade him from any absurd opinion of his own that all now fear to speak to him. He hath put four or five of his wisest bashaws to death only for counselling him to things fit for him and misliked by him, and he spared not his own mother but poisoned her.

The Turks hold traffic at home only with the English, French, Venetians and Poles. The wares that the English send are tin, lead, gunpowder, muskets, swords, copper, kersies, broadcloth, cony skins, brimstone, cordages, cables, steel and caviare. Some of these are laudable and good wares; but others abominable, and bring much slander to our nation and religion, which is, powder and other munitions for war and shipping, brought by the English in great abundance thither, and by no other nation. The English keep three open shops of arms and munitions in Constantinople, and the gain is very great, for gunpowder, which costs in England £3 the hundred, there is sold for 23 and 24 chickinoes (the chickinoe, or sequin, being worth 7s. 6d.); and so of tin. Muskets are sold for 5 or 6 chickinoes the piece, of which the best in England cost 18s. And so with copper and swords.

Noteth that the ruins of old Troy are yet to be seen; they are 30 miles in length between Gallipoli and the Castle at the mouth of the Straits. The walls are in some places a yard high, and many foundations of towers yet extant, and a great part of Helen's palace standeth.

15th. The three ships for Virginia under command of Capt. Christopher Newport which sailed from London on 20th December have been delayed in the Downs by contrary winds, but now are departed.

18th. Letters are being sent to the Deputy Lieutenants of the counties to encourage the planting of mulberry trees so that the making of silk may be established in the Realm. To that end at the next quarter sessions they shall persuade persons of ability to plant 10,000 mulberry trees, which the King will provide at the cost of ¾d. the plant, or 6s. the hundred; and further to each town there shall be made a supply of mulberry seed. A book of *Instructions for the increasing of mulberry trees* (with woodcuts), and the care and breeding of silkworms and for the making of silk in this country hath been written by William Stallenge.

21st. Thomas Morris, one of the yeomen of the King's Guard,

6

was slain in Chancery Lane by Humphrey Lloyd his kinsman. These two had quarrelled in the Half Moon Tavern about religion; whereupon Morris cast a cup of wine at Lloyd's face, and Lloyd threw a roll of bread at the head of Morris, but by their friends they were pacified. Today while Lloyd was standing at Lincoln's Inn gate with a friend, Morris with a friend of his passed by. Hereupon the quarrel broke out afresh, and both drew out their weapons. Lloyd gave Morris his death's wound and struck him also when he was down. He is now charged with murder. In former times he was touched with Watson's treason and also with the Gunpowder plot.

23rd. From the West comes news of a terrible flood three days ago caused by a mighty west wind which continued full 16 hours and with extreme violence brought in the sea, by reason whereof and of the spring tides furiously encountering the land waters swollen by a great rain, the River Severn, beginning as far as S. Michael's Mount in Cornwall, overflowed its banks and bounds all along both sides up into Somersetshire and Gloucestershire in some places 5 and in some almost 8 feet, and ran into the land almost 20 miles in length and 4 miles in breadth. In all places it came so fiercely that it was hard for man or beast to escape, for the waters came upon them with terrible noise and great mountains. Some who stayed to have their horses saddled or to set their houses in order or who would needs return home upon hope to save their wives, children, friends, jewels or evidences of their lands were overwhelmed. In some towns and villages the waters grew higher than the tops of houses, trees or churches. In many places some saved themselves by climbing to the tops of houses or by sitting on the new rivers of houses floating upon the water. Many cattle perished.

Some also with show of pity made out in boats pretending to relieve the distressed, but performed no such charity for they went only a boot-halling and made a prey of all they could lay hands upon. Among other things of note, upon some hills divers beasts of contrary nature had got up for their safety as dogs, cats, foxes, hares, conies, moles, mice and rats who remained together very peaceably without any sign of fear or violence towards one another. In the parts of Somersetshire there are drowned four score persons and damages done to the value almost of £20,000.

There are many stories of strange escapes of death, as of a maid that went to milk, and was forced by the vehemence of the waters with much ado to take refuge on a high hill whence she was saved by two lusty men who tied together two wooden troughs, such as they use to salt bacon in, and so using them for boats made great shifts to come at her. In another place a boy child of 5 or 6 years old was kept swimming by the space of two hours by reason that his long coats lay spread upon the top of the waters. Being at last on point to sink there came floating by a fat wether that was dead, very full of wool. The poor child caught hold on the wether's wool and with the wind he was driven to dry land and so saved.

28th. Now that the state of rebellion in Ireland hath given way to universal peace and obedience, the King sendeth certain general instructions to Sir Arthur Chichester the L. Deputy. Since there is no more effectual way to secure peace than an upright administration of justice, let the Deputy encourage the people by making them often taste thereof. For the planting of religion, worthy ministers are needed for whom competent livings must be provided. Let him inquire into the repair of ecclesiastical livings so that from England may be sent persons of learning and judgement to draw the people more towards religion. Of late many poor and vagrant persons from Ireland have transported themselves into France and other foreign parts, pretending to be banished for religion, whereby a scandal is raised against the King's government; such have so multiplied in France that the government there ordered them to be shipped into England, but henceforward they shall be landed in Munster whence they came. Strict course to be taken with merchants and ships of passage that no more of that kind be transported either into England or any other Prince's dominions, and to avoid the scandal.

30th. Of late the King of France jesting with a fool, the fool said he would be neither the Pope, King, nor pork. 'And wherefore?' said the King. 'Because,' quoth he, 'the Popes are no sooner chosen but they are despatched, for there have been three or four within less than three or four months. And as for Kings, they stand upon a ticklish state, for their own subjects go about to kill them; as for example,' quoth he, 'you and the King of England. And for a pork, he is no sooner fat but his throat is cut.'

2nd February. Sir Robert Dudley's licence to travel into foreign parts is revoked, for he is reported to have behaved himself inordinately, attempting many things prejudicial to the King and the Crown which cannot be endured.

6th. The King is said to have undertaken the debts of the L. Hay, the Viscount Haddington and the Earl of Montgomery to the value of £44,000, saying that he will once set them free and then let them shift for themselves. His own debts are stalled to be paid one half in May come two years, the residue in May following. Yesterday there was a great cause handled in the Court of Wards between the L. Treasurer and Sir John Leveson; at this first hearing the L. Coke was strong for Sir John.

13th. The Parliament reassembled on the 10th. Today certain remembrances of the late conference of the Committees of both Houses concerning the Union were brought in to be read, showing that it was there agreed that first to be repealed were hostile laws, such as that concerning passage into Scotland, and all Border laws, customs and treaties. As for commerce, so long as the Scottishmen continue their privileges in France, they shall undergo the customs of strangers in England, and no longer. Merchandises that are prohibited to be brought into England from foreign ports shall not be brought out of Scotland. Any Scottishman who shall sell to any Frenchman or stranger commodities of England, he shall pay double customs. The Scottish not to be debarred from the Merchants' Societies. A mutual exchange of all commodities to be allowed.

The Speaker offered to read the remembrances to the House but was interrupted by dispute whether they shall be read one by one and so debated, or all at once without distinction or pause. In this differences of opinion, Sir Christopher Piggott with a loud voice (but not standing up bare-headed as is the order) pressed to have them read generally at once. The House observing his earnestness and manner of sitting, for order's sake urged him to stand up and speak. So he rose, and pretending at first to deliver his reasons for the reading of the remembrances generally, he entered into invective against the Scots and Scottish nation, using many words of scandal and obliquy. He was astonished, said he, that any ear could be lent for joining a good and fertile country to one poor and barren, and in a manner disgraced by nature; and for associating frank and honest men with such as were beggars, proud and generally traitors and rebels to their King. There was as much difference between an English and a Scots man as between a judge and a thief. His speech was so sudden and unexpected that though there appeared in every man's countenance a distaste of what passed from him with such distemper, yet in the general amazement his speech was neglected, without tax or censure.

Thereafter it was moved that the remembrances of the conference were not agreed upon as set down and should be reserved only for private instruction and not entered as authentic by the House. It was then remembered that M. Attorney had the charge of a particular

9

report of the conference, wherein he laboured to excuse himself by a great cold that he had taken; but the House not being satisfied with his excuse, he entered into it particularly, agreeing in most part with the articles already set out. In the end M. Speaker moving for directions from the House, divers proposals were made but nothing agreed.

14th. The Scots in London are thrown into the utmost rage by Piggott's speech yesterday, but none dared to speak of it to the King until this morning Sir John Ramsay of his Bedchamber complained in the name of his countrymen. Hereupon the King sent for my L. of Salisbury and blamed him for not having spoken of this last night and because he and the rest of the Councillors had shown so much coolness and indifference as to wait till his return to punish the offender. The Council also was summoned, to whom the King spoke very harshly, declaring that he was a Scot himself and that nothing could be applied to the nation in general in which he had not his share; and that one of the express commands which he would give the Prince (who was then present) should be to do the same, and from that hour he would give him his curse if he should fail in this point.

In the Lower House the articles of the Instrument concerning Naturalization were debated. Hereupon 'M. Nicholas Fuller made a long speech against it, alleging many reasons, as that God had made people apt for every country, and the several countries He hath fitted for their several natures and qualities. One man is owner of two pastures, with one hedge to divide them, the one base, the other fertile and good: a wise man will not pull down the hedge but make gates. Before we admit the Scottishmen, consider what place and room we have for them. Look in the Universities; there many of our own, very worthy, are not provided for. Amongst our merchants there hath been no success, no fruit these 3 years, labour and travail all they can; our traders are already too many; impositions are laid upon our English while the Scots are discharged. Our merchants venture to sea with great vessels furnished at great charge; they, with little bottoms and little charge, carry their wares up and down in packs, and by this means have taken away all the trade of Dieppe already. That Kingdom is miserable where the rich men are exceeding rich, the poor men exceeding poor. If King Philip had had a son by Queen Mary, he would have been King of Spain, Sicilia, etc.: would it have been fit to naturalize all those subjects? It is not good to mingle two swarms of bees under one hive upon a sudden.

10

16th. The Lower House entered upon the case of Piggott's speech which the King so much mislikes and taxes the neglect of the House that the speech was not interrupted in the instant and the party committed before it became public. This matter having been long debated, the Sergeant was summoned to bring in Sir Christopher with his mace. He was thereupon called to the bar to be heard, where he laboured to explain his words and to clear himself of malice and disloyalty. So he was commanded to retire to the door, and after much dispute, was called back again, and kneeling at the bar judgement was pronounced upon him by the Speaker: that since his offence was so apparently heinous, the House did not hold it fit that any particulars should be given for their judgement, which is that he shall be carried to the prison of the Tower and there remain during the pleasure of the House, and that he be dismissed from his place of knight of the shire for Buckinghamshire, and a new writ issued for a new election.

17th. The Venetian Ambassador being lately in the antechamber waiting to be introduced into the Presence, the King sent out to him the little Duke of York with an arquebus on his shoulder, who goes right up to the Ambassador declaring that he is thus armed for the service of the Republic. To whom the Ambassador replied that the Republic would be very proud of so big and brave a Captain, and that under his leadership was sure to win a great victory.

Today in the Lower House Sir Fr. Bacon answered those who are opposed to the naturalization. Of the inconveniences alleged, the first being that of naturalization there may ensue a surcharge of people upon this Realm of England, he declared that for numbers of the Scottish nation to plant themselves amongst us is a thing rather in conceit than in event; for though the similitudes of a tree that will thrive better if removed into a more fruitful soil, or of cattle that will break through a hedge into more fruitful pasture, be plausible, yet there longeth more to a family that shall remove from one nation to another. The first coming of the King was the greatest spring for the entrance of that nation; but now in these four years' space, how many families of Scottish men are planted in the cities and towns of England? Apart from persons of quality about the King's person at the Court and in London, and some inferior persons that have dependency upon them, the number is extremely small. Nor is this Realm peopled too full, for there are manifest badges and tokens rather of scarceness than of press of people, as drowned lands, commons, wastes and the like, which is a plain demonstration that howsoever there may be an overswelling of people about

11

London, yet the body of the Kingdom is thin sown with people; the Realm was better peopled in former times, and in proof thereof let the House remember hỏw many of them serve for desolate and decayed boroughs.

Then he spoke of the difference of the fundamental laws of the two Kingdoms, and of those who would begin by first demanding that the Scots should be subject to our laws. He would have naturalization first, and in nature separable from union of laws; for naturalization doth but take out the marks of a foreigner, but union of laws makes them entirely ourselves. Besides, we do not deny those of the Kingdom of Ireland the benefit of naturalization, nor those of Jersey, Guernsey and the Isle of Man, where our common law is not in force. As for the inequality of the fortunes of the two nations, that by the commixture thereof may ensue advantage to them and loss to us, this difference consisteth but in the external goods of fortune. For to do them right, we know that they are 'a people ingenious, in labour industrious, in courage valiant, in body hardy and comely.

He treated also of the inconveniences that would occur if they proceed not with the naturalization, alleging sundry records of Kingdoms united only in sovereignty, whereby followed rebellions and insurrections. So likewise hereafter these two Realms will be in continual danger to divide and break again, whereas the Kingdom of England, having Scotland united, Ireland reduced, the sea provinces of the Low Countries contracted, and shipping maintained, is one of the greatest monarchies, in forces truly esteemed, that hath been in the world.

20th. This morning Robert Drury, a Benedictine friar, was indicted at the Old Bailey before the Lord Mayor, the Recorder (Sir Henry Montague) and other justices, that in contempt of the statutes he had departed out of this land and at Valladolid in Spain had been made a priest by the Bishop of Leon by authority derived from the Pope. Sithence he had returned to this land to reconcile and to withdraw away his Majesty's subjects from their natural allegiance to a foreign service and obedience. In his defence he began to justify his priesthood, when it was answered that priesthood solely was not imputed him for treason for he might exercise it overseas; but here in this kingdom it was by law treason for any made priest by the Pope's authority to come home again to seduce loyal subjects' hearts from their duty to the service of a foreign government. Divers papers were shown which were taken in his custody, as Parsons' opinion concerning the Oath and the like. Drury was found guilty of high treason.

12

At this same session also Humphrey Lloyd was found guilty of the murder of Thomas Morris; and it was observed that Drury after his condemnation as he passed by Lloyd in the docket gave him absolution with his hand crossing him and using some close speeches. At his own condemnation Lloyd openly confessed himself to be a Catholic.

At noon today a woman servant in the house of Sir Jerome Bowes was set upon by two men who struck her on the head with an iron bar and then dragged her down into a cellar by a cord put about her neck. Then these two ascended into the house and took therefrom four bags of money and certain gold buttons. As they came downstairs, hearing the woman cry out, one of them descended again into the cellar, stopped her mouth with a glove and slew her with another blow. It is believed that the men are Edward Wilson (formerly a servant to Sir Jerome) and Robert Tetterton, and that they are gone towards Chester whither the hue and cry is being sent after them.

22nd. Today there is conference between the two Houses concerning the *post nati* (that is, those born in Scotland since the King's coming to the Crown of England), whether they be already naturalized, or aliens as most in the Commons maintain. The case was opened by Sir Francis Bacon; after whom spake Sir Edwin Sandys, Sir Roger Owen and Sir John Bennet, Doctor of the Civil Law. The L. Chancellor declared that it was not a case of *de bono* but *de vero*, not what was fit but what was the Law of England. Then Sir John Doderidge, the King's Solicitor, and other professors of the Common Law continued, urging many reasons against the *post nati*, as that since they are not subject to the Law of England, they should not have benefit therefrom; that every nation hath a precinct wherein the laws have operation, and naturalization is an operation of the law and cannot extend the places outside that precinct; that a man cannot be born a subject of two allegiances, nor by birth natural of two kingdoms; that inconveniences would ensue in honours, privileges and things of value which would be confounded without order. The conference is adjourned till tomorrow when the Judges are to attend to deliver their opinions concerning the point of law.

24th. When Lloyd was drawn in a cart with others to Tyburn, all the carts were stayed at S. Sepulchre's Church for the customary prayer and exhortation founded by M. Dove. All the while the preacher was speaking, Lloyd stopped his ears, but said that if any Roman Catholics were near he desired them to pray for him.

25th. In the Lower House, Sir Thomas Lowe, one of the knights for the City of London, produced a relation in writing of the cruelties done by the Spaniards upon our English merchants, and especially concerning a ship belonging to divers merchants of London called the *Trial.* This ship, being of 120 tons with but 18 men aboard, being in trade in the Levant seas and last of all re-loaded at Alexandria with indigo, spices, drugs and other commodities to the value of 40,000 ducats, two years since was met at sea by a fleet belonging to the Viceroy of Sicilia, which commanded the purser to come aboard the Admiral who questioned him, saying they were commanded to search for the goods of Turks and Jews, which if they found none aboard they would dismiss them. Yet, notwithstanding their promises, finding none of those goods aboard they alleged that they had taken from a Frenchman a piece of ordnance, a sail and a hawser. When this was denied, they put the purser to grievous torture and hanged him up by the arms upon the ship's deck, and the more to increase his torments they hanged two hundredweight of iron at his heels. As he still denied it, they put him the second time to the torment, and to add to it they tied a goat to the rope which with her struggling in grievous manner increased his pains. At the third time they brake his arms, yet he still denied it. At length the master and all the mariners were sent to Sicilia, where some were put in prison and the others in the gallies, by which cruel usage in a short time the master, the merchant and the purser died; and being dead they would afford them no other burial than in the fields and sea-sands. All the men, save four, being wasted, these four by continual torment and starvation were so consumed by their miseries that in the end they resolved to set their hands to a piece of writing that they had taken away from the Frenchman the piece of ordnance and the rest. Long since his Majesty hath written to the Duke of Feria, Viceroy of Sicily, to restore the ship and goods again, but notwithstanding the King's letters and the care of the Lords of the Council still there is no satisfaction.

Sir Thomas also offered a petition to the King concerning the Spaniards' cruelties that letters of mark may be given to recover these damages upon the Spaniards.

26th. All the Judges, but only Sir Thos. Walmsley, have declared in favour of the *post nati*, declaring that allegiance extendeth further than the law national and is not tied to the body politic of every kingdom, whence it is manifest that Scots born in Scotland since the King of England is also King of Scotland are not aliens but subjects, and so be accounted in England.

14

Robert Drury, the Benedictine priest, was condemned to death as a traitor; and being asked if he had anything to say, he replied that he took himself not to be convicted of treason but only for his priesthood; if the Law made that treason he had nothing to say but appealed to the King's mercy. It now appeared that in the interim since his trial he had offered to take the Oath privately before M. Recorder, who deferred it to a more public occasion. Moreover, in a letter to a person of great honour he had written that he thought all honest Catholics might safely take it. Being now required to take the Oath he refused, saying that since he was condemned to death it would do him no good. The like was also offered to another priest by name Davies who likewise refused. Sentence of death was passed upon them both.

27th. This morning Drury, having dressed himself after the manner of the Benedictine friars abroad in a new suit of apparel of black stuff with a black new priest's gown or cassock buttoned down before with buttons and loops and a new corned cap on his head, was drawn on a hurdle to Tyburn. Being brought up into the cart and prepared for death by the executioner, he used some speeches to the same effect as before. He confessed himself a Catholic and a priest, and desired all Catholics to pray with him and for him. As the cart went from him, he caught fast hold with his left hand on the halter and very hardly was enforced to let it go, which was by some taken to show that he had hope of life. He hung until he was quite dead, and afterwards his body was quartered.

In the Lower House M. Speaker interposed a message from the King to the effect that it is a great contempt for any member to absent himself from the House; and he wished that no lawyer or other man of note might depart the town until this great matter of the Union is brought to more ripeness. It is resolved upon Monday next come sennight in the afternoon the House shall be called.

28th. Yesterday M. Martin Lister, a member of the Lower House, informed that Sir Christopher Piggott, remaining a prisoner in the Tower, is sick of a burning fever and in danger of his life, and petitioned for his release. Today comes a message from the King, commending the House for the action taken in the case and wishing he may be free from prison if the House think good. Upon this ensued a motion that he might be restored to his place again, which was not assented; but it was ordered that he shall be enlarged, and to this end a letter sent by M. Speaker to Sir William Waad, the Lieutenant of the Tower. Meanwhile Piggott hath written to my

L. of Salisbury, protesting that his distasteful speech was made through his gross ignorance, he being unaccustomed to discourse in so grave an assembly. The ground of his speech was a zealous and tender respect to secure the preservation of the King, the Queen and the Prince; and the suddenness of the matter and his want of artifice and amazedness transported him so that he said he knew not what; but of his soul he made an absolute distinction between the well-deserving Scots (who had been God's good instruments) from them which proved false, with a humble suit to the House not to make such account of them as of our dear natives.

1st March. Sir Edward Baynham is now in Madrid and there presented his service to Sir Charles Cornwallis, the Ambassador Resident, denying with large oaths all that had been alleged against him. He is said to be much in the company of Anthony Cresswell the English Jesuit who resideth there and hath written a book, which he dedicated to the Spanish King, alleging that this late Powder Treason (howsoever undertaken by the intemperate heads and hands of certain ignorant young people) yet was plotted and devised by some Councillors in England for the overthrow of the Catholic Religion in England.

3rd. This day the Speaker made a motion concerning the manifold miseries fallen upon the subject by reason of the great overflowing of waters in Devon, Somerset, Gloucester, Monmouth and Glamorgan, and a committee is named to consider all convenient courses for the relief of the calamities caused by so extraordinary an accident, whereof the like hath not been heard of in many ages.

5th. Sir Robert Johnson complaineth in the House of a turbulent clamour and outcry of certain women against him as he walked the streets for speaking against the Bill touching wherrymen and watermen. M. Speaker is directed to write to the Justices of Middlesex to prevent disorders in this matter.

6th. Breton has a little book, called *A murmurer*, dedicated to the Lords of the Council, taxing our many murmurers, and especially those who rail against the King for that it is a horrible vice; concluding that the Union of the two Kingdoms is a kind of marriage wrought by the hands of God.

7th. At a conference between the Committee of the two Houses concerning the Union sundry objections were urged by the Lower House. As for the word 'naturalization', it is very large and new, and they would not have it extended too widely. There be two kinds of

16

union: the one perfect importing the consolidation of both countries into one body by laws and uniform government; the other imperfected, united in the head, yet severed in the body. Though they would allow of the perfect union, yet they offer certain cautions and restrictions; for if at the first the Scots should have all our privileges and benefits, it may be feared they will never proceed to the perfect union on their side. Between France and Scotland there is an ancient league wherein we are always considered the common enemy. Such leagues should be abrogated, for ancient friendships will not suddenly be forgotten; since the King's coming, the French King hath erected a band of Scottish horsemen. As for inheritance: they should be given leave to purchase and inherit lands among us which should be subject to all charges and forfeitures as ours; and provision made against the exportation of our wealth and coin. In ecclesiastical matters, no Scottishman should become a Bishop (for he sits in Parliament and has judicature under him), nor Head or Master of a College (for the Universities are contained under the ecclesiastical). Of all other dignities, they should be capable of one tenth at most. And no Scottishman should be capable of two dignities or benefices or above; nor of a dignity unless he have taken the degree of B.D. in one of our Universities; or of a benefice without the degree of B.A.

8th. In August last year eight ministers from Scotland, who protested against the restoration of Bishops in that country, were commanded to come to London, and summoned to the presence when they spoke to the King very boldly, especially M. Andrew Melville. About a month later they were bidden attend a service in the Chapel Royal, where Dr. Andrewes preached upon Numbers 10, of the Two Trumpets, proving that the convening of assemblies pertained to Christian Kings. The next day, which was the Feast of Michael, the ministers were again brought to the Chapel and there saw on the altar two books, two basins, and two candlesticks, which moved M. Melville to make certain satirical verses for which he was called before the Council. Being rebuked by the Archbishop of Canterbury, Melville broke out very invectively, and declared that his Grace was burdened with corruptions and vanities and superstitions, profanation of the sabbath, silencing and imprisoning of true and faithful preachers, and holding up of antichristian hierarchy and popish ceremonies; and further, taking hold of the white sleeves of the Archbishop's rochet and shaking them, he called them Romish rags and a part of the Beast's mark. He was therefore sent to the Tower; and the rest of the ministers kept in the houses of divers divines about London. They have now petitioned that they may be sent back to Scotland.

17

9th. Sir Christopher St. Laurence greatly complaineth to my L. of Salisbury that coming to Gravesend, he is arrested and lodged in jail by one John Somerfeld, mercer in Cheapside for a debt which was repaid a year last Easter; but by means of his man's drowning which had his quittance Somerfeld came into Ireland and would have him pay the money again. Whereupon the mercer complained to the L. Deputy, but Sir Christopher declares that his bonds were not delivered because they were in Ireland with Somerfeld's agent. Notwithstanding his warrant from the L. Ambassador for his free pass, they have used him as if he had been the arrantest traitor in the world, and robbed him of £60 in gold and a diamond worth £24.

14th. There is much complaint of the inconveniences of long conferences between the Lower House and the Lords, for that these committees are forced to stand bareheaded the whole time of the conference. The matter being referred to a committee of the Lower House, M. Fuller reported that in the time of Edward III the two Houses sat together, and that upon any occasion of conference the Lords came down to the Lower House; and it is urged that in all commissions, though the persons be unequal in degree yet if they be equal in commission let all sit alike, all covered or all bareheaded; for this present custom is found a great hurt and danger to the bodies of the Lower House, almost impossible for the strongest body to endure, considering the length of the conferences and the crowding and thronging. Upon this report it was moved that Sir Fr. Bacon or some other be sent in message to the Lords about it; but upon further debate, resolved to forbear, because it is probable that the Lords will hear of the motion and provide accordingly.

17th. A tomb is to be erected in Westminster for the Lady Sophia, who died last June, by Maxmilian Poutrain, the King's Master Sculptor.

20th. The King of Denmark hath signified that he would have Thomas Cutting, who is servant to the Lady Arbella and a man well skilled in playing upon the lute. She hath despatched him with her high commendations of his art and character.

21st. There is a poem by M. Richard Pricket called *The Jesuits' Miracles or new Popish Wonders* deriding certain miracles claimed in England by the Jesuits, as Garnet's straw; denying that papists (such as Campion) put to death in England be martyrs; and inveighing against the Pope as Anti-Christ. Of the Oath saith:

Who dares not swear allegiance to his King,
But vows himself unto the Pope's behest,

Will at the Pope's command do anything.
And such a one hides treason in his breast;
Let not their country unto them do good,
Who Popes to please will suck their country's blood.

23rd. This week past the Speaker hath been sick of a great pain in his head and neck and unable to attend, and so the business of the House hindered. Today M. Fuller propounded that since in the absence of the Speaker business of great importance is neglected they might enter into debate of those things which they might do without a Speaker, which is referred to the Committee upon Privileges, the mover saying that he had heard of precedents that upon such accidents a Speaker might be chosen from day to day. Another said that the Speaker was not their head but one of themselves, and they had power to choose a Speaker, for he is only to moderate; to which it was answered that there is no such precedent, and that the King must give leave. The matter was further argued but the House was not divided.

24th. M. Speaker, being now recovered and in his place, moved that since this is the anniversary of the beginning of his Majesty's happy reign, commonly called Coronation Day, the House should adjourn to hear the sermon in the Abbey, which was applauded. So the Speaker with the more part of the House went to the sermon which was preached by Dr. Ravis, Bishop of Gloucester, upon Matthew xxi. 42.

At the Tilt Sir James Hays sent, as is the custom, to present his shield and device to the King, and to this end made choice of a young Scottish gentleman, M. Robert Carr. But as he was dismounting, his horse being full of fire and heat threw him down before and broke his leg. When the King learnt that the gentleman's name was Carr, he remembered that on his first coming into England he had a page of that name, which this proved to be, for the pages the King brought with him to wait upon his coach in the French manner were discharged and footmen according to the English way supplied their places. M. Carr was instantly carried into M. Rider's House in Charing Cross, where the King, who had little desire to see the triumph, so soon as it was ended went instantly to visit him. The King is so much moved by this accident that he sendeth his own physicians and surgeons to use their endeavours for his recovery. This M. Carr since his first discharge from the King's service hath travelled in France and is but newly returned. He is a very handsome and well bred gentleman.

26th. There is a rumour in Court that a truce for 6 months has been made between the Archduke and the States, which has been affected without informing our King. Hereupon my L. of Salisbury sent for the Agent to the States, who said that he had no knowledge that a truce was concluded, but the States dismissed the first envoys of the Archduke with the answer that unless they were recognized as independent, and also that the name of the King of Spain appeared in the treaty, they would have no more to do with it.

28th. Yesterday the Lords sent a message to the Lower House concerning the point of conveniency of naturalization, as it might concern those born before the King's coming to the Crown, and those born after, which had been discussed in a committee of the two Houses but without that success and effect as was desired. The Lords wish the conference renewed so that the business may have a speedy conclusion. Today the message was discussed in the Commons but though many motions were made this way and that, there are no conclusions.

30th. Dr. Richard Vaughan, the Bishop of London, is dead. He came hither from Chester when the present Archbishop was translated to Canterbury. In his younger years very prompt and ready in speech and withal facetious; but since his coming to London he grew heavy and corpulent of too little exercise, and was taken with an apoplexy. He was held a mild man and well spoken of in the City.

31st. This afternoon at 2 o'clock the Lords and Bishops of the Upper House, the Speaker and the Commons assembled in the great chamber at Whitehall where the King sitting in state spoke to them concerning the Union of the two Kingdoms. After the King's speech ended, M. Speaker with the Commons returned to the Lower House which is adjourned to 20th April.

1st April. The Company of Merchants trading in the East Indies have set forth a third voyage and today three ships, viz., the *Dragon*, the *Hector* and the *Consent*, departed, with Capt. William Keeling as their commander.

2nd. About the middle of February Sir Robert Dudley, calling himself Earl of Warwick, came to Leghorn. He was married at Lyons to his Mistress Southwell, and had the Pope's dispensation for it, procured by one Capt. Elliot. The Great Duke of Florence entertains him very handsomely, and has written to my L. of Northampton declaring that Sir Robert has come to his dominions to live quietly in his religion; he is very faithful to his King and desirous to remain his faithful vassal. Since my L. is regarded as a father by Sir Robert, the Duke would have my L. treat him as a son and keep him in the King's good graces in spite of the calumnies of his enemies.

3rd. Prince Henry was confirmed today in the Chapel Royal at Whitehall by the Archbishop of Canterbury, with the Dean of the Chapel assisting him, both in rich copes. Six Bishops attended the Archbishop, the King remaining the while in his great closet.

5th. The Prince with the King his father received the Holy Communion in the Chapel at Whitehall, a cushion being prepared whereon he kneeled at the left hand of the King and somewhat lower. After the Dean had ministered the communion to himself and his assistants, he ministered to the King and then to the Prince who received the bread first and then the cup, bread and cup being prepared for each separately.

7th. Sir Thomas Shirley is a suitor to the King for the Jews, for one of three courses: the 1st, that they may have free privilege to inhabit in Ireland because doubtless their being there would make that country very rich. They are willing to pay a yearly tribute of 2 ducats for every head and they would bring great store of bullion of gold and silver by issuing of Irish commodities into Spain, such as salted salmons, corn, hides, wool, and tallow. The 2nd course is to give them privilege to inhabit in England and have their synagogues, for which Sir Thomas supposes he could draw them to a greater annual tribute because their chief desire is to be here. But since the King is not willing they should have any synagogues in his dominions, they should give a fine for leave to trade, which they will purchase at a high rate; for the Jews banished out of Spain desired to trade in Naples, and to that end gave the King 100,000 ducats for one year. Many extraordinary commodities may be reaped out of the Jews; and the first and greatest is that if the Eastern Jews once found a liking of the King's countries, many of them out of Portugal (which call themselves Morani) will come fleeing hither; and they will bring more wealth than all the rest, and by them the most part of the trade of Brazil will be converted hither; wherein the King may give the King of Spain a greater blow in peace than Queen Elizabeth did with all her long and tedious war. Moreover, if the King shall have any occasion to be at an extraordinary charge, he may at any time borrow a million of the Jews with great facility, where the merchants of London will hardly be drawn to lend ten thousand. Besides, daily occasions will be offered to make greater commodities out of them if once the King has hold of their persons and goods; but at the first they must be tenderly used, for there is great difference in alluring wild birds and in handling them when they are caught, for they are a very subtle people. The politic Duke of Florence will not leave his Jews for all the other merchants whatsoever.

12th. A truce between the Archduke and the States for eight months by land is now confirmed, the Archduke having used the ministry of a Franciscan friar, who went privately to the Hague disguised as a captain with offers of peace or truce. The States find it strange to be acknowledged a free people by their enemies, and the Archduke's condescending to so unexpected conditions may be suspected as not sincerely intended or a cloak for some greater design. There never happened more sudden alteration beyond all wise men's expectations. The King would not at first believe the terms until the Agent of the States showed him the letter of his masters, which are that the Archduke treats the States as free provinces over which he has no claim: each party to keep what they now hold; and meanwhile the Dutch to have time to deliberate, making known their determination by September; and all warlike actions to cease. The King has no great liking for this truce since it is concluded unknown to him, and moreover the continuing of the war protected him from Spain.

15th. My L. of Salisbury is now at Theobalds which he will shortly exchange with the King for Hatfield, which he also hath visited with the Earls of Worcester and Southampton to view the place where he will place his new habitation.

17th. This day M. Henry Hudson and his company, consisting of eleven seamen and a boy communicated with the rest of the parishioners at S. Ethelburg's church in Bishopsgate before they set forth on a voyage of discovery towards the North Pole at the charge of certain merchants of London.

19th. Of late accusation was laid against the old Lady Montague for default of conformity in religion in her County of Sussex; but upon representation to the King, the Council now require the Attorney General to have the case removed into the Court of King's Bench and thereafter all further process stayed, for that the Lady is a noblewoman, aged, and never called in question for her fidelity in the late Queen's time.

20th. There is printing that allegorical play of Dekker's called *The Whore of Babylon* which the Prince's Players played, wherein is shown, saith the author, the greatness, magnanimity, constancy, clemency and other incomparable virtues of our late Queen; and on the contrary part, the inveterate malice, treasons, machinations, underminings and continual bloody stratagems of that purple Whore of Rome, to the taking away of our Princes' lives and utter extirpation of their Kingdoms. Presenteth the late Queen Elizabeth under Titania the Fairy Queen and Rome under the Empress of Babylon; and bringing in also Dr. Parry, Campion and Lopez as Paridel, Campeius and Ropus. Complaineth that the players marred his lines in the playing, and justifieth his writing (against those who critically tax him that he falsified the account of time) that he wrote as a Poet, not as an Historian, and that these two do not live under one law.

Upon Friday morning last (17th) between 8 and 9 of the clock in the morning there was a sudden great flood in the City of Coventry which was all unexpected for there was neither rain nor thunder. The water came so abundantly into the suburbs and city that it rose in some places three yards and better, and entered into the streets near the river, and houses to the number of 257, causing great damage and loss of household goods, especially to the tanners, whittawers, dyers, bakers and brewers.

Wilson and Tetterton who were condemned for the robbery and the murder of a servant woman in Sir Jerome Bowes's house have been hanged. They were taken at Chester whither the hue and cry followed them, notwithstanding they called themselves by feigned names. Being condemned to death, both resolutely refused to admit their guilt until at the last upon the ladder Wilson admitted the fact and accused his fellow, and Tetterton confirmed that he had given the fatal blows. Being asked to make confession of the Faith in which he died, he said he would die in the faith of God Almighty; but he refused to say the Apostles' Creed and denied some of the articles therein, from which it is concluded that he was of the sect called Brownists.

21st. The Parliament came together again yesterday, but no Bill was read and the Lower House adjourned at 10 o'clock, there being present not above three score. Today because of the small assembly the House is adjourned till the 27th.

25th. There is a little pamphlet of news from Venice (printed for Francis Burton) reporting that the preachers in Venice preach loudly against Free Will, teaching the people that we have free will only to evil, and that if we do good, it cometh not from us but from God; that our justification cometh only by the death of Jesus Christ, and we cannot be saved by any merit or intercession of Saints; that the

Church is not tied to any particular place and he that maintaineth it is a devil and son of perdition; that it is altogether necessary that the people read the Old and the New Testament to know the will of God, and it is no more time to put their subjection to the discretion of their confessors who are become cozeners, jugglers, merchants of their souls and shopkeepers of their bodies; that sermons are more needful than Masses, for many have been converted by hearing of sermons but none by Masses. Declareth that the Senate doth permit this doctrine to be preached to take away the errors of the people and to put down the authority of the ecclesiastics who command Princes as their pages and slaves. These proceedings in the heart of Italy (saith the writer) 'by the Pope's arrogancy occasioned, may be a means to shake to the ground the false foundation of the Church of Rome and her doctrine which is ready to fall'.

29th. When the Venetian Ambassador heard of that pamphlet of news from Venice, he sent to the Earl of Salisbury to require that it should be taken and burnt, and the printer punished. My L. of Salisbury therefore caused all copies that were to be found with the printer or the booksellers to be burnt, and no others sold upon pain of death; but as for the printer it appeared upon examination that he had his Grace of Canterbury's licence to print. The Ambassador, on hearing of this, grew very hot, saying that he could not understand how a man of the Archbishop's prudence and virtue could have allowed such lies to be coloured under the King's name; but his indignation was caused in part because he would give a check to those churchmen who are always ready to use both tongue and pen against the Catholic religion, and also to show his zeal to other Catholic Ambassadors that they may report his doings to Rome and to their own Courts.

1st May. The King often times visits M. Robert Carr, the young gentleman whose leg was broken at the Tilt, sometimes for an hour or more discoursing with him to sound him and know what he is; and though he finds no great depth of literature or experience, yet such a smooth and calm outside that there might be good anchorage for his most retired thoughts. Every courtier now concludes him to be the new favourite, and so many great men flock to see him and to offer to his shrine that the King hath laid a restraint upon them lest it may retard his recovery by spending his spirits.

2nd. These five days past there is much debate of the Union in the Commons but nothing resolved. This afternoon the House attended at Whitehall where the King spake to them to explain certain points in his former speech and to set before them some course of proceeding, in these words: 'I propounded ever, and so I crave at your hands, an absolute and full union, but not a perfect union; such an union as must have that preparation which is made. And because I spake of an absolute union, to say or think I wished nothing in the meantime were absurd. I wished such an union as there might be *unus Rex, unus grex, una lex.*

'It is merely idle and frivolous to conceive that any imperfect union is desired, or can be granted. It is no more unperfect, as now it is projected, than a child that is born without a beard. It is already a perfect union in me, the Head. If you wanted a Head, that is me, your King over you all; or if you were of yourselves no body, then you had reason to say it were unperfect; but it is now perfect in my title and descent, though it be not an accomplished and full union, for that Time must ripen and work.'

Of certain speeches which he misliked: 'I looked for no such fruits at your hands; such personal discourses and speeches; which of all other I looked you should avoid, as not beseeming the gravity of your assembly. I am your King. I am placed to govern you, and shall answer for your errors. I am a man of flesh and blood, and have my passions and affections as other men. I pray you, do not too far move me to do that which my Power may tempt me unto.'

His conclusion: 'I would wish you to proceed with order and with diligence, and above all love to your Sovereign. I say, with the more diligence; because now the Sickness increasing, the heat of the year, yea, your own hay-harvest do persuade you to make haste into the country. Make no more doubts than is needful. Where everything is made doubtful, there nothing will ever come to perfection. If any doubts do arise, make me acquainted with them; pour them into my bosom; I will strive to give you satisfaction. If I cannot answer or satisfy them, let the blame rest upon me. And to conclude, I desire that your travails may be such as you may procure strangers to reverence us, our enemies to fear us, our friends to be glad, our subjects to rejoice with you and me; that the world may see there is an union still in working and proceeding; that you beware of all fanatical spirits, all extraordinary and colourable speeches; that there be no distractions nor distempers among you; that you breed not contempt to the great work so well begun, and discouragement to others that wish well; that you tempt not the patience of your Prince; and finally, with all speed you proceed with as much as can be done at this time, and make not all you have done frustrate.'

There is a long poem by Christopher Lever of the sufferings of Queen Elizabeth in the bloody time of Queen Mary, setting her among the Saints and Angels, as one far exceeding all others, the Virgin Mother only except.

4th. The Speaker reminding the House of the caution in the King's speech not to spend the time in idle discourse, declared that he had received a Bill which he directed the Clerk to read, entitled 'A Bill for the continuance and preservation of the blessed Union of the Realms of England and Scotland, and for the abolishing and taking away of all hostile Laws, Statutes and Customs that might disturb or hinder the same'. The House then gave special order that no man should go forth; yet M. Attorney went forth without leave, at which exception was taken that it was a great contempt and that he ought to be sent for by the Mace. Much was spoken *pro et contra*, but upon a motion taken the House divided with the Noes 133 and the Yeas 110; so he was not sent for.

6th. The Bill for the Abolishing of hostile Laws was read the second time in the Commons; whereupon much debate concerning those members whose discretion the King had taxed in his speech, and it was agreed to make known to the King their desire that he would not suffer himself to be traduced by any private suggestion or reports but either by M. Speaker or some other means be pleased to receive information from the House itself; that he would give leave to such persons as had been blamed by him to clear themselves in his presence; and by some gracious message make clear to the House they could with all liberty and without fear deliver their opinions.

7th. The matter of the King's censure upon members of the Commons being renewed by Sir George More, the Speaker said that the King had already taken notice of yesterday's debate and commanded him to let them know how apt they would find him to entertain their petitions; and touching liberty of speech, he should not think him worthy of his place that did not speak freely what he thought, so it were bounded with modesty and discretion.

10th. The Scottish ministers, except for M. Andrew Melville who remains in the Tower, are commanded to depart to Newcastle upon Tyne and there to remain under peril of rebellion.

The Bishop of Cork, being demanded of the Council to certify the state of his diocese, lamenteth that all over the country in his charge no marriages or christenings are done, except by Popish priests, only Roscarboy excepted, where he remains and may command, for he suffers none to inhabit there unless they conform. The country is waste since the route of the rebels and the Spaniards at Kinsale. They that escaped the sword died through famine, and out of parts of his diocese 4,000 or 5,000 have departed for France or Spain. Five or six livings must therefore be united till the country be better inhabited. An English minister must needs be beholden to the Irishry; his neighbours love him not, especially his profession and doctrine, they being compelled to hear him. Moreover the spiritual livings are uncertain, for the cultivators occupy the land three or four years and then are gone to other ground. There is an abbey at Buttevant under the L. Barry where divers friars in their habits go up and down the country. Every gentleman and Lord has his priest, who is called 'Father'.

Sir Henry Brounker, the Lord President of Munster, hath proceeded very hotly against the recusants, who have complained to the Privy Council by whom he is admonished to avoid extraordinary courses but to proceed rather by instruction and the due execution of the Law, for the popish religion is deep rooted, the people but lately reduced from rebellion and prone to a relapse, so that extraordinary rigours must stir evil humours to a desperate resolution. Seminary priests and Jesuits may be apprehended and punished by Law, the others who show example of contemptuous behaviour, but not those who merely show recusancy of coming to church or secret exercise of their religion in their private houses. As for their complaint that the President hath entered their houses, taken their goods, or kept their wives or children from relief, the Council cannot believe that it is true; or if there be any such matter, let him take present order for its redress. The Lord Deputy himself complaineth that some of the heads of the clergy are very remiss, especially the Archbishop of Munster, who holds four bishoprics.

12th. Sir Charles Cornwallis, the Ambassador in Spain, being of late received in audience by the King there complained much of the honour done to Garnet the Jesuit who was executed last May, for they have procured a painter to make pictures of Garnet, under it setting the words 'Henry Garnet, an Englishman, martyred in London', signifying thereby that King James is a tyrant, for none but tyrants execute that kind of cruelty upon the Saints and witnesses of God. Moreover in the Low Countries the Jesuits have set out a book of the supposed miracle of Garnet's straw, but the Archduke hath caused it to be suppressed.

15th. From the Counties of Northamptonshire, Warwickshire and

Leicestershire comes news of a sudden insurrection of a great number of common persons who have assembled themselves together. They violently cut and break down hedges, fill up ditches, and lay open enclosures of commons which of ancient times were open and employed in tillage. In some places, 1,000 have come together of men, women and children; at Hill Norton in Warwickshire there were 3,000, and at Cottelbich 5,000. They bend all their strength to level and lay open enclosures, without exercising any manner of theft or violence upon any man's person, goods or cattle; and wheresoever they come they are generally relieved by the near inhabitants who send them not only carts laden with victual but also good store of spades and shovels.

In Devonshire an earthquake was felt in divers parts, as Barnstaple, Tiverton and Bampton, at which last also there was a little lake which ran by the space of two hours, the water whereof was as blue as azure, yet notwithstanding as clear as might be.

16th. There is a poem called *Barley-break: or a Warning for Wantons* of the lewd love of Streton and Euphema whereby both lovers and the old father come to violent ends, dedicated to the virtuous maiden Mistress Elizabeth C, daughter to Robert C, Esquire; whereof the author, W. N. Gentleman, would have nothing constrained against his simple meaning.

18th. A committee of the Commons is appointed to consider a petition upon the better ordering of the laws in force against Jesuits, seminary priests and recusants; of some course to be taken touching non-residence and pluralities of beneficences; and for the more free preaching of the Gospel.

22nd. The King today took possession of Theobalds which my L. of Salisbury hath exchanged for Hatfield House. The King and the Queen with the Prince Henry and the Prince Joinville (the brother to the Duke of Guise) were entertained to dinner; and afterwards being entered into the gallery there was seen nothing but a traverse of white across the room, which being suddenly drawn, was discovered a gloomy obscure place, hung all with black silk, and in it only one light which the Genius of the place held as if sadly and drooping at the departure of his Lord; but soon the black vanishing, there was discovered a glorious place, figuring the seat of the household gods, and in one corner a boy hovering in the air with wings displayed. Hereat Mercury cheers Genius, and the Three Fates tell him that he must now be servant to the Bel-Anna, whereat he delivers the keys to the Queen. This device was made by Ben Jonson.

28

24th. Dr. John Rainolds, President of Corpus Christi College in Oxford, died three days ago. By his will be leaves forty books to the public library of the University, first of all to be chosen by Sir Thomas Bodley, if there be so many fit for that place wherewith it is not furnished already, and the rest of his books to other Colleges and to his friends. It was Dr. Rainolds who in the Conference at Hampton Court urged upon his Majesty the new translation of the Bible.

25th. By the mediation of the Cardinal Joyeuse (sent from the French King) the quarrel between the Pope and the Venetians is now ended; which began upon three principal reasons. The City of Venice, fearing that most of their land would in the end fall to the clergy, made a law that if any Venetian at his death gave land or solid possession to a religious Order, the State of Venice is to possess the land, giving the Order its worth from S. Mark's treasury. Also, they made a prohibition that no man should build a religious house without the consent of Signory and only in such places as the Senate should appoint. The third reason was that since the Pope and his officers had been very slack in punishing the offences of the Clergy, they themselves inflicted punishment upon some ecclesiastics, which the Pope would not endure. Peace is made upon the terms that the ecclesiastics be now handed over to the Pope who revokes his interdict; the decrees are to remain but to be used moderately; and all Regular Orders departed or banished return to their convents in the State, except the Jesuits. There was no ceremony or public note of gladness.

27th. A week since the Speaker signified that it was the King's pleasure to adjourn the House till the 27th. This matter being called in question, today the Speaker defended himself against those who declare that he adjourned the Court without the privity of the House, saying that it is in the King's power. Further it had come to the King's ear from the ordinaries in town (not from the House or any member of it) that the House had been adjourned so that the fewer members resident in town might overcarry the question in hand touching the remanding of malefactors upon the Border from one country to the other, whereby the King thought himself much touched in honour. He would have some course taken for recalling absent members and their better attendance.

28th. There is news of a notable fight at sea in the Road of Gibraltar, where on the 24th April a fleet of Hollanders entered the Road and there burnt and destroyed sundry Spanish ships and galleys,

29

although they were in their own harbour and under shot of the town and the castle. The Spaniard with the second shot he made slew a young gentleman, and the bullet passing on by misfortune struck off the Admiral Hemskirk's left thigh close to the body; and the same bullet struck off a gunner's hand wherewith he was ready to give fire. The valiant Admiral feeling death approaching encouraged them that were about him all he could, and bade them choose out another in his place; and so died. Many trust that this seafight will put an end to the truce, but Sir Noel Caron (the Agent for the States) hopes that the King will be hereby encouraged to warmer action; yet the Archduke labours all he can to conclude a peace, and even how liberty of conscience can be allowed.

29th. The Ambassador at Venice delivered to Sir Robert Dudley his letter of recall under the Privy Seal, but observing that the superscription did not give him his pretended title of Earl of Warwick, he would not open it, and so returns it to my L. of Salisbury with the answer that whatsoever his Majesty shall command he will most willingly obey. He protesteth that those commanded to deliver the privy seal said that he was in such disfavour with the King that the English merchants were commanded not to come to him, so that there is spread abroad over Italy a report that he is a traitor. As for his being a Catholic, there are 20,000 of them in England, and good subjects. That he made a questionable marriage: so did the Earl of Devonshire, one of his Majesty's Council, and like marriages are in the Arches daily without offence to the State. For his taking upon himself his titles abroad: he has better right to them than the L.'s of Westmorland and Beauchamp, or L. Mounteagle at home. Sufficient testimony has been given that he is son and heir of his father, and subsequently Earl of Warwick and Leicester. Begs that he may not be recalled through the malice of his enemies to his great disgrace, for he would serve the Great Duke of Florence in his designs against the Turk.

2nd June. Sir Anthony Mildmay and Sir Edward Montague went out to Newton where a 1,000 riotous persons who call themselves levellers were busily digging, but were furnished with half pikes, long bills, bows and arrows and stones. These gentlemen, finding great backwardness in the trained bands, were constrained to use all the horse they could make and as many foot of their own servants and followers as they could trust. First they read the proclamation twice, using all their best persuasion to make the rioters desist; but when nothing would prevail, they charged upon them both with horse and foot. The first charge they stood and fought desperately, but at the second charge they ran away. There were slain some 40 or 50 and a great number hurt. Sir Harry Fooks that led the foot is very sore hurt and more likely to die than to live.

3rd. The Earl of Huntingdon is now required by the King to take charge against the rebels. He shall assemble the principal gentlemen and resolve what course is to be taken. Although the King would spare blood, yet some special persons should be made examples to the others; yet if the resistance is likely to be such as the subduing of them will cost too much blood, he shall publish by proclamation in the King's name that if they acknowledge their offence and submit themselves to his mercy, they shall have pardon of their lives, excepting only the first movers and inciters of others.

Sir Henry Brounker, Lord President of Munster, is dead in Ireland, after an illness of three months. He died without any show of impatience, contrary to the reports spread against him that he died raving and eating his flesh from his arms lamenting his rigour against recusants. The Earl of Thomond for the present has his place, to whom my L. of Salisbury writes that he knows the late President to have been faithful to his King, of a sound religion, and honest to his friends, though in the matter of recusancy somewhat extreme yet far short of the complaints against him which arose more of a malicious prejudice against his person as one more fervent than others.

4th. Because there hath been argument concerning the giving of evidence for a defendant in a case at law, a note is delivered to the Speaker touching the customs of the Scottish courts, for the better satisfaction of certain doubts made about the present Bill. In Scotland, in civil causes witnesses are admitted for probation, but only in favour of the pursuer, for the defendant would prove against the libel if he had benefit of witnesses, which is altogether unlawful; and therefore in many actions the defendant will press by all means, either by a cross libel or some trick or other, to change the motion from a defender to a pursuer. In Scotland in criminal causes, ordanes and juries pass upon the life or death very near to English law; for their jury is chosen out of places near to the fact committed, for the Law presumes that such a jury may better discern the truth of the fact by their own knowledge; and they are not bound to examine witnesses, unless they please in favour of the pursuer, which is seldom used, but not lawful to be done in favour of the defendant. Howsoever, the judge may privately examine beforehand such witnesses as he thinks may inform him of the truth, and these may be examined or their depositions read in the presence of the parties and the jury, but never in the defendant's favour. To admit witnesses in favour of the party defendant and in criminal causes is against English Law, Scottish Law, the Civil Law and the Law of all nations.

8th. There is a book, written by Anthony Nixon, of the travels of the three sons of Sir Thomas Shirley, who was formerly Queen Elizabeth's Treasurer for Wars. Sir Thomas Shirley, the younger, in 1602 served the Duke of Florence by sea, and thereafter with three ships of his own warred against the Turks. But his men growing mutinous for lack of good success, he attempted to surprise an Island. The inhabitants, who were both Greeks and Turks, after their first surprise came against his men who fled and abandoned him to the enemy. Now for three years he was a prisoner of the Turks, who kept him at Constantinople, where he was very vilely treated and often in danger of his life; nor would the English Ambassador stir greatly to aid him until letters came from his Majesty, and then he so bestirred himself that Sir Thomas was given his freedom in December 1605. He remained in Constantinople till February 1606, and thence returned to his father and his friends in England this present year.

Of Sir Anthony noteth his adventures, as formerly known by that book printed in 1601, adding thereto his service with the King of Spain, whom he now serveth in the Levant Seas.

The third brother, M. Robert Shirley, after the departure of Sir Anthony from Persia remained behind, serving most valiantly against the Turk. He is now married to a Persian lady, cousin german to the King, by whom he hath two children, both baptized Christians; and he hath good hope he may in time bring the King also to become a Christian.

9th. Today the House was called by the general book of names. As the Clerk called each name, the party called (if present) rose bareheaded and answered. If absent, and excused by some in the House, he was noted absent for special reasons; if no man excused him, he was noted *deficit*. The names of the deficiencies to be presented to the House tomorrow.

10th. While the Court of Star Chamber was sitting, news was brought that John Popham, the L. Chief Justice of England, was dead, some said of an ulcer in his bladder, others that he had taken pills (supplied him by the Empiric Ralegh) and the physic wrought on him, for he died suddenly in the same hour, just after he had signed several warrants; others that he died of grief for sharp words from the King. Some regard him as a most worthy man, a main pillar of the Gospel and religion, a severe and upright justice, and the only supporter of the Common Laws of England, an infinite loss to the law and its professors; yet though the godly lament, the lewder sort of people rejoice.

The L. Chancellor in his speech delivered to the Judges and Justices of the Peace did show how the King had an incessant care for the good of his people and the quietness of the country, and hath given commandment that all persons shall depart to their countries not for their idle pleasures but to have special care for the peace of the country which is disturbed either by papists or sectaries. These usurpations and anarchies are dangerous, and the magistrates must have care that the people be not idle nor stir up discontent by prophecies or pamphlets, and there be order in ecclesiastical governors, and that there be not a Pope in every parish. It is the part of a Justice of the Peace to foresee and provide against these things and to withstand the beginnings, as now in these late depopulations, a great and wicked offence that the Justices and Sheriffs should have prevented and foreseen. They must look therefore to all seminaries and their followers, and to their conventicles and to all vagrants strong to labour yet idle and gentlemanlike in approach, yet without means, libellers and devisers of plots. They should look also to the Justices of the Peace that are turbulent or neglect their duties.

From Spain it is reported that Sir Anthony Shirley is turned Catholic by persuasion of Cresswell the Jesuit. He is a great magnificator of the straw miracle, for being lately in the company of divers Englishmen who were commending the late book of the proceedings against the Powder Plot traitors, Sir Anthony said that there were indeed many eloquent and well-set speeches in that book but one poor straw had made them all or nothing.

11th. Richard Johnson hath written a little book in form of a dialogue between a Country Gentleman and a London Citizen concerning the walks in Moor-fields, and many other antiquities and customs of the City. Noteth that the dagger in London's arms remembereth Sir William Walworth, Mayor, who with his own hands slew the rebel Wat Tyler.

12th. The King, attended with divers Lords of the Privy Council, came privately to the house of the L. Mayor (Sir John Watts); and after dinner Sir John presented him with a purse of gold which the King very graciously accepted. As he was ready to depart the L. Mayor besought him that he would be free of the Clothworkers, which the King accepted. Then he descended into the dining chamber and went into the Clothworkers' Hall, the Lord Mayor bearing the Sword before him; and being entered into the Hall he was received by the Master and the Wardens, and when he had learnt that the Master of the Company was Sir William Stone, the King said, 'Wilt thou make me free of the Clothworkers?' 'Yea,' quoth the Master, 'and think myself a happy man that I live to see this day.' Then the King said, "Stone, give me thy hand, and now I am a Clothworker.' After that, he walked in the garden and into the great parlour; and whilst he sat there the Earls of Cumberland and Shrewsbury, both being free of the Company, presented him with bread and wine. So the King drank to the Company and in proof of his especial favour gave them two bucks yearly for ever against the time of the election of the Master and the Wardens.

When the Earl of Huntingdon came into Leicestershire, he found all quiet; but on the 6th there assembled about 80 in tumultuous sort, of whom he dispersed the greater number, but apprehended the principals, of whom one John Reynolds is sent up to London as a base ringleader and turbulent varlet. Yet my Lord is blamed of the Council because he did not make example by the deaths of some few of them; to which he replies that he did indeed take some 8 or 10, very poor creatures, of whom he caused two or three to be brought to a windmill (no tree being near) where he commanded halters to be put round their necks. Finding them penitent, he spared their execution, intending to deal very sharply with them if the least stir had again risen; but since that time all is quiet.

This Reynolds is either a pedlar or a tinker, a base fellow, whom they surnamed Captain Pouch because of a great pouch which he wore by his side, wherein (said he) was matter to defend them against all comers; but when he was searched there was found only a piece of green cheese. He told them he had authority from the King to throw down enclosures, and that he was sent and directed by the King of Heaven; yet he kept them in good order and forbad them to swear or offer violence to any.

Until the offenders were examined it was generally bruited that the cause of these discontents was religion; some saying that it was the Puritans because they were stronger and sought to enforce their pretended reformation; others that it was the Papists thereby to obtain restoration or toleration; but it is now manifest that the sole cause was only for the laying open of enclosures.

14th. At Colyton in Devon three days since rain fell, being as it seemed a thunder shower, among which were certain drops like blood which stained those things it fell on: and a partlet was slain by it.

15th. The body of the Dutch Admiral slain in the fight at Gibraltar was embalmed and brought to Holland. On the 8th he was interred with an honourable military pomp, the body being carried by 12 captains, and followed by all the chief magistrates, colonels and citizens.

16th. The petition against recusants, framed by the committee of the Commons, was pressed to be read in the House, but M. Speaker made answer that the King had taken notice of it, and saith he will be careful to execute those laws, and it shall be needless to press him. Hereupon sundry members urge that the petition shall nevertheless be read, for it is a great wound to the gravity of the House to deny it. M. Speaker replied that there were many precedents in the late Queen's time when she restrained the House from meddling in petitions. Upon this it is moved that Sir Robert Cotton, a known antiquary, and M. Robert Bowyer, Keeper of the Records in the Tower, shall search the records and bring precedents concerning messages from the Sovereign, and petitions. Further, the Speaker is pressed to let his Majesty know how much this refusal grieveth the House.

The Levellers in Northamptonshire have now surrendered. They had fortified themselves and resisted those sent there against them, but being terrified by the death of some of their leaders who were taken prisoners and hung in their sight they yielded. It is said that only the leaders will be punished, for their ill deeds were caused by those who misused them, so that while the King blames the manner, he cannot blame the cause of their action. This rising grew so fast out of Northamptonshire where it began that, but for lack of a leader, it would soon have become a rebellion, and it is suspected by some that some great ones must have encouraged them. There is great vigilance in the City where the watch has been strengthened and all suspected persons, especially Catholics, closely observed.

17th. In the Commons Sir Fr. Bacon delivered a report on the conference with the Lords concerning the complaints of the merchants against the Spaniards; and especially of the speech of my L. of Salisbury, who said that complaints of merchants were usually subject to much error, for they spake, for the most part, upon information, and that carried through many hands, of matters done in remote parts, so as a false or factious factor might oftentimes make great tragedies upon no great ground; further, though the wealth and welfare of the merchant is not without a sympathy in the general stock of a nation, especially an island, yet the particular profit of the merchant should not be the public case of the Kingdom. Though their grievances are great and do multiply, yet are they often the authors of their own miseries; for they commit many errors and in the pursuit of their own remedies and suits, they do it so impoliticly that except Lieger Ambassadors should become merchants' factors their causes can hardly prosper. And such is now the confusion in trade that shop-keepers become merchants, seek base means by gifts and bribery to procure the favours of officers in foreign places. Nor are the wrongs so great, considering trade in those parts was never greater; whereas if the wrongs were so intolerable as they propound them it would work a general discouragement of trade. As for their complaints in fact, the injustices are not of the highest order, being rather delays in justice, which proceed not so much from malice as the proud and dilatory nature of that people, which are a by-word throughout the world. Concerning the complaint of trade into the West Indies: the right of the Crown of Spain to the Indies was never confirmed nor denied in the late Treaty; yet the offences and scandals of those who voyage thither maketh the point worse. This very last voyage to Virginia, intended for trade and plantation where the Spaniard hath neither people nor possession, is already become infamed for piracy; witness Bingley, who first insinuating his purpose to be an actor in that action of plantation is become a pirate, and his ship taken in Ireland. As for the remedy of letters of mark: the remedy is incompetent and vain, and dangerous to the merchants and so to the whole state; for the stock of goods of the Spaniard in this kingdom is a trifle, whereas the stock of English goods in Spain is a mass of mighty value.

The making of war and of peace is the indisputable prerogative of the Crown, and great prejudice might come of handling and debating of this matter in Parliament. There is no King who will providently enter into a war but will first balance his forces, seek to anticipate confederacies and alliances, revoke his merchants, find an opportunity of the first breach and many other points which if they once do but take wind will prove vain and frustrate; and therefore this matter is *arcanum imperii* and must be kept within the veil.

Sir Francis also reported the speech of another Earl who said he was persuaded that the two Houses differed rather in credulity than in intention; for their Lordships did not believe the information so far, but yet desired the reformation as much as they. Further, he said that the Lower House in its first foundation was merely democratical, consisting of knights of shires and burgesses of towns and intended to be of those places for which they serve; and therefore to have a private and local wisdom, and so not fit to examine or determine secrets of state which depend on a variety of circumstances. He alleged other reasons of the same kind, concluding that it may cast some aspersion upon his Majesty, implying as if the King slept out the sobs of his subjects until he was awakened with the thunderbolt of a Parliament.

18th. The Speaker interposed a message from the King that if the House think good to have the petition concerning recusants read, he is not against the reading. It is therefore read at large. Noteth sundry abuses in the Church, as of ignorant curates, ministers scandalous and offensive in life, the great discontent caused to students in divinity by pluralities. Petitioneth that there may be restored to their ministry those suspended and silenced ministers whose refusal of ceremonies proceedeth only from conscience and fear to offend God. In the dispute it is declared that in England there are 8,000 parish churches; not 2,000 preaching ministers; not 1,000 that preach once in a month; not 500 single beneficed; 300 deprived or silenced; 400 Jesuits and seminaries in England; 40 simple people converted by one Jesuit in a year; 300 convicted recusants in a shire at the Queen's death, now 800.

20th. The Bill for the Abolition of all memory of Hostile Acts etc. was this day, after so many day's debate and amendment, passed by the Commons and sent up to the Lords.

25th. In Ireland of late one Robert Lalor, a priest, has been convicted under the Statute of King Richard II known as *Praemunire*. This Lalor received order of priesthood above 30 years since and was made Vicar-General of the Apostolic See of Dublin and the bishoprics of Kildare and Fermer, which jurisdiction he exercised boldly for many years until the proclamation commanding Jesuits and priests to depart the Realm. Thereafter he began to lurk and to change his name. Howbeit he was at last apprehended in Dublin and committed to prison, and being examined before the L. Deputy himself, he was afterwards convicted and so rested in prison for two terms. He then made petition to the L. Deputy to be set at liberty, and subscribed to a voluntary confession in which he acknowledged that he was not a lawful Vicar-General, that King James was now lawful and supreme governor in all causes ecclesiastical as well as civil, and neither the Pope nor any other foreign Prince hath any power to control the King in any cause ecclesiastical or civil in his Kingdoms; that all bishops ordained and made by the King are lawful bishops; that no bishop made by the Pope had any power to control any act made by the King's authority. After this confession Lalor was given more liberty than before, and many of his friends had access to him, to whom he protested that he had only acknowledged the King's civil and temporal power, without any acknowledgement of his authority in spiritual matters. These words being reported to the L. Deputy, Lalor was indicted under the Statute of *Praemunire* and charged before a jury of the city of Dublin, the trial by reason of the man's reputation and the nature of the cause drawing many of the principal gentlemen of the Pale and the provinces.

At his indictment Lalor pleaded not guilty. Whereupon the Attorney General, before descending to the particular evidence, spoke at great length of the various Acts made before Henry VIII's time against the Pope. When he came to the evidence against Lalor, the Attorney demanded of him whether he had not professed to divers of his friends that he had not acknowledged the King's supremacy in ecclesiastical causes. Lalor's answer was that he had indeed said to some of his friends that he had not confessed that the King was supreme governor in spiritual causes, for in his confession there was no mention made of spiritual causes but of ecclesiastical.

'This is a subtle evasion indeed,' said the Attorney General, and demanded what difference he would make between ecclesiastical and spiritual causes. To which Lalor replied that the question was sudden and unexpected, and that another day should be taken to dispute the point. But the Attorney refused, and thereupon spoke upon the distinction made between causes spiritual and ecclesiastical and others temporal and civil. Truly, saith he, they were so called not from the nature of the causes but from the quality of the persons whom the Prince made judges in these causes. The clergy did study spiritual things, and therefore the causes wherein they had jurisdiction were called spiritual causes. And therefore where M. Lalor hath acknowledged the King's Majesty to be supreme governor in all ecclesiastical causes, he hath also acknowledged the King's supremacy in all spiritual matters.

The jury having found the prisoner guilty of the contempts whereof he was indicted, judgement was given according to the statutes.

29th. At the Curtain the Queen's Players have a play called *The Travels of Three English Brothers*, founded on the late book and written by Day, Wilkins and Rowley. Showeth their many strange adventures and the treacherous dealings of Jews, Turks and Persians. In one scene presenteth Will Kempe the Clown playing an extemporal merriment with an Italian Harleken and his wife.

30th. Dr. Thomas Morton on being made the new Dean of Gloucester sent for M. John Donne (to whose learning he is much indebted in his late works of controversy) to urge upon him to waive his Court life and enter into Holy Orders, adding thereto the promise of a rich benefice, To which, after some day's consideration, M. Donne replied that some irregularities of his life had been so visible that he feared he would bring dishonour on that sacred calling. M. Donne now liveth at Mitcham, much straitened, with his wife and three children. He fell into such melancholy that he wrote a treatise called *Biathanatos*, or a thesis that self homicide is not so naturally sin that it may never be otherwise.

1st July. Of late the Prince declared to the Venetian Ambassador that had he been of riper years he would have come to the aid of the Republic. The Ambassador was therefore required to deliver his Highness the thanks of the Senate for that offer, which was done at Nonesuch, where the Prince showed him all the delights of that Palace. On his departure the Prince said that this day he had shown his amusements, but thereafter the Ambassador should see his studies and exercises so that he might bear testimony of his pains to reach that high estimate which the Senate had taken of him.

3rd. Today the King repaid to the citizens £60,000 which they lent to the late Queen on 3rd February 1599.

4th. This afternoon the Speaker with the Commons came up into the King's Presence in the Upper House, where after sundry speeches made, the Parliament is prorogued until 16th November. The chief statutes enacted in this session are:

An Act for the utter abolition of all memory of hostility between England and Scotland whereby all Acts of former times directed against the Kingdom of Scotland shall be abolished, provided that Acts made by the Parliament of Scotland shall likewise be abolished; and treating of offences that shall be committed by the subjects of one kingdom that shall pass into the other. No Englishman shall be sent out of England to take his trial for offences committed in Scotland until such time as both Realms shall be made one in laws and government. And because the partiality and corruption of many that live upon the Borders cannot but produce much and frequent perjury, the jurors shall be chosen of persons of better condition and quality than hitherto, who shall according to their conscience and discretion admit only such witnesses for or against the party arraigned as shall appear to them to be free of hatred or affection.

An Act to restrain the utterance of beer and ale to alehouse-keepers and tipplers not licensed.

An Act for the repressing of the odious sin of drunkenness which is of late grown in common use, whereby any one convicted shall be fined 5*s.* for every offence, to be paid to the churchwardens of the parish where the offence is committed; and if any constable or other officer do neglect the correction of an offender, he shall be fined 10*s.* And anyone who shall remain tippling in any inn or alehouse shall be fined 5*s.* and if unable to pay then to be set in the stocks for the space of four hours.

An Act for further explanation of the former Act concerning the bringing a fresh stream of running water into the northern parts of the City of London by the New Cut or River, whereby the commissioners shall have power to cause to be made a trench not exceeding ten feet in breadth, and (where needed) to erect a trunk or vault of brick or stone for the passage of the water.

5th. Sir Julius Caesar, Chancellor of the Exchequer, was sworn a Privy Councillor. His father was a physician from Padua in Italy, by name Aldemare Cesare, who came to England and was physician first to Queen Mary and afterwards to the late Queen.

7th. Some days since the Archpriest Blackwell was taken and brought before the Archbishop of Canterbury and the Dean of Westminster, by whom he was examined eight times. At his examination the Archbishop gave him copies of the Pope's Breves and of his answers thereto, and he was asked whether he still held his former opinion of the Oath. Now, seeing the hatred Catholics incur for the refusal of the Oath, and how that Parliament did avoid to call in question the authority of the Pope to excommunicate but only intended to present the danger which might ensure by such an inference as is mentioned in the Oath, he admitted the Oath of his private opinion; and he hath taken it word for word as is set down in the Statute. Afterwards falling into speech of excommunication, he said that he thought his Holiness would not at any time excommunicate his Majesty; further, if such excommunication should come, whereby subjects were discharged of their allegiance or bound to bear arms against the King or offer violence to his person, he would hold himself bound by the laws of God to continue his Majesty's loyal and faithful subject. He would have all good Catholics concur with him, and take the Oath; for no lawful excommunication can be denounced by the Pope which can inculcate such an offence. Now he writes to the priests over whom he has charge that they should take the Oath as he has done, and instruct lay Catholics that they also may do the same.

Sir Toby Mathew, the Archbishop of York's son, returned to England a few days since after three years' travel in France and Italy where he was reconciled to the Roman Church in Florence to the sorrow of his particular friends, especially M. Dudley Carleton and Sir Fr. Bacon. He spoke so openly of his falling away from the Anglican Church that he was sent for by the Archbishop of Canterbury, who finding little hope of reducing him by conference, the Oath was tendered him, which he refused and is now sent prisoner to the Fleet. His best fortune will be a banishment. His father the Archbishop he hath not seen, for he has gone down in Yorkshire to comfort his mother who is little less, as they say, than dead for grief.

9th. About a month since, a lewd fellow named Bartholomew Helston went about the town giving himself forth to be Queen Mary's son, oftentimes gathering the people about him. Sir William Waad caused him to be apprehended and examined him. He declared that he was stolen from Hampton Court where he was born, and spake words savouring rather of a seditious disposition than of lunacy. So he is committed to Bridewell but because the masters of that prison wearied of him, Sir William again sent for him, and finds that he takes this course out of a malicious and knavish humour, being in want and a tall lusty fellow. It is left to my L. of Salisbury whether he remain in Bridewell or be sent to Bedlam.

10th. The attainder of the priest Lalor, being the first case of *Praemunire* in Ireland, breeds no small terror not only to the priests and Jesuits but to divers principal gentlemen of the Pale who have been maintainers of this priest, whereby they also have incurred danger of *Praemunire*, for it appeared upon the evidence that they had taken from him sundry dispensations for marriages within the degrees and for non-payment of tithes, and some had divorces and others presented clerks whom he instituted into benefices.

The Earl of Tyrone takes very ill the settlement of his country, for he knows it will reduce him to the moderate condition of other Lords in Ireland and England at this day; for when England was full of tenants at will, our Barons were then like the Irish Lords and able to raise armies against the Crown; and as this man was O'Neil in Ulster so the Earl of Warwick was O'Neville in Yorkshire. When the matter of Tyrone's dispute with Sir Donald O'Cahane was in question before the L. Deputy and the Council, Tyrone in passion

41

snatched out of O'Cahane's hands an instrument written in Irish and rent it in pieces, for which he afterward humbly submitted himself. When every man has his own, Tyrone will be owner of more land than he will thoroughly inhabit and manure as long as he lives; but it is not land but the bodies of men and the command over them that he desires. The cause of the dispute was that O'Cahane is much discontented with Tyrone's oppressions and would hold his country immediately from the King and not from Tyrone.

13th. The Vice-Chancellor and the Heads of sundry Colleges at Cambridge have petitioned my L. of Salisbury to aid them in the abuse of their free elections of fellowships and scholarships by the procurement of his Majesty's letters, which is a manifest inconvenience, being against the statutes of foundations, oaths of electors and free choice of the fittest. Such letters are procured partly by the boldness of unfit youths moving suit by their parents, partly by the partial affection of their tutors when they cannot have their pupils preferred as they would, whence grows faction in Houses.

16th. The King, the Prince and divers honourable Lords were today entertained by the Merchant Taylors in their Hall. At the upper end of the Hall there was set a chair of estate where the King sat and viewed the Hall, and a very proper child, well spoken, being clothed like an angel of gladness with a taper of frankincense burning in his hand, delivered a short speech of 18 verses, devised by Ben Jonson, which pleased his Majesty marvellous well. It had at first been intended that the Schoolmaster with his scholars should welcome the King but then it was doubted whether he was acquainted with such kind of entertainments. Upon either side of the Hall in the windows near the upper end were galleries of seats, made for music, in either of which were 7 choice musicians playing on their lutes, and in a ship, which hung aloft in the Hall, 3 rare men, apparelled in watchet silk like seamen, and very skilful, also sang; but the multitude was so great that lutes nor songs could hardly be heard or understood.

Then the King went up into the King's chamber where he dined alone at a table which was provided only for the King and the Queen (but she came not). In this chamber were placed a pair of very rich organs whereupon M. John Bull, Doctor of Music, did play all dinner time; and M. Nathaniel Gyles, Master of the Children of the King's Chapel, with Dr. Montague, Bishop of Bath and Wells and Dean of his Majesty's Chapel, and divers singing men, among them

William Byrde and Orlando Gibbons, and the Children of the Chapel did sing melodious songs.

While the King thus sat at dinner the Master and the Wardens with divers Aldermen and the Recorder of London humbly thanked his Majesty for gracing their fraternity and the Master presented him with a purse of gold of £100, and showed him the roll of those who had been made free of their Company. Whereat the King said that he was himself free of another Company yet he would so grace the Merchant Taylors that the Prince should be made free thereof. To the Prince also was presented a purse of £50. A like purse had also been prepared for the Queen; but since she came not, £50 was saved to the Company. After this the King came down into the Great Hall and sitting there in the chair of estate beheld the ceremonies of the election of the new Master and Wardens. Then he heard a song of farewell by the 3 men in the ship, which pleased him so much that he caused their song to be sung three times over.

The Company have admitted into their livery Dr. Bull and M. Gyles who with the rest of those that sang during the dinner gave their music gratis; but there was much complaint that the musicians in the Great Hall exacted unreasonable sums of the Company.

21st. Two Deputies recently sent over from the States have been received by the King and referred to the Council to whom they said they had come to seek the King's help for war or his counsel for peace. To which my L. of Salisbury demanded of them whether the peace was yet made. They replied it is still in the making, and they are under no necessity of making it save that they cannot carry on the war without aid. They will not make peace on any conditions unless their independence is granted. As for the French King they do not know his intentions. The Deputies have been told that the King is sending over two Commissioners (who are Sir Ralph Winwood and Sir Richard Spencer). It is generally believed that peace will be made because the Hollanders desire it, and the two Kings are so distrustful of each other.

24th. A proclamation is come forth promising pardon to all the late rebels that shall submit themselves and acknowledge their offence before the L. Lieutenant or his deputy in the county where they remain.

28th. Lodovic Lloyd hath written a poem dedicated to his Majesty called *Hilaria: or the Triumphant Feast for the fifth of August*, in four parts, treating of Temperance, Fortitude, Justice and Prudence, larded with many examples of these virtues, and ending:

Most liberal gifts I gave, O King,
If King will credit pen:
My heart, my life, my love, my self,
My book, and children ten.
But Caesar may, if Caesar will,
On me like Caesar look,
Make me to sing more sweeter notes,
Than Swan, on Severn brook.

29th. The two Deputies of the States have departed. They say that the truce is held up because the condition of independence is not clearly conceded in the ratification sent from Spain; whereupon the bearer of the ratification asked for six days in which he promised the Archduke would give them satisfaction.

There is come to London an Ambassador from the Turk, by name Mustapha, recommended by Murat Rey, Admiral of Algiers, a man of 70 years old who heretofore was as much renowned for his exploits in the Levant Seas as ever Drake was for his attempts upon the Ocean. This Mustapha is a man of a goodly presence and a gallant spirit, sociable, affable and full of entertainment to all comers, and to give better content to those that come to see him is content to dispense with some of his Turkish fashions, for being invited to accompany Sir Thomas Low, Governor of the Company, to dinner, he sat in a chair at the board's end and drank a solemn health to the King and to the Grand Signor.

He hath been two years in his journey, having accompanied M. de Brebis, the French Ambassador, through Anatolia, Armenia, Palestine, Egypt and Barbary as far as Algiers where they stayed 7 months, and the French Ambassador hoped to have obtained from the King and Murat Rey the coral fishing, but it was flatly denied. With this they went both of them to Marseilles where M. de Brebis promised he would make the French King acquainted with his message, and then come and fetch him. But the Mustapha heard nothing in 6 months. So he wrote to the French King saying that he had letters of the Grand Signor, and asked for audience as the Grand Signor is wont to give the Ambassador of all Christian nations. The French King wrote an answer persuading him to return, and sending a present of 1,000 crowns, which he refused, and did still demand an audience, which in the end was granted.

His errand to the French King was for the release of 150 Turks chained to the galleys at Marseilles, the greater part of whom were released by Count Maurice from Spinola's galleys at the winning of

Sluys. He saith he brought with him 80 French captives, whereof four were circumcised, and delivered them up freely, and yet in 7 months he could not get one Turk released. Reporteth many things of the perfidy of the French nation, liking neither their fashion nor their diet, their meat being so larded with hog's flesh that he could not eat of it. During his abode there, the King allowed him 15 crowns a day, and tried to dissuade him, as did also our Ambassador, from coming hither.

He is come but slenderly attended with some dozen Turks, whereof three only are civilly apparelled, the rest looking like the ambassadors that came to Joshua with old shoes and threadbare apparel. For his own person he hath many changes of garments very rich, and several turbants, and hath brought with him either for presents or for a pledge in time of necessity, twenty-one pieces of cloth of gold and silver, valued at 1,000 marks. Our merchants allow him £4 a day. It is said that he will complain of the losses caused by the English pirates in the Mediterranean sea and also will seek an export of powder and arms for the Turk.

The Turk reporteth much talk at Constantinople and Marseilles of English pirates in the Levant Seas. Capt. Ward hath combined with the Turks at Algiers, where the French Ambassador requested Murat Rey to move Ward to be favourable to the French. 'I favourable to the French?' quoth he; 'I tell you if I should meet mine own father at sea, I would rob him, and sell him when I had done.' Then Mustapha asked him whether he would command him any service into England for the procuring of his pardon. He answered that he would never see England again but would be buried in the sea.

31st. On the 24th Verreyken came to the Hague with the agreation (or agreement) of the Spanish King to the truce, but because neither the form nor the words were agreeable to the States they would not accept it. It is sent back for further consideration and amendment. There are divers opinions about the truce. Many hold that it is not proposed *bona fide* by the King of Spain and the Archduke, for it seems incredible after such treasure and blood spent. Others say that without peace the Spaniard will be put to far greater expense for the great charges to hold the far distant islands whence he draws his treasure. Yet the wiser sort of the Netherlanders grow fearful lest the common people once they have tasted peace will not again be brought to arms, and so being overcome they will fall again under the Spanish subjection.

The King's Men have a play by George Wilkins entitled *The Miseries of Enforced Marriage*, of one John Scarborrow who is betrothed to a maid in Yorkshire, but being a ward is forced by his guardian to marry another. Hereupon the maid dies, and Scarborrow growing desperate lives dissolutely until at the death of his guardian he is reconciled with his wife and brethren.

2nd August. The French King by his Ambassador sent to the Prince a present of armour and arms, in return for which the Prince sent a letter written in his own hand in French. When he received it from our Ambassador, the French King immediately opened it and compared the writing of the name with the rest of the letter to judge whether it were all of one hand, which he seemed at first to doubt because of the neatness of the character, on which he soon satisfied himself. That King ever speaketh with great show of passionate affection towards the Prince accounting him as of his own son; for he is resolved to cultivate that young plant since it promises to produce fruits much more favourable to France than the stock from which it is raised.

5th. The King and the Court are still on progress and so the Turk who remains in the City cannot get his business done. It is now known that he has come about the pirates, to which the answer is that if the Turk cannot restrain his subjects nor can the King of England, especially as they are already outlawed for their acts. There is much indignation among the merchants that one English ship has been taken by the Venetian great galleys.

8th. The Turkey merchants have written to my L. of Salisbury reminding him of the great charge of this Turkish Chauss and of his retinue, and requesting that since there is a ship shortly to depart for Constantinople he may soon have his audience of the King. They say he is a man of very good sort and has been five times Ambassador to the Signory of Venice; and since he is the first that ever came from the Grand Signor they would have his entertainment made better for the more credit of his Majesty's Ambassadors on the other side.

12th. A Prince of Moldavia, by name Stephen Bogdan, came to the Court some days since. He is one of many who claim a right in that country, and it is thought that he is now come here because of the presence of the Chauss. The Chauss has not yet received his audience as the King, who knows the nature of the Turk, would receive him in a place where great pomp may be displayed.

14th. The Archbishop of Dublin this summer having caused a

46

visitation to be made of the dioceses under the Archbishop of Cashel finds many foul disorders, enough to induce the people in those parts to think that among the Protestants there is no religion. Many churches are in decay, among them the cathedral at Cashel; many livings have no curates, and the profits are received by the Archbishop or his sons or kinsmen. He himself receives the profits of twelve livings without order taken for the services of the church; other livings are leased out and the profits go to the Archbishop. Upon this the L. Deputy declares that the insufficiency and cold devotion of the clergy and want of education of youth is a very uncomfortable impediment, and a reason to despair of seeing any good effects in the matter of reformation. As for the complaints made against Sir Henry Brounker, the severity was rather verbal than actual, for though the fines imposed amounted to £7,000, not above four score pounds were levied, and though the gentleman porter or other officers demanded their fees (or more perhaps) yet they took little.

15th. In Rome the Cardinal Borghese has complained to the Venetians that the excommunicated theologians who supported the cause of the Republic in the late disputes frequent the house of Sir Henry Wotton in Venice, and there speak ill of the Pope and of the Apostolic Chair, and that Sir Henry is a cause of scandal in Venice. All this is denied by the Senate.

18th. Capt. Newport is come from the adventurers in Virginia, having left them in an island which is in the midst of a great river 120 miles into the land. They write much commendation of the air and soil, and the condition of it. Silver and gold have they none; and they cannot be at peace with the inhabitants. They have fortified themselves and built a small town which they call James-town. One Capt. Warnam, a special friend of Sir Walter Cope, was taken last week in a port in Kent, shipping himself for Spain, with intent (as is thought) to have betrayed his friends and showed the Spaniards a means to defeat the Virginian attempt. The Council hath voted a double supply to be sent thither with all diligence.

19th. The King and his Court are now at Salisbury, but few of the Council are with him, for most of the Lords have gone to their own country places, and nothing will be done till the King returns. There is much murmuring these days against progresses, which were first made that the needs of the subject might be known and satisfied, but now they are become a great burden insomuch that the King will have them short. When he returns, it is said that much care will be taken to raise money and to increase the numbers of the fleet.

The Grand Duke of Tuscany is now employing many English, shipwrights and others to build ships for him and to teach others. This is ill taken by our Turkey merchants, for it cannot but anger the Turk against our nation, and they would persuade the Chauss, if they could, to protest to the King.

20th. Those who have returned from Virginia say that they cannot yet be at peace with the inhabitants of the country. There hath been much discontent amongst them, and but for the patience and godly exhortations of M. Robert Hunt their preacher the whole business had been overthrown.

After leaving the Downs they watered at the Canaries and thence traded with the savages at Dominica. Going from the West Indies towards Virginia they were not a little discomforted when the mariners had passed three days their reckoning and found no land, so that Capt. Ratcliffe would have borne the helm to return to England but for an extreme storm, which made them hull at night and the next day drove them to land. Their first entry, in a bay called Chesupioc, they called Cape Henry; and here 30 of them were recreating themselves on shore when they were assaulted by 5 savages who hurt Capt. Archer and another very dangerously. That night the box was opened and the orders read in which Bartholemew Gosnold, John Smith, Edward Maria Wingfield, Christopher Newport, John Ratcliffe, John Martin and George Kendal were named to be the Council, and to choose a President among them for a year, who with the Council should govern; matters of moment to be examined by a jury but determined by the major part of the Council, in which the President had two voices.

Until 13th May they sought a place to plant in, and then the Council was sworn, and M. Wingfield chosen President, but Capt. Smith was not admitted of the Council, for since their landing at the Canaries, he had been restrained as a prisoner upon the scandalous suggestion of some of the chiefs that he intended to usurp the government, murder the Council and make himself King, and that his confederates were dispersed in the three ships and divers of them would affirm it.

Now falleth every man to work, the Council to contrive the Fort, the rest to cut down trees to make place to pitch their tents; some to provide clapboard to relade the ships, some to make gardens etc. The savages used at first often to visit kindly; and such was the President's overweening jealousy that he would admit no exercise at arms nor fortification except the boughs of trees cast together in the form of a half moon by the pains of Capt. Kendal. The new plantation is called Jamestown.

Newport, Smith and twenty others were sent to discover the head of the river. They passed by divers small inhabitations called Powhatan, consisting of 12 houses pleasantly seated on a hill; before it three fertile isles, and about it many cornfields. The Prince of this place is also called Powhatan, and his people Powhatans. To that place the river is navigable, but higher by reason of the rocks and islands there is not passage for a small boat; this they call the Falls. The people treated them kindly till they were within 20 miles of Jamestown on their return; and had not God blessed the discoverers otherwise than those at Jamestown there had been an end of the plantation; for at the Fort they found 17 men hurt and a boy slain by the savages; and had it not chanced that a crossbar shot from the ships struck down a bough from a tree among them that caused them to retire, our men had all been slain, for they were securely at their work and their arms still in dry fats. Hereupon the President was content that the Fort should be pallisadoed, the ordnance mounted, and his men armed and exercised; for many were the assaults and ambuscadoes of the savages, and our men often hurt by their disorderly straggling.

Six weeks being spent in this manner and the ships about to return to England, it was proposed to refer Capt. Smith to the Council in England to receive a check rather than by particulating his designs to make him odious to the world. But Capt. Smith so utterly scorned this charity and publicly defied his enemies that all the untruths alleged against him were clearly disproved; which begat such a general hatred against M. Wingfield, the President, that he was adjudged to give him £200; so all he had was seized upon, which Smith returned to the store for the general use of the Colony. Nevertheless, M. Hunt reconciled them and Capt. Smith was admitted of the Council; and the next day all received the Communion; and the day following the savages desired peace, and on 15th June Capt. Newport sailed for England, leaving behind a hundred, of whom, as well as the Council, there are 47 gentlemen, 4 carpenters, 12 labourers, sundry tradesmen, some boys and others.

25th. The L. Advocate of Scotland hath written to the King concerning the silver mine in the lands of Hilderstoun. His search began in June of last year upon discovery of spar powdered with lead, and in February last they found ore holding silver. Since then they have won 3,500 stone of ore of varying quality. The King's tenth hath been received by the Earl of Tullibardin by the King's gift. Of the rest, there is fined 16 or 17 stone of silver, which has rendered £12,000 Scots, and the work is very chargeable. As to the worth of the mine, Sir Bevis Bulmer, who is thought one of the most skilful mineral men of the Isle, bound himself to pay £4,000 rent as owner, and £1,500 more yearly to such others as he useth in the works, besides the King's tenth.

27th. Toby Mathew hath leave to go as often as he will to Sir Fr. Bacon with his keeper, and is put in good hope of further liberty. Nick Fuller hath been pitifully trounced by the High Commission and cannot yet get himself out of the briars. Many and most of our Puritan Parliament men are put out of the commission of the peace. Commissioners are going to enquire into enclosures and depopulations, most of them lawyers taken out of Kent, Surrey, Sussex and such places as are least interested in that business. They shall find out how many towns, villages, churches, hamlets, parishes, farms and the like have been wasted or stand depopulated since 20 Eliz. (1578), and by what means: and how many people were maintained thereon before the depopulation. Also what quantities of ground have been turned from the use of husbandry and tillage into pasture for sheep and other cattle by unlawful enclosure or otherwise. Also what highways have been stopped up or straitened. It was thought by the bells last week that the sickness would have again risen, but by the bills the number is lessened.

31st. These two months past the deaths from the plague have been more than ordinary, for in July there died of it in the City and the liberties 191; and this month of August the weekly returns are 77, 69, 76, and 71.

2nd September. The King has come to Windsor from his progress, and is expected to come to Whitehall in a few days. The Councillors who are to raise the subsidy are here already, but the needs of the Court will come before the increase of the navy. The Archpriest Blackwell has given much satisfaction to the King by taking the Oath of Supremacy, and advising others to do the like. By the King's command he is well treated in prison.

6th. There are many seditious sermons these days; and in one of them lately the preacher brought out this prophecy:

> Henry the 8 pulled down abbeys and cells,
> But Henry the 9 will pull down bishops and bells.

7th. The French King has sent the President Jeannin and others as his ambassadors to the States complaining that they have dealt very secretly with their enemy without his advice, and offering them further aid if they continue the war; or if they make peace that he may deliver his advice therein.

9th. The Court is still at Windsor and there remains because of the increase of the Plague. The Chauss has been given his audience, being received by the Court and the Council with much pomp. He presented letters from the Grand Signor, but made only one request: that provision should be made against the damage caused by the English in the waters of his master. He is to be given a private audience in a few days.

12th. By order of the Council, young Sir Thomas Shirley has been arrested and is now lodged in the Tower, upon which some surmise, that some plot against the State has been discovered; others say he has turned Turk, and some that the Chauss is the cause of it, because Sir Thomas was once arrested in Constantinople and of revenge has done an ill turn to the Chauss, declaring him to be an impostor and a spy. The Prince of Tangier, son to the Duke of Luxembourg, has come with a large train, but merely to see the country. The King is now at Theobalds, and the Queen at Hampton Court, very sad at the illness of the little Princess, whom the King loves so sincerely that it is thought he will give up his hunting to go to her.

15th. M. Hudson and his company are returned from their voyage to discover a passage by the North Pole to Japan and China. They went as far northward as 82° of latitude, and they have found a great inlet or bay at 78°. They endured much peril from ice and fog. M. Hudson reports that between 78° and 82° he can find no passage but that the land may be profitable to those that will adventure it; they found abundance of seals.

16th. Sir Oliver Lambert is come from Ireland in post. He brings word that Tyrone and O'Donnel with their wives and children are fled into Spain and that Macguire brought a ship from Dunkirk, whither they are all embarked and gone. It is thought they have practised by their Jesuits and seminaries with Spain, but unlikely that they will procure the King of Spain suddenly to declare himself in any open invasion, seeing that he is now occupied with this treaty.

The King in passing through London from Windsor touched at Whitehall to visit his new building, which he could scarce see by reason of certain pillars set before the windows, and he is nothing pleased with his L. Architect for that device. He was likewise with the Archbishop at Lambeth to hearten him in his conflict with Nick Fuller who had procured an inhibition from the Judges to the High Commission to proceed no further upon that course, but upon better advice they sent a retractation of their inhibition, and poor Nick is nicked as before. A French captain, one Fierebras, was taken last week by two who prosecuted him out of France. He hath long since in many places been hanged in effigy for notable murders and villainies, but now the original is like to follow the copy. Help was given by our officers in catching and conveying him. The Parliament in Scotland is ended; and in general they are no more fond of the Union than we here; yet they please the King better by their quick despatch.

17th. The little Lady Mary, the infant daughter of the King and the Queen, died yesterday morning at Stanwell, the L. Knyvet's house. She was aged 2 years and 5 months. She had a burning fever for 23 days and a continual rheum fell to her lungs and putrified there which she had not the strength to avoid. The news was brought by my L. of Worcester to the Queen who desired that he would go to Stanwell to see the Lady opened, for she was extremely desirous to know the cause of her death. She desired also that the King should be acquainted with her death which he takes as a wise Prince should do. She will be buried on the 21st but without any solemnity or funeral.

Sir Thomas Shirley is now said to have been committed to the Tower for overbusying himself in the traffic of Constantinople, to have brought it to Venice and the Florentine territories. The Turk had audience at Windsor; he had no business but the compliment. The term is like to be rejoined to *mensis Michaelis* if the sickness continue, which increases and is pitifully dispersed in and about the City.

21st. A certain English gentleman by name M. Richard Cave last month died at Venice. Thereupon Sir Henry Wotton and the other English gentlemen of the Religion conferred about his burial, for although the body might have been buried in one of the churches with the ordinary solemnities, yet they feared that it would be given out he had died in the Romish faith. Nor would they consent to have him buried in the cemetery at Padua where the Almains of all religions are buried with Popish rites. They concluded therefore they would carry the body to the port of Malamocco and there in the gulf they committed it to the sea, and thereafter met privately at Sir Henry's house at a sermon for the solemnization of his remembrance.

27th. My L. of Salisbury rebuketh Sir Charles Cornwallis the Ambassador in Spain because in his letters he neglects those things done on the sea coasts, such as what number of ships are in the Groin, Seville and Lisbon, nor hath he gained one natural Spaniard to reveal a secret for a reward, insomuch that his advertisements are either generalities or things rather to be accounted news than intelligences. As for his treating with the Spanish King in the matter of Tyrone, he shall make light of it, saying that without the King of Spain those Irish are poor worms upon Earth; and if the King of Spain should think it time to begin with Ireland, our King will show the Spaniards that he sends there as fair a way as they were taught before.

28th. It now appeareth that Tyrone, before his flight, came several times to the L. Deputy complaining of his journey into England (whither he had been summoned because the Deputy had referred his cause against Sir Donald O'Cahane to the King and the Privy Council) because between the shortness of the time and his present poverty he was not able to furnish himself as became him for such a journey. He took leave in a more sad and passionate manner than he used at other times, and thence went to Mellifont, Sir Garret Moore's house, where he wept abundantly when he took his leave, giving a solemn farewell to every child and servant in the house. From thence he went to Dundalk, where he rested two nights, and on the next travelled all night with his impediments (his wife and children). It is likewise reported that the Countess his wife, being exceeding weary, slipped down from her horse, and weeping said she could go no further. Whereupon the Earl drew his sword and swore a great oath that he would kill her in that place if she would not pass with him and put on a more cheerful countenance. Next day he came to Lough Foyle where the Governor invited him and his son to dinner, but such was their haste that they went over to Rathmullin where the Earl of Tyrconnell and his company met them. There Tyrconnell sent for the foster father of his brother's son, bidding him bring the child with him, but he being met by the way by the Baron of Dungannon and the child's father, they took the child violently from him, which terrified the foster father so that he escaped by the swiftness of his horse. Of this child they have a blind superstitious prophecy because he was born with six toes upon one foot; for they affirm a prophecy that when such a one, being of the sept of O'Donnel, shall be born, he shall drive all Englishmen out of Ireland.

Nevertheless in many ways this departure is providential to make

the King repair the error committed in making these men pro-
prietary Lords of so large a territory without regard of the free-
holders' rights or of the King's service. Wherefore the Deputy pro-
poundeth that the King shall take their countries into his possession,
divide the land amongst the inhabitants (to every man of note as
much as he can conveniently stock and manure), and bestow the rest
upon servitors and men of worth in Ireland, and withal bring in
colonies of civil people of England and Scotland with condition to
build castles and storehouses upon their lands; and further that the
forts shall be repaired and new forts built. Then will there be no
need to spend the revenues in the reducing and defence of that Realm
from time to time as has been customary for many hundred years
heretofore.

29th. The Council have written to Sir Arthur Chichester, the
L. Deputy, to seize the fugitive Earls' lands, taking their peaceable
inhabitants into his protection. A proclamation shall be published
to declare to the world the justice of the King's proceedings, for
he mercifully pardoned their former treasons and bestowed great
honours on them: they had no grievances, not even in that cloak for
all treasons, Religion. Tyrone, on being sent for to England, hath
declared his own conscience guilty of treasons which can be proved
upon their indictments. For the plantation which is to follow upon
attainder, the King approves the Deputy's project and is resolved to
make a mixture of the inhabitants, as well Irish as English and
Scottish; and in the plantation generally to observe two cautions: that
such as be planted shall not be needy but of reasonable sufficiency
to maintain their portions, and that none shall have a vast but only
a reasonable proportion. Before this plantation can be digested and
executed, much must be prepared by the Deputy so that the King
may be better informed of the lands to be divided.

30th. The plague is much increased this past month, the weekly
deaths being 105, 121, 124, 177. For this reason the Parliament which
was to have come together on 18th November is now prorogued till
10th February, lest if Term and Parliament meet together and draw a
double concourse of people, the sickness be dispersed into the Realm.

2nd October. Many persons who offended in the late seditious insurrections about enclosures have submitted themselves according
to the proclamation, whereof in the county of Northampton alone
there were 143 this past month, of whom 62 are labourers and 21
husbandmen.

7th. Robert Carr is now likely to win the King's affection and doth it wonderously in little time. The King leaneth on his arm, pinches his cheek, smooths his ruffled garments, and when he looketh at Carr directeth discourse to divers others. The young man doth study all art and device; he hath changed his tailors and tiremen many times, and all to please the King who wisheth for change every day. The King teacheth him Latin, and some wish another would teach him English too, for he is Scottish bred and hath much need of better language. The King doth much covet his presence, and all the Ladies too, for he is straight-limbed, well-favoured, strong-shouldered and smooth-faced, with some sort of cunning and show of modesty. The older courtiers labour to gain his favour, but in vain. Speedy honours are talked of for him.

10th. About the 10th of July Sir Anthony Shirley departed from Barcelona with all his crew, in the ship of Sir Edwin Rich called the *Violet* of London, who also carried them from Genoa to Naples where he landed about the end of July, and should have received 1,000 ducats for his passage, but Sir Anthony paid him with one of his Aleppo tricks with just nothing. It is said that he intends to get in Capt. Ward to serve him, for *similis simili gaudet.* At his coming to Naples, for his welcome within five days he had his gaskins in the night stolen out of his window, and in them a 'sedula' of the King for 7,000 ducats and a jewel of his own worth 4,000·ducats which left him *sin blanca.*

12th. The new Banqueting Hall in Whitehall, in place of the old rotten building pulled down last year, hath now been rebuilded, very strong and stately and larger than the former, with many fair lodgings.

Proclamation has again been made forbidding the building of houses in the City of London, and commanding that all the forefronts that shall be built to be made with the outer walls of brick or stone.

13th. Tyrone with his company is landed in France, whence he is resolved to pass through the Archduke's country, where his son is, towards Rome. He was shrewdly tossed at sea and met with contrary winds from Spain. When the French King heard he was in Spain, he spoke much of the discourtesy the King of Spain would offer if he should give them any favour, but now being wished to stay them in his own country till our King might be advertised, he changed his style and said that France was free.

14th. The Chauss has at last been received by the King in private audience, in company with the Prince of Moldavia. The Turk complained of the English pirates, and more especially that they took service with the Grand Duke, and begged that the King would take such order as would distinguish loyal subjects from others, to which the King replied that those complained of are outlaws, and he can do nothing except punish them if they are caught.

An English merchant who was at Tunis two months ago reports that Ward the pirate and all his followers to the number of 300 wish to return to England if they can first be pardoned, but knowing that he cannot hope for pardon unless he first satisfies the Venetians he offers to restore three of their ships which he now holds, together with the merchandise, worth 30,000 or 40,000 crowns. Ward is now making ready to do worse damage. The Turks support him for they make great profits from his takings.

14th. On 7th and 8th August the Jesuits at Lyons had a play of the Last Judgement that lasted two whole days. There were galleries built round about and at the four corners tents pitched as a tiring-place for the actors. There were many players but the spectators infinite. First, at the four corners, figuring the four winds, four trumpets sounded, when straightway the drums rattled like thunder, fireworks flew forth like lightning, hell did seem to open, at which many in the shape of fiends rose from below, some having whips in their hands, some snakes, some forks, all roaring. Then a cloud seemed to divide, and on the top were seen stars of gold, infinitely rich, on top of which sat a reverend Jesuit, Petronia de Silva, a Spaniard, Prefect of the Jesuits' College, presenting the Person of God, from whose mouth all things were determined. On his right hand sat another Jesuit of beautiful presence, representing God the Son. And on the left a beautiful fair nun, taken out of the nunnery of S. Clare, who represented the person of the Virgin Mary. All about them thronged angels in white crowned, and beneath their feet Prophets, Apostles and many figuring Martyrs.

After much music and many hymns of joy all was whist, and Time entered, who was called upon to turn back the rolls of his records and show the present world. This Act consisted of the destruction of cities, the ruin of kingdoms and the downfall of Princes, *videlicet*, Agathocles, Dionysius, Cressida, Tamburlane and Lais. The moral of all was that Time is uncertain, beauty but a strumpet, and strength but a reed.

The Act being ended, instead of music to prepare another, the devils roared. Then the Judge above demanded the Book of the Register of men's actions, and Time which was Chorus, declared that Death had ended his sovereignty. The four trumpeters summoned again to awake both the old and the new dead from their tedious sleep. Then were brought in by the hand of angels divers Popes, and Jesuits, such as have been put to death in England, as Parry, Campion, Summerfield, Ballard, Babington and Lopez, and that Friar James Clement that killed King Henry III, King of France. On the contrary part, on the left hand of the Judge, were the Turks with their father Mohamet and his janissaries, Prester John, the Emperor of Persia, and Protestant Princes, Queen Elizabeth, the Grave Maurice, and Lutherans, Hugonites, Calvinists and Protestants (from the word *protest*, meaning they profess much and do nothing).

Then were presented also in dumb show or in action, the Inquisition in the Low Countries, the slaughter of the Hollanders, the attempts against us in '88, and many more. At length the Judge arose to pronounce sentence against them, and to make his speech more terrible, fire was thrown out from under his seat. The effect of his speech was that for disobeying the authority of the Pope and his faithful servants and pastors, they were now to lose the joys of Heaven and to be thrown straightway into Hell. Whereon Lucifer and his whole synod of fiends took hold on them, and in turn led them away, among them Henry VIII, whom they named under Lucifer the first founder of the heretics, Edward VI and our late Queen and many others.

But the end of the play was marred by reason of a great storm, with great darkness and rain, which much pleased the Protestants, who saw in it a sign of God's anger.

15th. Some have given out that the Breve which the Pope wrote admonishing all English Catholics not to take the Oath of Allegiance was not written of his own accord but at the instigation of others, and therefore to be disregarded. He hath therefore sent a second Breve straightly declaring that his first apostolic letter concerning the prohibition of the Oath was not only written upon his own instruction but after long and weighty deliberation upon all things contained therein; and therefore all Catholics are bound fully to observe them, rejecting all interpretations persuading to the contrary.

16th. In the Court of Star Chamber one Louche a cook and Robert Holland a scrivener were charged with erecting new buildings contrary to the proclamation. Louche is fined £200, imprisoned, and his house to be plucked down, but Holland in respect of his mild and modest carriage is fined £100, imprisoned, and the forefront of his house to be new built with brick before Whitsuntide, or else plucked down. Sir Fr. Bacon, the King's Solicitor, informed against them. He said that we have need of a law against inmates in London and out-mates in the country, for depopulations have destroyed and decayed all other good towns, and servants for husbandry are now not to be found. It was also said that these cases are infinite. The Court appointed a commission two years ago and found three hundred faulty. In four large houses they found 8,000 inhabitants, and in the last great plague out of one of them 800 died of the pest.

20th. Of late L. Thomas Howard wrote to Sir John Harington who hath in mind to come to Court, advising him of certain things to be observed toward gaining the King's good affection. The King doth wondrously covet learned discourse. He doth admire good fashion in clothes; so let Sir John be well trimmed, with a new jerkin well bordered and not too short. Of late many gallants have failed in their suits for due observance of these matters, and eighteen servants were discharged and many more will be who are not to his liking in these matters. In his discourse, let him not dwell too long on any one subject and touch but lightly on religion. Let him not say of himself 'This is good or bad', but 'if it were your Majesty's good opinion, I myself should think so and so'. One thing is most weighty: the roan jennet whereon the King rideth every day must not be forgotten to be praised, and the good furniture above all, which lost a great man much notice of late. This nobleman came in suit of a place and saw the King mounting the roan, and delivered the petition which was heeded and read, but no answer was given him then nor the next day. The L. Treasurer being pressed to move the King's pleasure therein, the King replied in some wrath, 'Shall a King give heed to a dirty paper when a beggar noteth not his gilt stirrups?' For it fell out that the King had new furniture to his house that day. But above all, he should see Robert Carr before he goes to see the King, for Carr was with him a boy in Scotland and knoweth his taste and what pleaseth.

21st. The Lady Penelope Devereux, sister to the unfortunate Earl of Essex, is lately dead. She was married against her will to the L. Rich, whom she deserted to live with her former lover, the late Earl of Devonshire; and upon her first marriage being annulled, she married my L., to the great scandal of the King. In her young years Sir Philip Sidney wrote his *Astrophel and Stella* to her. She died a Catholic.

24th. Samuel Rowlands hath a book called *Democritus, or Doctor Merry-man his Medecines against Melancholy Humours*, being a collection of sundry short merry tales in verse.

27th. The Deputy complains that of late, and especially since the flight of the two Earls, priests and Jesuits daily flock into Ireland in greater numbers than ever before, so that they vaunt they have more priests than the King has soldiers. They land secretly in every port, a dozen of them together sometimes, and afterwards disperse themselves into every town and county. They have so gained the women that they are in a manner all recusants. Most of the mayors and principal officers refuse to take the Oath of Supremacy. In many places the people resort to Mass in greater multitudes, and if it chance that a priest known to be factious be apprehended both men and women will not stick to rescue him. These priests have so far withdrawn the people from all fear of the law and loyalty towards the King that such as are conformed and go to church are everywhere derided, scorned and oppressed by the multitude.

31st. Sir Francis Vere is married to the daughter of Sir Julius Caesar's wife, which bred some wonder at Court. The lady is aged 16. His friends pity at it, and others smile for she is not of the fairest.

The weekly deaths by plague grow less, for this month past there died 150, 113, 110, 82 and this past week 68.

1st November. On news that the Archpriest Blackwell had taken the Oath, the Cardinal Bellarmine hath addressed him a letter showing his disquiet at the fall of his constancy; nor, saith he, could that Oath be lawful because it was in some sort tempered and modified, for those kind of modifications are nothing else but sleights and subtleties of Satan that the Catholic Faith touching the Primacy of the See Apostolic might either secretly or openly be shot at, for which Faith so many worthy martyrs even in England itself have resisted even unto blood. For certain it is that in whatsoever words the Oath is conceived by the adversaries of the Faith it tends to this end that the authority of the Head of the Church in England may be transferred from the successor of S. Peter to the successor of King Henry VIII; for that which is pretended of the danger of the King's life, if the High Priest should have the same power in England which he hath in all other Christian countries, it is altogether idle, for it was never heard of from the Church's infancy until this day that ever any Pope did command that any Prince, though an heretic, though an ethnic, though a persecutor, should be murdered, or did approve of the fact when it was done by any other.

This Oath is so craftily composed that no man can detest treason against the King and make profession of his civil subjection but he must be constrained perfidiously to deny the Primacy of the Apostolic See. But the servants of Christ, and especially the chief Priests of the

Lord, ought to be so far from taking an unlawful Oath where they may endamage the Faith, that they ought to beware that they give not the least suspicion of dissimulation that they have taken it lest they seem to have left any example for prevarication to faithful people. The Archpriest should therefore take heart, and considering the weightiness of the cause not trust too much to his own judgement; and if peradventure his fall have proceeded not upon want of consideration but through human inferiority and fear of punishment and imprisonment, let him not prefer a temporal liberty to the liberty of the glory of the Sons of God, nor make the faces of his brethren ashamed, for upon him at this time are fixed the eyes of all the Church. Let him not so carry himself in this last act that he leave nothing but laments to his friends and joy to his enemies but rather display gloriously the banner of faith and make to rejoice the Church which he has made heavy, so shall he not only merit pardon at God's hands but a crown.

2nd. From Venice: Fr. Paul Sarpi was attacked by three murderers who wounded him in three places and one left a dagger sticking in his cheek bone; which has caused great anger in all, from Senator to gondolier. From Padua they fetched Aquapendente (the most excellent surgeon of the world). Though he was rendered senseless the Friar's wounds were not dangerous and he is now recovering.

3rd. There is a new book by Thomas Dekker in his customary vein called *The Dead Term, or Westminster's Complaint for long vacations and short terms*, in manner of a dialogue between the two Cities London and Westminster. Containeth also the complaint of Paul's steeple (which was fired by lightning in 1561 and still headless) of what is committed in her walks which echo with such knavish villainy; what whispering there is in Term times how by some sleight to cheat the poor country clients of a full purse; what plots are laid to furnish young gallants with ready money (which is shared afterwards at a tavern) thereby to disfurnish him of his patrimony; what buying up of oaths out of the hands of knights of the post, who for a few shillings daily sell their souls; what laying of heads together as it grows towards eleven of the clock where for that noon they may shift from Duke Humphrey and be furnished with a dinner at some meaner man's table; what damnable bargains of unmerciful brokery; what shuffling, shouldering, justling, jeering, biting of thumbs to beget quarrels, braving with feathers, bearding with mustachios, casting open of cloaks to publish new clothes, muffling in cloaks to hide broken elbows, such spitting, hawking, and humming, every man's lips making a noise, yet not a word to be understood. 'For at one time, in one and the same rank, yea, foot by foot, and elbow by elbow, shall you see walking the knight, the gull, the gallant, the upstart, the gentleman, the clown, the captain, the apple-squire, the lawyer, the usurer, the citizen, the bankrout, the scholar, the beggar, the doctor, the idiot, the ruffian, the cheater, the Puritan, the cut-throat, the high-man, the low-man, the true man and the thief; of all trades and professions some, of all countries some.'

It is to be noted that there be three judgement seats in the Great Hall at Westminster, *videlicet*, at the entry on the right hand the Common Pleas where civil matters are to be pleaded, specially such as touch lands or contracts; at the upper end of the Hall on the right hand (or South east corner) the King's Bench where pleas of the Crown have their hearing; and on the left hand (or South west corner) sitteth the Lord Chancellor accompanied with the Master of the Rolls and other men learned in the Law and called Masters of the Chancery.

The times of pleading in these Courts are four in the year, called Terms. The first is Hillary Term, which beginneth the 23rd of January (if it be not a Sunday) and endeth the 12th of February. The second is Easter Term and beginneth seventeen days after Easter and endeth four days after Ascension Day. The third Term beginneth six or seven days after Trinity Sunday and endeth Wednesday the fortnight after. The fourth is Michaelmas Term, which beginneth the 9th of October, if it be not a Sunday, and endeth the 28th of November.

5th. The Archbishop of Cashel has complained that divers in Ireland have plotted by indirect courses to bring him into question and hazard of his life for his good service to the State and his profession; but the Privy Council knowing how church livings are ordered generally in Ireland doubt whether (if he be as faulty as he is charged) it would be convenient to proceed so strictly against him, his old age considered and the many faults of the like kind so common in Ireland; for many ill-affected subjects would be glad that one of his place and profession should be deprived for such faults and frauds.

7th. My L. Danvers prepares to go to Munster with all speed and great care is taken for the safety of Ireland to prevent the conspiracies and invasion of Tyrone who yet stirs not. There has been an unkindness at Court between the two Welsh Earls, Worcester and Pembroke, grounded upon differences in Wales, but my L. of Salisbury takes an honourable care they shall content them both by maintaining good works. The Turk and the Prince of Moldavia are now going away.

10th. From Cambridge cometh a book called *The Interpreter*, made by Dr. John Cowell, the King's Professor of Law in the University. Herein is set forth the signification and true meaning of such words as are mentioned in the Law writers or Statutes of the Realm which require any explanation, exposition or interpretation. These words are set out in the order of the alphabet, each being defined, with the authorities therefor quoted and noted.

12th. Two days since M. Phineas Pett, who is now Master of the Company of Shipwrights, presented the model of the new great ship to the Lord Admiral, who well approved it and commanded it to be carried to Richmond where the Prince now lies. Moreover the L. Admiral (who greatly favours Pett) told the King, who this afternoon journeyed from Whitehall to Richmond only to see the model, accompanied but with the Prince, the Admiral and one or two attendants. The King was exceedingly delighted and spent some time questioning Pett, and demanding whether he would build the ship in all points like the model, for (said he) 'I will compare them together when she shall be finished'.

13th. Blackwell from his prison in Lambeth hath answered the letter of the Cardinal Bellarmine, justifying his taking the Oath and maintaining that the Supreme Pontiff hath no imperial or civil power unlimited and at his own will to depose our King, as Cardinal Allen and other writers not to be condemned have noted in their writings; nor is it denied that the Pope is the Supreme spiritual leader. When the Oath is propounded, it is understood of the magistrate to refer only to the ordinary power of the Pope. Nor if the Cardinal could conceive the ruin of Catholic families which follows upon refusal of the Oath would he think otherwise, for there will ensue not only dejection of mind but even the most lamentable extirpation of the whole Catholic faith. He seeks therefore that the Cardinal shall change his opinion of him, and that the voices of his adversaries shall be silent, for he is now an old man, cast into prison for his Catholic faith and in daily peril of his life.

15th. There is come forth a proclamation concerning the flight of the Earls of Tyrone and Tyrconnell, declaring that the only cause of their flight is the knowledge of their own guiltiness, and denying that any proceedings against them were intended for cause of religion, nor was there any question of their rights and possessions. Affirmeth that they had entered into a combination for stirring up sedition and rebellion, and directed divers instruments (priests and others) to make offer to foreign States and Princes; and this proclamation is set forth to discredit all untruths to the contrary.

17th. The second agreation from the Spanish King was brought to the Hague by Friar John Neyen who made a long speech of the sincerity and uprightness of the King of Spain: yet it caused general dissatisfaction because it omitted certain points and promises formerly made. Nevertheless it is agreed to submit the agreation to the several States whether the treaty shall proceed. A Low Country captain newly come over saith that the issue of the treaty is still uncertain; that the people of the country are much divided upon it, some very inclinable to it, some contrary, as their places of habitation are subject to offence by the enemy or otherwise; that the soldiers all do fear it. Declareth that the Hollanders are marvellously strong at sea, and by their ungrateful carriage to Englishmen and not acknowledging any favour done them by this nation, we are like to find them very hollow hearted friends.

The old Countess of Southampton is dead and hath left the best of all her stuff to her son, and the greatest part to her husband, Sir Thomas Heneage.

18th. The Chauss has left England at last, having been here four months. He parted in high displeasure and declared publicly that he would do all the damage he could, for he was disappointed of the gain he had expected, for he received no present neither from the Levant Company nor from the King. Shortly before he went, the late Ambassador at Constantinople, M. Henry Lello, arrived in London who advised the King that this Chauss is a person of no importance, and if presents were given him, others of his kind would be encouraged to come here. The merchants thought likewise, for they have already been at great charges to entertain him, and they have no hope that the King will repay them seeing that he grows so careful of his spendings. Moreover they send him back in a ship at their own charges.

19th. Some days since one Pemly, a minister in Kent, was sentenced by the Star Chamber because he set up on a post of an inn gate in a market town in Kent a libel against Bishops and the government of the Church. Today he was first degraded by the Archbishop of Canterbury and then put to his punishment. First he had 25 jerks, and then stood in the pillory and had papers, and one of his ears cut close from his head, and after he had 25 jerks more. He is also fined £2,000.

20th. In answer to that letter which my L. of Salisbury wrote to the

King's Ambassador in Spain, Sir Charles Cornwallis protesteth that he can rely for intelligence of sea matters only upon the English Consul at Lisbon who advertises him once a fortnight, but in other places there are no Englishmen of diligence and ability, only young factors. Nor can he by rewards obtain intelligences from Councillors of War or Secretaries. To the under-officers rewards are due by custom, but nothing is to be gained from them. Others, indeed, upon offers only, and those not directly but collaterally, took such offence that he was in peril to lose all good will.

25th. The States have proposed that before they come to treat with Spain our King shall enter into an alliance with them, and a like proposal is believed to have been made to the French King.

27th. In the Star Chamber was heard a cause between Thomas Edwards, a physician of Exeter, and Dr. Wootton and other physicians and apothecaries. Edwards and Dr. Wootton falling out and using bitter terms, Dr. Wootton writes a letter beginning 'Master Docturdo and Fartado', and more than two sides of vile matter, ribaldry and defamation, which he subscribes and sends to Edwards; and keeps a copy thereof, and likewise delivers copies to divers others who also publish it. This was greatly to the defaming of Edwards, who was brought up an apothecary and allowed a physician by the College of Physicians in London upon examination, and otherwise reputed a very honest and discreet man. The defendant, Dr. Wootton, pretended that Edwards had himself first published this libel. Moreover Wootton had gone around administering interrogatories to the principal men of the Country against the credit and reputation of the plaintiff. There were 80 of these interrogatories, on four yards of parchment which the Lord Chancellor measured.

The question was whether this was a libel or no; and it was resolved by the Judges and all the Court that it was a libel; for if a man write a private letter defamatory and not otherwise publish it either before or after the writing, he shall not have an action. But forasmuch as the publishing doth provoke malice, and breach of the peace, and revenge, it shall be punished severely in the Court. The L. Coke therefore began a very sharp sentence, and the greatest number agreed. He would spare Wootton corporal punishment because of his degree, but he fined him £500, and the other defendants £40 a piece, and £200 damages to Edwards. Then L. Coke spake very sharply of the sin of libel. Further it was decreed that the Doctor at a public market at the next general assizes at Exeter shall be set up in some eminent place, and wear about his neck for a tippet the four yards of interrogatories, and confess his faults, and then the interrogatories should be returned to the Court to be defaced and cancelled. Moreover he shall be imprisoned and bound to his good behaviour.

28th. Tyrone and the rest of his company are not fled to Spain as was thought but landed in France. Thereupon our Ambassador presented himself to the King to demand that they might be stayed till his Majesty might be advertised of it and his further pleasure known therein. To this the French King replied that France was an open country for passengers, and besides it appeared for anything he knew that they were retired out of this country for matters of religion and private discontent. Thereupon they are gone into the Archduke's country without coming to Paris or speaking to the French King. When Sir Thomas Edmondes likewise insisted upon their staying he received the like answer. Moreover they were carried to the Archduke's presence and have been publicly feasted at Bruxelles by the Marquis Spinda and are now placed at Louvain. Thence it is said, leaving their wives at Louvain, Tyrone with Tyrconnell and M. Guyre are to take their journey to Rome, and so to Spain.

29th. Of late in Venice there was a practice of a priest discovered to blow up by a train of powder Pietro Paulo, his books and him; but it was discovered by a stranger passing by who espied a light in a vault in the night time.

The King went to Newmarket about two weeks since and it is thought will follow his sport there till it be near Christmas. He is indifferent well pleased with the hunting. He is not so earnest as he was to go his hunting and hawking in all weathers, and is more apt to take hold of an excuse to play at maw all day. There are many gentlemen at Court, but all of them cannot satisfy the King why a white gerfalcon of his lately flew away and cannot be heard of again.

30th. The plague deaths this past month are but 21, and in the months previously 66, 55 and 46.

1st December. My L. of Salisbury greatly complaineth that his son, the L. Cranborne, is so backward in his progress under his tutor at the University that he cannot speak six words in Latin; in any part of story without book he is not able to show memory of four lines, neither is his manner of repeating anything like to those whom tutors teach to speak distinct and ornate; for his logic, a month would beget more knowledge than he hath in one of no greater capacity; nor doth he show any capacity in the mathematics, language, music or any other gentlemanlike quality; nor is he able to write a fair hand.

6th. The King hath granted £600 in yearly rent to the new favourite, Robert Carr.

9th. The King remains at Royston for the hunting, but he is said to be living in retirement with a Dean who is very learned. A book by Parsons the Jesuit has recently appeared, urging the freedom of the Catholic religion in England, and the King out of a certain rivalry in learning to Parsons is preparing an answer. The Queen and her Ladies at his request are preparing a new Masque.

10th. Certain sums of money have been given for the better maintenance of sermons at Paul's Cross for gratuities for unbeneficed preachers. The L. Mayor and the Court of Aldermen have further provided that as well as the gratuity everyone that preaches at the Cross shall be freely entertained for five days from Thursday before the day of preaching until Tuesday morning following, with sweet and convenient lodgings, fire, candle and all other necessaries.

24th. This evening at Whitehall the King knighted Robert Carr who was lately sworn Gentleman of the Bedchamber. It is said by those who dislike the new favourite that the King has no other reason for his choice but handsomeness, and that this love is so amorously conveyed as if he had mistaken his sex; for the King's kissing him after so lascivious a mode in public and upon the theatre of the world prompts many to imagine things done in the tiring-house which posterity will call by some other name than love. Sir Henry Rich, who might also have won the King's favour by reason of his face and complexion, lost his opportunity by turning aside and spitting after the King had slabbered on his mouth.

28th. This winter there is a great frost, which began on the 8th of the month and continued for 7 days, but thereafter thawed gently for 5: but these 4 days past it has again been very cold so that many persons now walk half way across the Thames upon the ice.

31st. Sir Thomas Bodley is as ever busied with the procuring of books for his library in Oxford. Each week he sends down books by barge in pipes and hogsheads, and these he would have very exactly entered in the Catalogue. He now urges Dr. James the Librarian to get the help of a Jew that is in Oxford for the Hebrew Catalogue.

OTHER BOOKS AND PLAYS PRINTED 1607

i. In 1604 and in 1605 M. Thomas Bell set forth two books, the one called *The Downfall of Popery* to which Father Parsons wrote an answer called *The Forerunner of Bell's Downfall;* to which M. Bell wrote another book called *The Pope's Funeral* challenging an answer, full of scurrility against the teachings of the Church of Rome and the Jesuits. From Rouen is now come forth an *Answer* from 'B.C. Student in Divinity' (who is held to be Parsons) at great length retorting upon Bell point by point, wherein, saith the author, 'his manifest untruths, gross corruptions, cunning sleights, vain cavils, immodest railing, insolent challenging and idle excursions are noted, examined and refuted'.

ii. *The Optic Glass of Humours,* discovering such matters as self knowledge; the sympathy of the soul with the body; diet and surfeit; the temperaments and diversity of wits according to the divers temperatures of the body; of the spirits; the four humours; of dreams which accompany each complexion. Noteth many strange examples of the melancholic humour, as of one that thought himself dead and would not eat until cured after a strange manner. His friends furnished a table with variety of dishes and caused three or four in white sheets to sit down and eat in his presence; who demanded what they were. They answered that they were ghosts. 'Nay then,' replied he, 'if spirits eat, then I think I may eat too'; and so fell roundly to his victuals.

iii. A poem by Henry Raymond entitled *The Britain Shepherd's Tears for the Death of Astrabonica,* written in penential verse in 21 cantos; also *The World's Vanity,* a poem on the brevity and uncertainties of this mortal life.

iv. There have been many plays entered for the printing this past year, some old but for the most part new, far more than ordinary. Of the King's Men: *The Miseries of Enforced Marriage, The Revenger's Tragedy, The Devil's Charter* (by Barnaby Barnes), *The Merry Devil of Edmonton, The Tragedy of King Lear* (that was played before the King on S. Stephen's day last year), *Volpone.* Of the Paul's Boys: *The Phoenix, Michaelmas Term, The Woman Hater, Bussy D'ambois, The Puritan, Northward Ho!, What You Will, A Trick to Catch the Old One.* Of other Companies: *The Whore of Babylon, Cupid's Whirligig, The Travels of the Three English Brothers, The Family of Love, The Woman Killed with Kindness.*

1608

4th January. M. Nicholas Fuller pleading for two clients in the Court of High Commission declared that the Court had no power to imprison, to put to death or to fine any subject, for which he was forthwith committed to the Fleet and fined £200. He paid his fine but the submission tendered him was such that he would not at first digest it; then having subscribed it and sent it to the Archbishop, he afterward sought to recall it. His Puritan brethren have also done him an ill turn for they printed his argument to his great prejudice, but at length by the persuasion of his friends he said that he would stand to his submission. Now he is released, having made submission *modo et forma*, and went home as quickly as he could over the ice.

5th. All the holydays there were plays at Court, four by the King's Men and three by the Prince's but with so little concourse of strangers that they wanted company. The King was very earnest to have a play on Christmas night but the Lords told him it was not the fashion, which answer pleased him not a whit, and said he, 'What tell you me of the fashion? I will make it a fashion.' Yesterday he dined in the Presence in great pomp, with two rich cupboards of plate, the one of gold, the other that of the House of Burgundy pawned to Queen Elizabeth by the States of Brabant, exceeding massy, fair and sumptuous. The reason for this extraordinary bravery is said to have been that he would show himself in glory to certain Scots that were never at Court before.

7th. On Twelfth Eve there was great golden play at Court, no gamester admitted that brought not £300 at least. My L. of Montgomery played the King's money and won him £750, which he had for his labour. The L. Mounteagle lost the Queen £400, and so of the rest, only the King and Sir Francis Wolley who got about £800. The Queen's new Masque which was to have been put on last night is postponed till Sunday, by reason of the quarrels of the Ambassadors; for the French Ambassador learning that the King intended to invite the Spanish Ambassador complained hotly that since the matter of precedence is still undecided, the honour of his Master would be impeached. In this great cold London is almost like a besieged city. The posts are so greatly delayed that there is no news from overseas, neither from the Low Countries nor from Ireland. Yesterday the Archbishop came from Lambeth over the ice to the Court.

From the Tower my L. of Northumberland continueth to petition for his release to the King by means of the Countess his wife; to whom the King said he would take his time, but let him first prove that Thomas Percy had given him no warning of the intended crime. To this my L. replies that his Majesty who is so great a scholar and so judicious cannot but know how impossible it is to prove a negative.

11th. There is a proclamation proroguing the Parliament for divers causes till 27th October next.

14th. The Queen's *Masque of Beauty*, which Ben Jonson devised, was presented this night at Whitehall as an answer to that Masque of 4 years since; for as that was a *Masque of Blackness*, so this is of Beauty, with 16 masquers of whom the chief are the Queen, the Lady Arbella, and the Countesses of Arundel, Derby, Bedford and Montgomery. The principal scene is a Throne of Beauty, divided into eight squares in each of which are set the masquers in couples, and the ascent to the throne consisting of six steps is covered by a multitude of Cupids, chosen out of the best and most ingenious youth of the Kingdom, noble and others. The colours of the masquers varied, one half in orange-tawny and silver, and the other in sea-green and silver, with bodices and short skirts in white and gold. The Masque was very greatly admired and applauded for the cunning of the machines, the abundance and beauty of the lights and the well ordering of all, but what caused most wonder and was beyond all expectation was the wealth of pearls and jewels that adorned the Queen and her Ladies, especially the Lady Arbella who exceeded her. At the end the King said that he intended by this Masque to consecrate the birth of the new Great Hall, which his predecessors had left him built merely in wood but he had converted into stone.

15th. The great frost still holds, and these last days many have set up booths and standing of sundry things to sell upon the ice, and some shoot at pricks and play at bowls. Many fantastical experiments are put in practice, as certain youths burnt a gallon of sack upon the ice and made all passengers partakers; but the best is of an honest woman (they say) that had a great longing to have her husband get her with child upon the ice. Amongst other things are two barbers' shops, in the fashion of booths with signs and other properties of the trade, to which many resort and are there trimmed so that another day they may report they lost their hair between Bankside and London.

17th. There is a great lottery being held in the City, the prizes all of plate as gilt spoons, cups, bowls, ewers and the like, for which many venture their skill if haply they may draw out a prize of £40, £50 or even £100. For every prize there are put in some forty blanks; there are 7,600 prizes and 42,000 blanks. Multitudes crowd about the doors, and the room is continually filled with people, every mouth bawling for lots, and every hand thrust out to snatch them. The lots are in papers, rolled up like wafers. One crafty knave, taking up on him to play the good shepherd, gathered money from several men and women, and so crowding through the press, he comes back and delivers so many blanks as he hath received shillings, but these blanks are not of the lottery but cunningly made up by himself.

19th. On the 9th a day of prayer and fasting was held throughout the United Provinces for the peace or long truce which is about to be negotiated.

20th. Sir Henry Wotton hath sent the King a portrait of Padre Paulo Sarpi by the hands of Capt. Pinner, saying that it may give some pleasure to his Majesty to behold a sound Protestant in the habit of a friar. This is the second portrait, for the former was taken by the officers of the Inquisition at Milan and there stayed.

21st. Tyrone begins to find himself cheated of his hopes and is trying to obtain pardon. He has not only written to the King, attempting to justify his flight, but he has also approached the English Ambassador in the Low Countries. The King of Spain has not yet granted him access to Spain, and the Archduke has fixed the time of his departure. Nothing remains for him but the Pope who, it is said, shows little wish to receive him in Rome lest greater trouble be caused in Ireland, and also because he would be spared the expense of keeping him.

22nd. There is much hope and joy conceived of the great mine in Scotland, for the Commissioners advertise the greatness of it; and for the goodness, upon an assay made this day, 100 ozs. of ore makes 60 ozs. of pure silver. The Commissioners have laden in Scotland a bark wherein 12 tons of this ore is embarked and comes for London. If this proves true, the King's empty coffers will be filled and his great debts paid.

26th. The frost continues in very strange manner, and the Thames so hardly frozen that it is made a beaten highway to all places of the City, but the bridges are in great danger upon a thaw. A great part of Kingston Bridge is down, and all the merchants that dwell upon London Bridge have removed their goods of value, fearing they know not what. The Council have written to the L. Mayor requesting that some relief may be given from the City to the poor watermen for they cannot labour in this extreme weather. The King has given £200 to be distributed among them.

The Ambassadors of the Archduke are now come to the Hague, conducted there by 500 horse of the States. Spinola arrived in a most royal fashion, having 20 companions of good sort, and 40 in a livery; hath brought with him great store of plate and rich hangings, and many jewels of all prices to bestow as he thinks good. It is verily believed that a peace will be concluded for the Spaniard denies no propositions or demands of the States. Tyrone is still at Louvain, nothing well pleased with his reception which at first was good but now careless.

The King has newly gone to Theobalds for six days. The Spanish Ambassador hath invited the 15 Ladies that were of the Queen's Masque to dinner, and they to bring with them whom they please without limitation. The great Masque intended for my L. Haddington's marriage is now the only thing thought upon at Court. There are to be 5 English and 7 Scots, and it will cost them each £300. The Lords of the Council have sat every day for this week past to borrow money of the citizens of London who appear before them. The sum desired is £100,000. The citizens are greatly troubled with it, and the best protest they have no money, but are willing to give their bonds, some for £4,000 and some for £2,000.

28th. The fugitive Irish Earls and their adherents have been indicted in two counties in Ireland and a true bill found against them by a jury of 23 gentlemen of best quality, whereof 13 were of the Irish nation. The bill was read publicly both in English and in Irish, and the evidence delivered. The jury were readily persuaded to find the bill against both Earls. But because the rest of their followers named in the bill were charged with the treason in as high a degree as the Earls themselves, 16 jurors conceived a doubt because it was very probable that many of them knew not of the Earls' practices; and some were reported to have left the Kindom unwillingly. To satisfy them on this point they were told that an indictment was but an accusation and no conviction; and that such as adhered to a known traitor might justly be accused to be partakers of his treasons. They made another scruple, that the indictment charged the Earls that they imagined the destruction of the King's person, whereas no part of the evidence proved so much. To this it was answered that if the Earls practised to deprive the King of his Crown (which every rebel endeavours to do), it follows as a necessary condition that they imagined the death of the King; for he that would take the King's crown from his head, would likewise (if he could) take his head from his shoulders; and he that would not suffer the King to reign, if it lay in his power, would not suffer him to live. Being satisfied on these points, the jurors within an hour found the bill true, and returned it subscribed with their names.

2nd February. The great frost which has continued very violent from the 24th December began to thaw 3 days ago. Yesterday the ice began to break little by little, and today all the great rocks and overspreading ice are quite dissolved or sunk. In all, this frost has endured for the space of 7 weeks, off and on, yet the ice was not so delicate and smooth as was the great frost of 1564 by reason that the frost then held firm from the beginning unto the ending.

7th. (Sunday.) This afternoon Sir Toby Mathew was called before the Council Table and after sundry schooling by the Earl of Salisbury (who told him he was not privy to his imprisoning which he did no ways approve as foreseeing so light a punishment would make him rather more proud and perverse), in conclusion they allotted him 6 weeks' space to set his affairs in order and depart the Realm, and in the meantime willed him make choice of some friend of good account and well affected where he may remain, but not to go abroad till he depart out of the Realm.

The second ship is now returned from Virginia with no more news than the first, other than the extremity of the weather; but their health is exceedingly good, though their clothes are but thin and their diet poor. But they are full of idle proceedings and divide themselves into factions, each disgracing the other, even to the savages.

9th. From the press of Robert Barker, the King's Printer, comes forth a book printed *Auctoritate Regia* and entitled *Triplici nodo, triplex cuneus, or An Apology for the Oath of Allegiance*, with no name of the author but generally known to have been written by the King himself, invectively countering the two Breves of Pope Paul V and the late letter of Cardinal Bellarmine to Blackwell the Archpriest. Herein it is declared that the Oath of Allegiance was framed so that a separation might be made between good subjects (who although they were otherwise popishly affected yet retained in their hearts the print of their natural duty to their Sovereign) and those like the late Powder-Traitors who thought diversity of religion a safe pretext for all kinds of treasons. The Oath was taken by many, as well priests as others. But this sending out of a Brief by the Pope forbidding all of his persuasion to take the Oath sows new seeds of jealousy between the King and his subjects by stirring them up to disobey the lawful command of their Sovereign and giving him just ground to punish them, so that they are in this strait: either the loss of their lives and goods by renouncing their natural Sovereign, or the condemnation of their souls by renouncing the Catholic Faith.

Thereupon giveth in full the Pope's Brief wherein he praises those who cheerfully undergo all kinds of cruel torments rather than offend the Majesty of God, shining no less in their martyrs than in the first beginning of Christianity. To which the King maketh answer that the late Queen never punished any papist for religion but that the punishment was for their own misbehaviour. For himself, the King declareth that he has shown many favours to Papists, and that none were or are put to death since he came to the crown for cause of conscience, except that now this discharge given by the Pope to all Catholics from taking the Oath of Allegiance be the cause of the punishment of many; which, if it fall out so, let the blood light on the Pope's head.

As for the second Brief, he calleth it 'the craft of the Devil', for now that many Catholics, and the Archpriest himself, have taken the Oath, they must renounce and forswear their born and sworn allegiance to their natural Sovereign.

As for that letter of Cardinal Bellarmine to Blackwell, declareth that those who refuse the Oath must of necessity hold that King James is not the lawful King of England; that the Pope may depose him, give authority to some foreign Prince to invade his dominions, discharge his subjects of their allegiance, give them leave to offer violence to his person or government or subjects; that the Oath is not lawful and may be taken with equivocation and mental reservations. Quoteth authorities of Councils of the Church, and inveigheth merrily against the Cardinal for seeming to rejoice at the supposed martyrdom of his old friend Blackwell. But, saith the King, as for the Catholic Faith, there can be no word found in the Oath tending to the matter of Religion. As for the Cardinal's saying that the Popes have never meddled against Kings, noteth many examples to the contrary, as of our Henry II after the slaughter of Thomas Becket, who besides his going barefooted in pilgrimage was whipped up and down in the chapter house like a schoolboy and glad to escape so.

Further argueth that the Pope is no Universal Bishop, and that Kings are warranted both by the Old Testament and the New within their own Kingdoms to govern their Churches as well as the rest of their people. Concluding that he has nothing to answer Bellarmine's

73

letter, save by way of regret 'that so many good sentences taken out of the Scripture, so well and so handsomely packed up together, should be so ill and naturally applied.

'But an evil cause is never the better for so good a cloak; and an ill matter never amended by good words. And therefore I may justly turn over the craft of the Devil upon himself, in using so holy-like an exhortation to so evil a purpose. Only I could have wished him, that he had a little better observed his decorum herein, in not letting slip two or three profane words amongst so many godly mortified Scripture sentences. For in all the Scripture, especially in the New Testament, I never read of *Pontifex Maximus*. And the Pope must be content in that style according to the law and institution of Numa Pompilius, and not S. Peter, who never heard nor dreamed of such an office.

'As for his *Caput Fidei*, which I remembered before, the Apostles (I am sure) never gave that style to any but to Christ: so as these styles, whereof some are never found in Scripture, and some were never applied but to Christ in that sense as he applieth it, had been better to have been left out of so holy and mortified a letter.'

Concludeth by asking all not to judge the speciousness of the words but the weight of the matter, and specially all good subjects that they may not be seduced from their natural duty.

The King hath sent copies of his book to the French and the Venetian Ambassadors by the hands of my L. of Salisbury's Secretary, who said that the book was a defence of the freedom and sovereignty of Princes in matters temporal, and does not touch upon the question of religion or of ecclesiastical jurisdiction. For certain private reasons his Majesty will not have his name appear as author.

10th. Yesterday the L. John Ramsay, Viscount Haddington, was married at Court to the Lady Elizabeth, daughter of the Earl of Sussex; and at night there is a masque by Ben Jonson called *The Hue and Cry after Cupid*. All, but especially the motions, were well performed, as Venus with her chariot drawn by swans coming in a cloud to seek her son, who with his companions Lusus, Risus and Jocus, and four or five wags more, were dancing a *matachina* and acted it very antiquely, before the Twelve Signs (who were the master-maskers) descended from the zodiac, and played their parts more gravely, being very gracefully attired. The maskers were 12, 5 English, the Earls of Arundel, Pembroke and Montgomery, L. Walden and Sir Robert Rich; and 7 Scots, the Duke of Lenox, the Ll. D'Aubigny, Hay and Sanquhar, Sir John Kenneth and M. Harry Erskine. The bride dined in state accompanied by the

Prince, the young Duke, the Lady Elizabeth, the Countess of Oxford, the Dukes of Saxony and other States to furnish the table. In the midst of the dinner the King drank a carouse in a cup of gold, which he sent to the bride, together with a basin and ewer, two livery pots and three standing cups, all very fair and massy, of silver and gilt, and withal a patent for a pension of £600 a year out of the Exchequer to the longer liver of them, with this message that he wished them as much joy and comfort all their life as he received that day the bridegroom delivered him from the danger of Gowry. Many other great presents of plate are sent from all sides, but Dunbar's went beyond all, being valued between £400 and £500.

11th. The treaty of peace goes on apace in the Low Countries. Spinola at their first meeting made a long speech in commendation of peace and touching the discommodities of war, persuading them to accept this fair offer of the King of Spain who had descended to treat with them as free States. But for all his fair words the States stood firm to have the point of sovereignty cleared before they would proceed any further; which was condescended to at the next session, and that in so free and ample manner as that neither the King of Spain nor the Archduke shall not so much as bear the arms of these Provinces. The next article is about trading into the East Indies (whence there is late news that the Hollanders have taken Malacca, a place of great importance), and this point it is thought will not soon be ended. But the hardest of all will be the free exercise of the popish religion in the United Provinces, which it is said will be resolutely stood upon by both sides. The negotiators sit at a board by themselves and the Ambassadors and Commissioners of France, England, Denmark, and other Princes sit looking on and as it were giving aim at another table. Many libels run up and down, and they talk of divers prodigies, as of a bell that rings two hours together when no one is near, and the bars of windows continually hammered as it were a smith's forge.

13th. One Sturtevant hath perfected a device to carry water in earthen pipes burnt, which are cheap, strong and convenient. The Romans and Grecians used such pots which have also been known in England, but the trouble in making them and fit joining hath been the occasion that we only carry water in lead, for hitherto 40 yards can scarcely be made by hand in a day. By this invention Sturtevant can cast 700 or 800 yards in a day, as just and even as a printer printeth his letters, which will be a great commodity. The King's Controller of Works is instant to have them put in use, for more water may be brought for 16*d.* in these pipes than in a pipe of lead worth a mark a yard.

14th. M. Julius Caesar, Sir Julius Caesar's son, a young man of 18 years, has been slain at Padua where he was a student. He used to frequent the fencing school of Bartholomeo Tagliaferro. Here he engaged in a bout with a pupil of the school, one Antonio Brochetta, and overcame him. Brochetta then challenged him again, but contrary to usage attacked most vehemently and wounded M. Caesar in the left hand, who then threw his dagger at Brochetta, but missed him. On hearing Caesar's complaints, the master of the school came out and told him never to come to his school again. So he went away and found an English doctor, who with much ado staunched the blood. Next morning Caesar comes early to the University, armed with sword and pistol, when he encounters Brochetta coming out of Tagliaferro's house with sword and buckler. Caesar shot at him with his pistol but missed; but as he was trying to draw his sword he fell. Whereupon Brochetta was upon him and thrust him through. Caesar rose, walked two paces, and fell dead. Others say that the pistol was discharged by accident from beneath his cloak which is pierced and burnt. The English students in Padua sent in great indignation to Venice to Sir Henry Wotton, the King's Ambassador, demanding the arrest of Brochetta, and complaining that although by order of the Podesta M. Caesar was given a public funeral in the church of S. Catherine, yet afterwards the body was taken up again and buried elsewhere because the clergy would not allow the body of a Protestant to remain in holy ground. On hearing the news the Venetian Ambassador here went to Sir Julius to condole with him on the death of his son; to whom Sir Julius acknowledged the exceeding rashness of the young man, for which reason he had sent him out of England to Padua where he hoped he would have acquired learning and good manners.

15th. Thomas Heywood has translated Sallust's *Histories* of the Conspiracy of Catiline and the war of Jugurtha against the government of the Senate of Rome, which are being printed by John Jaggard, with a long preface of the choice of history.

In London there is an apron worn by a young girl which when moved or rubbed ever so little casteth out flames; which is taken for a miracle, even (some say) by the Earl of Salisbury.

16th. After many ceremonies passed, the Deputies for both sides met for the first time in the Hague on the 6th. The Deputies for the Archduke and the King of Spain are Don Ambrosio Spinola,

General of the King's Army; Richardot, President of the Archduke's Privy Council; Sir John Mancicidor, the King's Secretary of War; Friar John Neyen, General of the Order of S. Francis in the Netherlands; and Sir Louis Verreyken, Principal Secretary to the Archduke. The Deputies for the States are William, Count of Nassau, and Walgrave, Baron of Brederode; and one for every of the seven Provinces, with Sir John Olden van Barneveldt for Zealand.

The Archbishop of York lately wrote to my L. of Salisbury that his son (for son he must call him though he might wish that he had never been born) might remain a prisoner rather than an exile, for never has any lay popish recusant abandoned the Realm, especially when not a persuader of others. For his parents' sake, his father being such as he is, he sought a little connivance, for if he should be cast out, there is no hope he may be reclaimed. To which my L. replied that he cannot help the Archbishop, for the King of his pleasure to the father hath granted the young man leave to travel instead of undergoing the penalty of *praemunire*; and he would leave it to God's Providence what may work in him when he shall see other parts of the world with some contentment rather than suffer him to be enclosed within stone walls where he will see no more of his native country than is contained in a prison.

17th. The old Countess of Shrewsbury, whom they call Bess of Hardwick, is dead at last on the 13th in her 90th year at Hardwick, greatly flattered, seldom deceived, and without a friend. She married four husbands and outlived them all; the first at the age of 14, and the last George Talbot, 6th Earl of Shrewsbury, and from each of them she was abundantly enriched. She was a woman of a masculine understanding, proud, furious and unfeeling, a builder, a buyer and a seller of estates, a money lender, a farmer, and a merchant of lead, coals and timber. The Lady Arbella is her granddaughter, being the daughter of her daughter Elizabeth Cavendish (a child of her second marriage) whom she married to the son of the Countess of Lenox. She was for ever building, 'tis said because of prophecy that she would die if she ceased from building; which happened in this late great frost. She is to be buried beneath a great monument which she built for herself.

23rd. Sir Charles Cornwallis, the Ambassador in Spain, complains that Fr. Cresswell receives communications from the Spanish Ambassador in London, by every despatch a packet, whereafter are whispered detractions of the King and his Government.

26th. The meetings of the Deputies continued for 10 days but now they are at a stand, the Netherlands as hotly insisting on their right of trade to the Indies as the Archduke's party would deny it.

27th. At the hearing of an English cause before the Council of War in Madrid a letter of his Majesty's was read wherein was specified his title of 'Defender of the Faith', at which the Spanish King's Fiscal of the Court rose and in extreme choler said that the Lords were all excommunicate for hearing so patiently so great an abomination, and that for his part he would rather give over his place than suffer his ears to hear that which was so derogatory to the honour of the Church of Rome. The Lords took him at his word and he hath lost his place and is sent to his country house.

28th. Toby Mathew is allowed 14 days' longer respite before he depart the Realm.

7th March. The Children at Blackfriars have a play about the late Marshal Biron which is very offensively taken by M. de la Boderie, the French Ambassador, for not only doth it present all the French Court but also the Queen uttering harsh words to Madame de Verneuil (the French King's Mistress) and giving her a buffet. Upon the Ambassador's complaint the play is stayed.

10th. Today was laid the first stone for the rebuilding of Aldgate at the charges of the City. Last year when the old ruinate gate was taken down there were found in the walls certain Roman coins, the forms and superscriptions whereof are to be carved and set over the conduit by the gate, viz., Clodius Alpinus, Vespasianus, Domitianus, Carusius, Valentianus and Trajanus.

11th. Notwithstanding the command to stay that play of Biron, the Children, now that the Court is removed, have again played it. Hereupon M. de la Boderie went to my L. of Salisbury complaining not only that the play has again been presented but that they added thereto matters of great moment which had nothing to do with Marshal Biron but were also plainly false. My Lord was much moved thereat and sent straightway to have the offenders taken; they found but three who are in prison, but the author of the play is fled away. One or two days before this, they made havoc of the King, the Scottish mine, and all the favourites in strange manner, for after showing the King curse heaven at the flight of a hawk and beating a gentleman for injuring his hounds, they played him drunk every day for a month. The King is so greatly enraged that he vows they shall never play more but shall first beg their bread, and he will have his vow performed. And to this end either the Lord Chamberlain or the Council shall take order to dissolve them and to punish the maker besides.

12th. Bogdan the Moldavian came to Venice and in the absence of the Ambassador took possession of his house. When Sir Henry Wotton returned, Bogdan declared that he went to recover his right under the protection of the Crown of Great Britain, and that he had letters from the King to the Ambassador at Constantinople. Sir Henry, at first uncertain whether this was a frenzy or cozenage, replied that it was not his fashion to believe men upon so small acquaintance, and if Bogdan could not show such order from the King, he must provide him with another host; whereat Bogdan asked wonderingly whether no direction had come from the Earl of Salisbury or the Lady Arbella.

14th. There is printing a book called *The Bellman of London*, discovering the idle vagabonds of England, their conditions, laws, degrees and orders, their meetings and manner of living. Herein the author first praising the country life, telleth how he wandered into a homely cottage where he espied great preparation of good cheer. Wherefore hiding himself to see who might be the guests, there came in a great company of rogues of all natures for one of their quarter-dinners. Falleth thence to discourse of the sundry kinds of rogue, as, upstart-man, ruffler, angler, wild rogue, palliard, choirbird, Abraham, patrico which last is a priest among beggars: the service he says is only the marrying of couples, which he does in a wood under a tree or in the open field; and the solemnity of it is that the parties to be wedded find out a dead horse or other beast, and standing one on either side, the patrico bids them live together till death them part, etc., and so shaking hands the wedding dinner is kept at the next alehouse. Noteth also the many laws of cheating and manner of each kind.

24th. Today being Accession Day the King, having first touched for the scrofula, with the Queen attended the accustomed ceremony of the Tilt. There is a report that a Bull has come from the Pope deposing the Archpriest Blackwell for the Oath, which he took, and excommunicating all who dare take it. The Bull has not yet come to the King's hands for the Pope has addressed his letters to the man who is to succeed Blackwell. 'Tis thought that this will breed much wrath in the King and the Council against the recusants.

25th. There is a rumour that the King of Spain will not grant any traffic to the Indies and will also have his Deputies insist on the free exercise of religion, and the grant of churches for those of the

Romish religion in the United Provinces, and that openly in all places; and otherwise they shall break up the treaty.

29th. The other four companies of players offer large sums for the removing of the late inhibition on playing, which (if granted) will be upon condition that they refrain from showing upon the stage any modern history, and from speaking of matters of the times, upon peril of life.

31st. Ward the English pirate taketh many ships of the Venetians to their great loss and fear. Of late one Moore, captain of an English ship that tradeth at Venice, was hailed by Ward without the Gulf, and answering that he was bound for Venice, 'Tell those flat-caps,' said Ward, 'who have been the occasion that I am banished out of my country that before I have done with them I will make them sue for my pardon.'

By his letters from Rome the Pope hath removed Blackwell from his office of Archpriest, appointing in his place George Birkhead, who shall admonish and warn all who have taken the Oath, or who have attended the places where the heretics assemble for their superstitious ministrations, or who teach that such things may be lawful. Further by this authority given him, the new Archpriest shall at his judgement declare them cut off.

1st April. Because of the many abuses and corruptions alleged against the officers of the Navy Royal a commission of fifteen is appointed to examine the matter, to punish the offenders, and provide a speedy reform. Among the Commissioners are the Earl of Northampton, the L. Admiral, Sir Henry Hobart the Attorney-General, Sir Francis Bacon the Solicitor-General, Sir Robert Cotton and others.

4th. One H.P. hath written a book of threescore and odd headless epigrams called *The More the Merrier*, as of a simple Justice—

> A simple Justice walking o'er the frozen Thames
> The ice about him round began to crack.
> He said to's man, 'Here is some danger, James;
> I prithee help me over on thy back.'

8th. The young Earl of Essex set out on his travels some days since, having left his wife behind him in the care of her mother, the Countess of Suffolk. He is now at Paris and hath been most favourably received at Fontainbleau by the French King, who led him out hunting and made other demonstrations of favour towards him. Because none of my Lord's own attendants were acquainted with the manners of that Court, M. de S. Antoine, who is riding master to Prince Henry, hath much steadied him.

9th. On the 31st March the Deputies, after many meetings, much dispute and exchange of articles, concluded to send the drafts of the articles into Spain by Friar Neyen. As for the traffic into the Indies, on which the greatest disputation arose, it is agreed that the Netherlanders may traffic for nine years to all places which are not under the power of the King of Spain. The next day the Marquis Spinola caused Friar Neyen to invite the eight Deputies of the States to dine with him, at which dinner they all drank deep, especially the Friar. He is now departed for Spain, and the truce continued for 40 days till his return.

10th. This morning about 8 o'clock in the Chapel of the Rolls, M. William Cavendish, the L. Cavendish's son, was married to the L. Kinloss's daughter, a young gentlewoman of 13 years of age; but the matter was so secretly conveyed that it was never generally heard of till done. The youth at first refused the Lady, albeit a pretty red-headed wench and her portion £7,000; but my Lord his father told him L. Kinloss was well favoured by the Queen, and if he refused it, he would make him worse by £100,000. The matter was so suddenly compounded that the settlements were only agreed upon last night.

George Gervase, a priest, for denying the Oath was quartered, bearing his sufferings very constantly, not one of the standers by offering to curse him. This persecution of Catholics is now very hot, not only in London but also in York where also a priest was lately put to death for refusing the Oath.

The Council has licensed M. Fuller to practise at the Bar till his cause be heard in the Star Chamber but to remain restrained.

11th. The Council has ordered that a clause be inserted into all passes that it shall not be lawful to go unto the City of Rome without special licence of his Majesty.

12th. Yesterday the town of S. Edmondsbury was burned. This fire started in an out malthouse, whence in a most strange manner through fierce winds the fire was carried to the farther side of the town, and as it went the flame flew clean over some streets and houses and did great spoil to houses furthest off. The fire ceased not till 160 houses had been destroyed, besides much damage of goods. Some of the inhabitants when they saw the fire to increase threw their household stuff into wells, whereby many that could otherwise have been saved wanted water in their extremity.

13th. The news of the new Archpriest is so spread about and so ill received by authority that in this general fear which has fallen on all Catholics he can hardly find a resting place; he is forced to change his lodgings almost every day. Nevertheless he has sent his Breve to Blackwell who received it with unwonted moderation though dumbfounded.

19th. Sir Thomas Sackville, Earl of Dorset and Lord High Treasurer died very suddenly at the Council Table, where much time had been spent over his dispute with Sir John Leveson, who had made complaint to the King for his countenancing his niece's cause against himself, and for certain wrongs done under colour of his office as if justified by law. The Lord Treasurer, intending to have Leveson punished for that scandal, was in the act of searching for a paper containing an opinion of lawyers against such accusers, when suddenly without any warning, he fell down and died instantly without a word spoken. In the opinion of the common people this is a terrible example, and a judgement on the King for his hardness of heart towards the poor, for the Treasurer was exceedingly wealthy, and too great a husband in the interests of the Crown, as the people say. He was aged 72. In his young years a poet; he wrote an Induction for *The Mirror for Magistrates*, and part of that tragedy of *Gorboduc* so highly praised by Sir Philip Sidney. He was made Privy Councillor by Queen Elizabeth in 1586, and L. Treasurer after the death of L. Burghley.

21st. There is another book of a century of epigrams called *Wit's ABC* by one R. West of Magdalen College in Oxford.

25th. Two epitaphs on the late L. Treasurer:—

1. Discourteous Death, that would'st not once confer,
   Or deign to parley with our Treasurer:
   Had he been thee, or of thy fatal tribe,
   He would have spar'd a life to gain a bribe.

2. Here lies a Lord, that wenching thought no sin,
   And bought his flesh by selling of our skin:
   His name was Sackville, and so void of pity,
   As he did rob the Country with the City.

28th. News is come from Ireland of a new revolt. On 18th and 19th April Sir Cahir O'Dogherty, seconded with Phelim Reagh McDavid, surprised the castle and fort of Culmore, took spoil of the little town of Derry and burnt it to the ground, and slew Sir George Pawlett. O'Dogherty first came to Capt. Hart (who commanded the fort at

Culmore), and amongst other things, tells him how unkindly his lady takes it that none of all the gentlewomen ever comes to see her; and yet she is well born and bred, amongst the best and civillest kind of ladies and gentlewomen in that Kingdom; and so desires Capt. Hart to bring his wife with him to dinner, which he does. After dinner, O'Dogherty draws Hart into an upper room, and there begins to declare that he is so hotly pursued by his enemies, especially Sir George Pawlett, that he is in great danger of his life; and now that Hart is in his hands he must either deliver the place or resolve to die. So the Captain is disarmed and left in custody.

Then O'Dogherty told Hart's wife that if she or he did not take present course for the delivery of Culmore into his hands, both they and their children should die, and as many as were therein. She, like one distracted, fell at his feet and cried for pity; but O'Dogherty uttered such bloody threats that she, being terrified and amazed, yielded to do what was in her power for the saving of their lives, choosing rather (as she said) to stand to the mercy of the King than to perish with her infants at his hands. So O'Dogherty made them both ride along with him; and when they came within a quarter of a mile of the house, being about 11 o'clock at night, he left Hart with 6 of his kerne in the bog, and took Hart's wife with himself and about 20 in his company, calling to the watch within to come forth and help their Captain, for he had broken his arm by a fall from his horse, and lay hard by not able to help himself. This the poor men did, not mistrusting any such treachery; and no sooner were they out of the door but they were taken, and the house immediately entered, and the rest that were lodged without surprised and taken in their beds. Then O'Dogherty sent for Hart, and put him and all the rest in the cellar and there locked them in.

From Culmore, the rebels, being about 90 in number, marched on and came to Derry by 2 o'clock in the morning, and there divided themselves into two bodies; the one, where O'Dogherty was, assaulted the nether fort; and the other, conducted by Phelim, entered on the backside of the Governor's, came into the court, and brake open the doors; whereat Sir George Pawlett escaped in the dark to Ancient Corbet's house, where in a short space Phelim killed him. Lieutenant Gordon, lying in his chamber, heard the shot and issued forth naked upon the rampier toward the court of guard with his rapier and dagger, where with one soldier of the company, he set upon the enemy and killed two of them; but the enemy being far more in number, one struck him on the forehead with a stone; whereat being somewhat amazed, they rushed upon him and killed him and the soldier also.

Ancient Corbet, meeting with Phelim within the higher fort, fought with and wounded him, and would by all likelihood have killed him if one of the rebels had not come behind him and cut off his leg; and so he too was killed by the enemy. The upper fort being taken by the rebels was immediately burnt. O'Dogherty with the other half of the rebels assaulted the nether fort, and finding the watchmen asleep, entered without resistance, and there killed M. Harris, Undersheriff of Donegal.

In the town Lieutenant Baker gathered together some 16 of the townsmen, one of the sheriffs, and 4 soldiers, and with these went to the nether fort with resolution to retake it, but in the gate he was wounded in the shoulder by O'Dogherty with a pike. Whereat, seeing his company but few and the rebels many, he retired into the town, and there gathered together 6 or 7 score men, women and children, and manned the house of Sheriff Babington, and kept the same. Likewise he manned the house of the Bishop of Derry with his own men and two or three soldiers, and brought the Bishop's wife and gentlewomen into the house, thinking them most safe with him. The two houses were kept until the next day about noon, in which time they killed 8 of the enemy and hurt 7, and lost but one of their company and one hurt. But the rebels being strong and increasing, the Lieutenant having many with him and destitute of victuals and munition, and seeing a piece brought by the enemy from Culmore and ready mounted to batter the houses, out of all hope of relief and wearied with the lamentable outcry of women and children, after much parley and many messages to and from, yielded the houses upon condition that every man should depart with his sword and clothes, and likewise all the women (except Mrs. Susan Montgomery, the Bishop's wife who is kept prisoner by O'Dogherty). O'Dogherty now returned to Culmore and there released his prisoners, declaring that it was not blood that he sought for.

The chief cause of this disaster is said to be Sir George Pawlett, who was regarded by the L. Deputy as unfit for command; for the discipline of nightly watching was altogether neglected by him, as was well known to the rebels. He was so odious to the soldiers and the rest of the townsmen that they would have done him a mischief in the tumult if he had escaped the rebels and come in amongst them.

29th. Proclamation has been made that the Oath of Allegiance shall be administered to all persons coming from beyond the seas.

6th May. My L. of Salisbury is the new L. Treasurer. Upon which he was heard to say that the Treasurership is a perilous place; for if the Treasurer consents to monopolies and to all the numberless devices for concealment and the proposals of new taxation, he gains for himself the people's ill will and their curses; and if he resists the same, he will be made odious to the suitors for monopolies and perhaps also to the King.

10th. One Andrew Battell of Leigh in Essex is returned to England, having been a prisoner of the Portugals near 18 years. He left England in 1589 with Abraham Cocks on a voyage to the River of Plate, but being on shore in the Isle of S. Sebastian was taken by the Indians and afterward sent prisoner by the Portugals to Angola in Africa, in 9° southward of the equinoctial line. He hath had strange adventures and escapes, and lived for many years among the negroes who never before saw white man. Speaketh much of a tribe called the Jaggs or Gagas. When the Jesuits brought news that the Queen of England was dead and that King James had made peace with Spain, the Portugal Governor gave him licence to return to England, but he broke his word. So Battell ran away and lived for three years with the King of Longo. In those parts he saw many strange beasts, whereof the most dangerous is the *pongo* or giant ape, in all proportion like a man but more like a giant in stature; for he is very tall and hath a man's face, hollow-eyed, with long hair about his brows. His body is full of hair but not very thick and of a dunnish colour. He goeth always upon his legs, and carrieth his hands clasped on the nape of his neck when he goeth upon the ground. These *pongos* sleep in the trees and build shelters for the rain; they feed upon fruit and nuts for they eat no kind of flesh. They cannot speak and have no more understanding than a beast. Battell had a negro boy which the *pongos* took and he lived a month with them unhurt. They go many together and kill many negroes; many times they fall upon the elephants and beat them with their clubbed fists and pieces of wood. They are never taken alive for they are so strong that ten men cannot take them. He saw also a beast called the *severa* or *zebra*, like a horse except for his mane, his tail, and strakes of divers colours down his sides and legs. These *severas* are all wild and live in great herds. Encountered many crocodiles whereof one was so huge that he devoured an *alibamba* which is a chained company of 8 or 9 slaves; but the indigestible iron paid him his wages for he died of it. These beasts will haul gennet, man or other creature into the water. Noteth also a kind of little people called Matimbas, which are no bigger than boys of 12 years old, but very thick and live only upon flesh which they kill in the woods with their bows and darts. They will not enter into any house, nor suffer any to come where they dwell.

14th. Tom Coryat of Odcombe has set out on his travels, being licensed thereto by the Council.

24th. Three days since Capt. Newport returned from Virginia, bringing with him M. Wingfield (that was the first President) and Capt. Archer. They report many disasters and much dissension in that plantation.

Within 10 days of Newport's departure in June last, the adventurers were in such a state that scarce 10 of them could go or stand, such extreme weakness and sickness oppressed them. So long as the ships stayed, their allowance was bettered by a daily proportion of biscuit which the sailors would pilfer to sell or exchange for money, saxifras or furs; but when these departed there was no relief but the common kettle from which the President allowed half a pint of wheat and as much barley for each man a day; and this having fried 26 weeks in the ship's hold contained as many worms as grains. Their drink was cold water taken from the river, which at flood was very salt, and at low tide full of slime and filth. With this diet and their lodgings in the open air, their extreme toil in bearing and planting palisadoes so strained them that between May and September 50 of their company died.

They complain that all this time Wingfield the President felt neither want nor sickness by ingrossing to his own use oatmeal, sack, oil, *aqua vitae*, beef, eggs and what not. Moreover he planned to escape from their miseries in the pinnace by flight; which being discovered, they deposed him and in his place have chosen Capt. Ratcliffe to be President; of the first Council Gosnoll being dead, and Kendal deposed.

Their provision being all spent, those who survived were forced to live upon sturgeon and sea crabs; but when all help was abandoned, the savages were so changed in heart that they brought such plenty of provisions that no man wanted.

The new President and Martin, who was also of the Council, are little beloved, being men of weak judgement in dangers and less industry in peace; they commit all things to Capt. Smith who by his own example and good words set some to mow, some to build houses, some to thatch them, himself always bearing the greatest task so that in short time most of them had lodgings.

After a while as the superfluity of the savages began to decrease, Smith took 6 or 7 with him in the shallop down the river to a place called Kecoughtan to search for trade, where at first the savages scorned him as a famished man, and would in derision offer him a handful of corn or a piece of bread for their swords and muskets. So

86

he let fly his muskets and ran his boat on shore, whereat they fled into the woods. He marched towards their houses and there found great heaps of corn, having much ado to restrain his hungry soldiers from taking it, for he expected (as soon after it happened) that the savages would assault him. Some 60 or 70 of them, painted black, red, white or parti-coloured, came on in a square order, singing and dancing, with their *okee* (which was an idol made of skins, stuffed with moss and hung with chains and copper). In this manner, well armed with clubs, targets, bows and arrows, they charged the English who so received them with their muskets loaden with pistol shot that down fell their god and divers lay sprawling. The rest fled to the woods; but soon they sent one of their leaders to offer peace and to redeem their *okee*. Smith told them that if only 6 would come unarmed and load his boat he would not only be their friend but restore their *okee* and give them beads, copper and hatchets besides; which on both sides was performed, they bringing him venison, turkeys, wild fowl, bread and what they had.

And now Smith perceiving that notwithstanding their late misery those at Jamestown still lived from hand to mouth caused the pinnace to be provided to get provision for the next year; and in the meantime he made other journeys in which he discovered the people of the Chickahamania. While he was thus absent, Wingfield and Kendal living in disgrace upon the pinnace, strengthened themselves with the sailors and other confederates and planned to take the pinnace and go for England. But Smith returning unexpectedly, that plot is discovered, and with shot of saker and musket, he forces them stay or sink in the river. At this time, one James Read their blacksmith, being chidden by Ratcliffe the President, not only gave him bad language but offered to strike him with his tools; for which rebellious act the smith was condemned by a jury to be hanged, but being upon the ladder and continuing very obstinate as hoping for a rescue and seeing no other way, he became penitent and revealed a dangerous conspiracy, for which Capt. Kendal as principal was by a jury condemned and shot to death.

Smith made a further journey, finding many towns of the savages and returning with corn. Moreover winter coming on, the rivers became covered with swans, geese, ducks and cranes, and what with good bread, Virginia pease, pumpions, fish, fowl and divers sorts of wild beasts, none of their tuftaffeta humorists now desired to go home; and they began to chide Capt. Smith because he had not accomplished more.

So once more he set out in the barge and proceeded as far as he could go. Then leaving the barge, himself with two Englishmen (who were named Robinson and Emry) he went up higher in a canow; and here, while he went fowling his two men were slain as they lay by their fire by the canow; and he himself being beset with two hundred savages, and falling into a quagmire was taken. For nearly a month these barbarians kept him prisoner, at one time tying him to a tree to have shot him, at another feasting him. At length they bring him to Powhatan their Emperor, where having feasted him in their barbarous manner, a long consultation is held, and the conclusion is that two great stones are brought before Powhatan. Then as many as can lay hands on him, drag him to them, and thereon lay down his head. Being ready to beat out his brains, Pocahontas, the King's dearest daughter, when no intreaty will prevail gets his head in her arms and lays down her own upon his to save him from such a death. Whereat Powhatan is content that he shall live to make him hatchets and her bells, beads and copper.

Two days after, Powhatan, dressed more like a devil than a man, with 200 as black as himself, came to Smith and told him now they were friends, and straightway he should go to Jamestown to send thence two great guns and a grindstone, for which he will give him the country of Capahowosick and for ever esteem him as his son Nantoquod. So to Jamestown they take him, and after quartering in the woods all night (when he expected they would have slain him), next day (which was 8th January) they come to the Fort where Smith shows Rawhunt, Powhatan's trusty servant, two demi-culverins and a grindstone to carry to Powhatan; but they find them too heavy, and when they see him discharge them loaded with stones among the branches of a great tree loaded with icicles, the ice and branches come so tumbling down together, the poor savages run away half dead with fear. But at last he sends them to Powhatan with such presents as gave them general content.

At this return Smith again found all in confusion at Jamestown, the strongest party determined to run away with the pinnace. For the third time Smith forced them to stay or sink. Some now plotted with the President to have put Smith to death by the Levitical law for the deaths of Robinson and Emry, pretending that he had led them to their deaths for his own ends; but his life was saved by the arrival that day of Capt. Newport and his ship. Thereafter every 4 or 5 days Pocahontas with her attendants brought him so much food provision as saved their lives, whereby their spirits were revived and all fear abandoned. The coming of Newport had been foretold to the savages by Smith, whom he had pretended to be his father, declaring that the whole world was under the command of Capt. Newport, insomuch that the savages every other day brought in great plenty of food, part of which they gave Newport as presents from the King, and the rest they sold at the price set by Smith who was their market clerk.

Ratcliffe the President and the Council so much envied Smith's estimation amongst the savages that they thought to advance themselves by their greater bounty in giving them four times more for their commodities than Smith had appointed. Moreover with the arrival of the supply they gave the mariners leave to truck and trade at their pleasures, so that in a short time there could not be had for a pound of copper which was before sold at an ounce. This ambition cut the throat of their trade but confirmed their opinion of Newport's greatness.

And now Powhatan desired to see Newport. So Newport sets out with Smith as his interpreter, and M. Scrivener (a man much respected) who had come out with the new supply, and some 30 or 40 chosen men for their guard, and were very well received by Powhatan who sat on his bed of mats, his pillow of leather embroidered with pearl and white beads, his attire a fair cloak of skins as large as an Irish mantle; at his head and feet sat a handsome young woman, and on each side his arbour house twenty of his concubines, their heads and shoulders painted red, with great chains of white beads about their necks; and before them his chief men in like order. Then Newport gave Powhatan a boy named Thomas Savage, whom he called his son, for whom Powhatan gave in return Nemontack, his trusty servant.

Some days being spent in feasting and dancing, Powhatan, who carried himself very proudly yet discreetly, then said to Capt. Newport that it was not agreeable with his greatness to trade for trifles in a peddling manner, but, quoth he, 'I esteem you a great Weroans; therefore lay me down all your commodities together. What I like I will take, and in recompense give you what I think their fitting value.' Smith, knowing the disposition of Powhatan, told Newport that it was his intent to cheat him, but Newport thought to outbrave this savage in ostentation of his own greatness agreed; whereat Powhatan valued his corn at such a rate that where they expected twenty hogsheads they received but four bushels. This bred some unkindness between the two Captains, but Smith smothering his distaste to avoid the savages' suspicions, glanced many trifles in the eyes of Powhatan, whose humour was for some blue beads, which Smith seemed so much to value that at their departure they took with them 200 or 300 bushels of corn, yet parted good friends.

And now a further disaster befell our adventurers; for while the new supply was being lodged, the quarters were accidentally set on fire, and so the town, being thatched with reeds was all burnt up, with their arms, bedding and apparel and much private provision. M. Hunt the preacher lost all his library and all he had, yet he never repined. This mischance happened in the great frost. Moreover the ship staying 14 weeks spent the beef, pork, oil, *aqua vitae*, fish, butter and cheese which was provided to be landed. Yet when they departed they left behind them such commodities as they could spare for those who had money, spare clothes, credit to give bills of payment, gold rings, furs or such commodities which they purchased at fifteen times their value. In this extremity of the bitter cold weather more than half of them died.

Smith and Scrivener did their best to amend what was amiss, but with the President went the major part. Their worst mischief was the hope of gold; there was no talk, no hope, no work but dig gold, wash gold, refine gold, load gold, in which Newport also showed himself most zealous. So the time is spent in loading the ship with certain shining yellow sand while all necessary business is neglected. On 10th April Newport sailed for England.

The L. Mayor is commanded to take care that the corn now being brought into the City from foreign parts be sold at reasonable prices and not bought up by ingrossers and such as will enhance the price.

26th. The officers of the ports are commanded to administer the Oath of Allegiance to all who return from overseas. If any would rather choose to depart back again rather than take the Oath, it shall be granted them without lingering, but they shall not be allowed under this colour to escape and come into the land.

28th. Tyrone is now in Rome receiving the pardons without any great comfort from the Pope though honourably received and brought with his company in coaches of the Cardinals that met him, and lodged and defrayed at the Pope's charges, whereat his friends are not much comforted because his usage is not answerable to their wishes. At Milan he received 6,000 crowns from the Count of Fuentes, and 300 crowns monthly from the Kingdom of Naples. His son hath dismissed all the English from his regiment as suspected, among them Sir Edward Baynham.

29th. O'Dogherty has removed with all his people into the fastness of Doe and Fanett in Tyrconnell where he means to abide. He now declares that all he has done is in zeal of the Catholic cause, and for no other discontent. He has left the fort of Culmore in the custody of Phelim Reagh with 30 warders and two gunners, but the Derry he has quitted altogether, leaving the forts (the houses excepted) entire as he found them. Some stirring loose fellows are now beginning to fall in with him. Sir Arthur Chichester has raised 400 men that for the most part served on our side in the last wars. He might have had many more but scruples to put arms in their hands, fearing lest the priests may seduce them into disloyalty at some time when it is least suspected.

1st June. The King in his hunting in Windsor Forest was heavily displeased at the great holes made by the swine, and gave orders that the keepers should kill any hogs they found there. But since it may be a heavy punishment for the inhabitants to lose their swine, the Earl of Nottingham warned the verderers to enjoin them to fill up the holes and to forbear to put their swine in the woods.

4th. Many seditious books and letters nowadays are landed in secret places, and above 60 persons this last fortnight. Moreover the pursuivants of the High Commission practise most dishonourable courses, for they will buy and sell priests and Jesuits for money. The bribes they take to overpass books, church stuff, and letters are infinite. Lay recusants also by annual pensions and bribes are withheld from charges.

5th. The King's Book is published again with certain words used against the Pope (declaring him to be Antichrist) now amended.

7th. To the end that the law concerning the *post nati* might be tried in the Courts, in November last there was a case made of one Robert Calvin, a child, born since the King's coming to the English Crown. This Calvin through his guardians, became possessed of a certain freehold in S. Buttolph's without Bishopsgate; whereupon two persons, John Bingley and Richard Griffin, refused to deliver up the evidences concerning the messuage, pleading that Calvin is an alien. Calvin's case being argued before the Courts, the question of the law is at last brought to the Court of Chancery, where judgement is today given at great length by the L. Chancellor Ellesmere, wherein he narrated all the proceedings concerning the *post nati*, from the King's proclamation of 20th October 1604, the many objections in Parliament since raised, and the precedents and cases in the Law. He said much, *obiter dicta*, of the Law, of allegiance and of naturalization, of which are to be noted: 'The Common Law of England is grounded upon the Law of God, and extends itself to the original Law of

91

Nature and the Universal Law of Nations.' 'There is a dangerous distinction between the King and the Crown, between the King and the Kingdom; it reacheth too far; I wish every good subject to beware of it.' 'Since there is but one King and Sovereign to whom faith and allegiance is due by all his subjects, can any human policy divide this one King and make him two Kings? Can *cor regis Angliae* be *in manu Domini* and *cor regis Scotiae* not so?' So judgement is given 'that Robert Calvin and all the *post nati* in Scotland are in reason and by the Common Law of England natural born subjects within the allegiance of the King of England'.

8th. John Marston the poet is by the Council committed to Newgate.

12th. In Ireland, the Marshal, the Treasurer and Sir Oliver Lambert have gone against the rebels, and came to Derry on 20th May where they found the forts and the church only standing, all other buildings, saving stone walls and chimneys, consumed by fire. Having left a ward in the church, the same evening they encamped near Culmore, but in the second night after Phelim Reagh burnt it, having first laid on board two or three barks all the pillage and munition he had there. He then withdrew towards the island of Tory, leaving the fort in better strength than he found it. The castle of Birt, within three miles of Culmore, still stands, but when Sir Ralph Bingley arrives with powder, munition and tools it should easily be taken. In that castle are O'Dogherty's wife and Mrs. Montgomery, the Bishop's.

Since the forces of the Marshal are too few to overcome the rebels, the L. Deputy intends to go against them in person with such forces as he can make. He would make this war thick and short, and he has no fears for the safety of the Pale unless the fugitive Earls return with or without forces. If the King send more men out of England or Scotland, he would have them sent with conductors only, and that captains and officers who have had former experience of these wars be preferred to strangers.

18th. The King hath knighted Thomas Overbury at the importunity of his familiar friend Sir Robert Carr. These two were first acquainted some seven years since when M. Overbury, with John Gilbey his father's chief clerk, were sent upon a voyage of pleasure to Edinburgh with £60 between them. There Overbury met with Sir William Cornwallis, one who knew him in Queen's College at Oxford. Sir William commended him to divers, and among the rest to Robin Carr then page to my L. of Dunbar. Our English Lords, who had hoped for an English favourite (to which end the Countess of Suffolk did look out choice young men whom she daily curled and perfumed their breaths) have now left all hope and turn to adore the rising sun; which is not hard to obtain for Carr is naturally more addicted to the English nation than to the Scotch; and especially since the Pythias to his Damon is Sir Thomas Overbury. There is much strife between my LL. of Salisbury and Suffolk who shall engross Sir Thomas and make him their monopoly, each presenting favours upon his kindred. Sir Thomas, who is naturally of an insolent spirit, is much elevated by being so intimate with the favourite and having so wholly ingrossed this commodity which cannot be retailed but by him and his favour.

20th. From Venice it is reported that Sir Anthony Shirley and his secretary are broken for want of gold, and that the Cardinal of Ferrara is publishing a discourse of Sir Anthony's sleights of wit played with divers Princes. His all-embracing fancy, like sand in a covetous man's griping fist, retains nothing to his benefit. The Emperor from whom he pretends his honour of Count of the Empire, disclaims him; Rome hath had sufficient acquaintance with his spirit; the Venetians have banished him; the Duke of Florence knows him and is too old a Tuscan to trust him. At Naples his credit failed with his money. He is now gone to Spain. It is said he is about a device to establish a peace between the King of Spain and the Turk; so his next voyage is voiced for Turkey, where if his brain save his skin, it may pass for a miracle.

23rd. Thomas Garnet, a Jesuit, was executed at Tyburn. He was offered his life if he would have taken the Oath but he refused it.

25th. Some days since died Sir Edward Stanhope, Doctor of the Civil Law and Chancellor of the Diocese of London, worth £40,000, and miserly in his expenditure. Whereon one wrote on his tomb:

A hundred and ten lies under this stone,
A hundred to ten to the Devil he's gone.

There is also put about this jest: 'News in Court out of Hell; that rich Doctor Stanhope put a case to the Devil. He said it concerned Common Law, and would be advised by Sir John Popham, who said it was an Exchequer case, and he would put it to Dorset, L. Treasurer.'

30th. The tenants and farmers of the shops in the Royal Exchange complain to the Lord Mayor of my L. of Salisbury's new building at Durham House for a place to buy and sell such wares as usually are bought and sold in the Royal Exchange, for it will doubtless be planted with many strangers, and being within the liberties of Westminster will occasion many of the nobility and gentlemen to buy there rather than go so far as the Royal Exchange.

5th July. The King's Men have a play called *Philaster*, written by Francis Beaumont and John Fletcher, both gentlemen. M. Beaumont is the son of M. Justice Beaumont, and M. Fletcher of that unfortunate Bishop of London who fell out of favour with Queen Elizabeth because of his second marriage, and died in 1596. The friendship between these two is much noted, for they live together on the Bankside, both bachelors, with one wench in the house between them, sharing the same clothes and the like.

6th. Dr. Richard Bancroft, the Archbishop of Canterbury, is chosen Chancellor of the University of Oxford to his great satisfaction. He hath appointed Dr. King, the Dean of Christchurch, his Vice-Chancellor. Requireth them above all things that the statutes for the frequenting of divine service, sermons and the catechizing of youth in true religion be diligently observed; also that old statute that no private tutor or reader be allowed for the instructing of youth unless first approved by the Vice-Chancellor and other divines which shall prevent popish or other schismatic corruptions in religion.

7th. The *Phoenix* with Capt. Nelson that hath been long missing is newly come from Virginia. She went out last year with Capt. Newport, and after much wandering found the port some three or four days after his departure for England. They report that upon Newport's departure the authority consisted of Capt. Martin and Ratcliffe the President. The spring approaching, Capt. Smith and M. Scrivener divided between them the building of the burnt town. The President would have had Smith and Scrivener to search the commodities of the Monachans' country beyond the Falls with 60 men whom Smith had so trained in arms that they little fear whom they may encounter; but there fell out a difference with Martin who was intent to fraught the ship with his fantastical gold, while Smith would relade her with cedar. There was also trouble with the savages. When Newport departed, Powhatan to show his love gave him 20 turkeys, for which Newport returned 20 swords. When Powhatan would have from Smith the like trade, finding his humour crossed he caused his people by ambuscadoes to take them perforce, surprising our people at work or any way, which was so long permitted by the peaceful President (who kept his house) that they became very insolent, until by chance they meddled with Smith himself, who without further deliberation hunted them up and down the isle, whipping and beating some, and keeping 7 of them prisoners. Whereupon in revenge they surprised two soldiers who were foraging and threatened to force Smith to redeliver his prisoners; but in less than half an hour he so hampered their insolencies that they brought back their two prisoners. The savages confessed that Powhatan had directed them to obtain the weapons to cut the throats of our men. Yet Powhatan sent his dearest daughter Pocahontas to excuse himself of the injuries done by his subjects, for whose sake Smith feigned to grant their lives. The patient Council would gladly have wrangled with Smith for his cruelties, but he has brought the savages into such fear and obedience that his very name affrights them.

10th. The L. Treasurer hath answered the complaints of the shopkeepers of the Royal Exchange declaring that by his new Bourse London will suffer (if it should so prove) but a little quill of profit to pass by their main pipe. All the moneys and merchandises of this Kingdom are possessed by the City of London, and it is but just London should contribute a small portion of commodity for Westminster which holds the persons of the King and the Queen and their royal issue, and the Courts of Justice. As for the petition of the Corporation of the Royal Exchange, in former times there were like complaints against that great work of Sir Thomas Gresham. In this project he is but bringing together shops into one handsome range in place of shops set up dispersedly in noisome stables and bare sheds. Remindeth the L. Mayor of the humours of men of occupation who will envy each his neighbour if he be but able to make a better window or a wider door than himself; and he would have him answer the petition as if he himself were in a like case.

The marriage of the L. Treasurer's young son, the L. Cranborne, with the L. Chamberlain's daughter is concluded and the books sealed.

13th. John Ward the pirate now is solely under the protection of the Turks and has given up all hope of returning to England. This Ward, commonly called Capt. Ward (concerning whom there is so much talk), is about 55 years of age. He is very short, with little hair and that quite white, bald in front. His face is swarthy and bearded. He speaketh little and is for ever swearing and drunk from morning to night. He is most courageous and prodigal, a great sleeper, a fool and an idiot out of his trade.

In his youth he was a fisherman upon the East coast. Then came to Plymouth where he won promotion in the wars with Spain. Upon a time he, with some sailors, stole a ship's boat and came to the Isle of Wight where they surprised a French ship and in her turned pirates, at last seeking shelter in Alarraca in Barbary. This was the beginning of the life he now leads. He now fell in with two English captains, the one named Bishop, the other Michael. Michael went home but left some of his crew with Ward, among them his lieutenant called Antony Johnson; and these two have been Ward's constant companions in drinking and robbing.

At Tunis there is a certain Osman, a captain of Janissaries. He began as a poor tailor but has since grown exceeding rich through the help of the pirates. Ward sold the cargo of the *Soderina* to this Osman for scarce half its worth. Last December Ward went out in the *Soderina* with 30 Christians, English, French and Flemish, and 350 Turks, having on board 55 bronze cannon and much ammunition; and in his company two other ships. On this voyage Ward's vice-admiral after attacking two English ships and taking from them 4,000 crowns, captured a ship from Marseilles of medium size and 22 guns, with 12,000 crowns and 29 Frenchmen who were made slaves in Tunis. Ward then transferred himself to the French ship and abandoned the *Soderina*, for she was leaky and rotten, in so much that soon after she sank with all on board, except for four men and a boy who were picked up at sea, floating upon some wreckage. When Ward went back to Tunis without the Turks, the Janissaries would have torn him into pieces, but were pacified by Osman. Ward now has a second ship, manned by 100 Turks, with 26 cannon; and a third also but very small.

· *14th.* At the exercises in the Music at Oxford, one Shepherd took upon himself a Cambridge quarrel, first upon a ballad made there in disgrace of the King's visit to Oxford; and then answering one Cecil, the Proctor of Cambridge who inveighed against a book set out by the Oxford Orator, touching the exercises performed before the King. For the first he said it was neither *cantus* nor *cantio*, *cantibula* nor *cantilena* nor anything but *Anglice* a ballad; those that made it may be called *balatrones*. As for Cecil, he recited all the invectives made by Tully in his oration against Caecilius, saying they were prophecies of this man; and in that mad merry vein went on for more than an hour before a great audience as well of Cambridge men as of others. There were like invectives by the Philosophers, and the Physicians against the Civilians, and the Civilians against women. The Divines also descanted against one another, as Dr. Thornton had his name divided into *spina* and *dolium*, and no

96

wonder he could not *perfecta implere legem* when *dolium* might be so easily filled and emptied; and many such young conceits not so well befitting their gravities and professions.

15th. One Lieutenant Copley hath been sent over prisoner out of the Low Countries for being lately 'perverted by a chaplain of Spinola's, and for some dangerous speeches, as for admiring him that slew the Duke of Orange, for commending Fawkes' enterprise and how honourable he died, and for giving out that if he got into England he would in short time be the most famous man in the world. On Monday (11th) a gentleman won a great wager for riding 5 measured miles between Brainford and Kensington 20 times in less that 5 hours. The wicked say that the Dean of Paul's wife was running away with Sir John Selby and had trussed up her trinkets and her husband's plate and what else she could come by; which being discovered by the neighbours was stayed, and she is returned from Ware being gone so far on her way.

16th. As the L. Deputy was at Armagh taking a review of his forces, news came that Sir Richard Wingfield (the Marshal) and Sir Oliver Lambert had encountered O'Dogherty in a strong fastnage where the horse could not be used. Whereupon the Marshal drew out 300 foot and for half an hour entertained a hot skirmish more bloody to the enemy though far greater in numbers, by which the traitor was beaten, and himself with his ensign and good store of his crew slain, and others taken prisoner. The Deputy hath made proclamation that none shall presume to relieve or protect any of O'Dogherty's followers upon pain to be adjudged traitors; and whoso shall bring in the body, dead or alive, of any of them (Phelim only excepted) shall have not only the King's pardon but also the goods of the person delivered.

20th. The Court has begun the progress from Theobalds whence the King came to Greenwich to see the works for the making of silk, which he would have done in England. He has brought over workmen from France, who promise that in a short time as much silk will be made in England as at present is imported.

21st. The Council have instructed Sir Arthur Chichester that since the most part of Ulster has fallen into the King's hands, he now intends to order it so that it may resound to his honour and profit, for which a fair opportunity is given by the absence of the fugitive Earls, the death of O'Dogherty and the imprisonment of Neale Garve O'Donnell. To prevent for the future any rebellious companion that chooseth to make himself head of any sept to disturb the peace and put his Majesty to the cost of prosecuting a company of wood kerne, there must not be so great a facility of granting pardons and taking submissions. The Deputy is therefore to abstain from making promises of any of the escheated lands or disposing of them till the survey is completed.

29th. One William Udall, an informer who declared that he could discover printing presses used for printing seditious books which will shortly appear, complaineth bitterly to my L. of Salisbury by whom he was referred to the Archbishop. This man intended to take a priest called Leeke, who is harboured near the Court and protected by four or five desperate persons. He therefore offered a goldsmith £20 to take Leeke. But when Udall attended the Archbishop he would not believe his tale; and suspecting that Udall's true intent was to warn the priest to avoid, he used threats and imputations against him and sent him to the Clink, albeit Udall told him that those who have his Grace's warrant to prosecute recusants have taken this same priest twice and let him go for money. Complaineth further that by his endeavours 800 seditious books were seized, with two suits of church stuff with silver plate, for which the pursuivant was offered £80 not to deliver it; yet when he went to the Archbishop and asked for some allowance from the takings, he was refused and threatened. His Grace, complaineth Udall, is content to give nothing but to receive all; whereas our Saviour saith *'beatius est dare quam accipere'*.

31st. Of late Capt. Newport sailed for Virginia bearing with him a private commission not to return without a lump of gold, a certainty of the South Sea or one of the lost company of Sir Walter Ralegh, together with a five-pieced barge to be carried over the mountains. He carries also a crown and a robe and other presents for Powhatan. There are 70 in the company; Capt. Peter Winn and Capt. Richard Waldo, two soldiers of experience, appointed to be of the Council; M. Francis West, brother to the L. De la Warr; 25 gentlemen; 14 tradesmen; 12 labourers, 8 Dutchmen and Poles to make pitch and glass; together with two women, Mrs. Forest and Anne Burras her maid.

1st August. Sir Stephen Proctor, who hath for some years been employed in gathering the debts due to the Crown, hath a project for reforming the abuses of informers and would have a patent for himself to be the King's especial officer to remedy the same whereby the King's coffers might be benefited. Noteth how an informer will exhibit an information into which he puts a hundred several subjects. Of this information every subject must take out copies and put in his answer; this will cost perhaps 100 marks. That done, no further proceeding, but the clerks have their fees, and the informer his dividend for bringing water to the mill. Informers receive pensions of divers persons to forbear them; and if any stand out and will not be in fee, then they will find means to have a dozen informations come upon a man at once. After an information is exhibited, the informer for the most part cometh to composition with the defendant whereby the King is defrauded.

7th. Of late there was a great stag carefully preserved for the King's recreation; but a little before his coming Sir William Dyer killed it, albeit he had been warned by the L. Lieutenant. Sir William is sent for to the Court, for the King will not let so bold a trespass go unpunished.

9th. Edward Kirkham and the housekeepers of the private play-house in the Blackfriars (where the Children used to play), growing weary of their many troubles have given up their commission under the Great Seal authorizing them to play, and have discharged divers their partners and poets. Their lease is surrendered to Richard Burbage (who had it by bequest of his father in 1597). Now the King's Players go about to use the private house for themselves, and to that end Burbage has taken into fellowship his brother Cuthbert, Hemings, Shakespeare, Condell and others of the company.

10th. There has been trouble in Constantinople between the French and the English. Some time since the French who serve in the army of the Turks complained that one of the household of the English Ambassador had carried off two of their women, whereat they were so angry that they went about looking for Englishmen to slay them; but since the English kept the house, the French resolved to attack the Ambassador's house. That night they made an assault and fired many shots, but without avail. Moreover one of the Frenchmen was slain; but our Ambassador is shut up in his house, for those Frenchmen are desperate and licentious villains whom no one can control.

12th. News is come from the L. Deputy that his soldiers have taken or slain most of those who were concerned in the late rebellion. The prisoners, after examination, he caused to be hung by martial law, the soldiers taking their arms, clothes, horses and whatever spoil they had. Others were taken or slain by one Hugh McShane and his brethren (who are a wild and strong sept of people dwelling

99

in the woods and glyns of Tyrone), not so much for conscience' sake as to expiate their own offences. The Deputy spares not to execute justice upon all who relieve the traitors if they are able to resist them; but many are excusable, living as they do in creaghts and poor cabins, and therefore unable to resist desperate and armed men.

During his stay in Dungannon, many of the rebels brought in daily were hung by martial law, and some by verdict of the jury, amongst whom Shane Carraghe O'Cahane was principal; who was executed as a traitor by justice of the common law, which was a kind of death seldom or never seen before in those parts of Ulster, and seems to terrify them more than hanging, a death which they despise more than any other nation living, for they are generally so stupid by nature, or so tough, or so disposed by their priests that they show no remorse of conscience or fear of death.

From Dungannon the Deputy marched through Glenconkeine which is the greatest fastness of woods and bogs in all the Province. There diligent searches made all Tyrconnell's men hasten back again out of Ulster, but the Marshal and Sir Oliver Lambert had so good watch and spial of them that many are lately discovered and slain, and some principal men taken, as O'Dogherty's base brother, another who slew Sir George Pawlett with his own hands, and Phelim Reagh the very firebrand of this rebellion, with 20 others who are reserved for public trial at the assizes at Liffer.

Phelim Reagh was discovered to be in a wood within 6 miles of the Marshal's camp. Upon news of it, the Marshal posted away with some 40 horse and environed the wood until some companies of foot came up. Upon the first search they missed him, and whilst they were thus in despair of him, another company came up and would needs search again; who found him. He made such resistance with his sword that it seems he would gladly have been slain, but he was badly wounded with a pike and beaten down before he could be taken. The Marshal takes great care for keeping him alive for his trial. This Phelim is one of the meanest in rank among the prisoners though for his malice and wickedness he has got himself a name beyond all his fellows. Now all that are known to have drawn blood in this late rebellion are either taken or slain.

Moreover in his journeying the Deputy hath held sessions (which could not be done without an army) and surveyed all the escheated lands in Ulster.

13th. One W. Battie hath a *History of Titana and Theseus* and their great love, strange adventures and happy ending in the vein of Lodge's *Rosalynd*.

The Prince today went by his barge to Woolwich to visit the *Ark Royal* which M. Pett is rebuilding, where being upon the poop 31 great brass chambers were discharged on shore, to his great content, and the more because he expected it not. Then the Prince commanded Pett to lead him into all the places of the ship, and so into the dockyard where the keel, stem and stern of his own great ship lie ready framed. Having partaken of a set banquet of sweetmeats and fruits, he then desired to be brought to the mount where the chambers were placed and now again loaded, with the train made ready. He was very desirous to have the train fired, but being informed of the danger, he gave order that they should be discharged at the holding up of his handkerchief in his barge, which was done at his departure to his great delight.

There is printing *A True Relation* of the colony in Virginia written by Capt. Smith in a letter to a friend, brought back by Master Nelson.

18th. Friar Neyen is still delayed in Spain, but 10 days ago President Jeannin came to the Hague from the French King, who had newly received the Ambassador from Spain. The French King now advises them to make a peace, if it may be on reasonable terms, and not stay any longer for the Friar; for no better terms are likely from Spain. The Spanish Deputies were therefore moved by the States to come to a final conclusion; but they would not until they had received further commission from their King.

19th. On the 12th there was executed in Edinburgh George Sprot, a notary, for high treason. This Sprot having given cause of suspicion by some words which fell from him, and afterwards by some papers found upon him, was accused of being privy to the plots of the late Earl of Gowry and Robert Logan, Laird of Restalrig, to murder King James in 1600, insomuch that he had read or heard certain letters which passed between the Earl and Robert Logan concerning the plot, but did not reveal the same; and further that he became possessed of the letter which was found in his chest.

When this indictment was read, Sprot confessed it to be true in every point, and was found guilty and condemned to be hanged upon a gibbet until he was dead, and thereafter his head to be stricken from his body and affixed upon a prick of iron upon the highest part of the Tolbooth where the heads of Gowry and the other conspirators stand.

When Sprot was brought to execution, he died very religious and penitent, fully confessing his offence and praying that the ministers

101

who were present would proclaim his confession in their pulpits. Being upon the upper part of the ladder he desired liberty to sing the 6th Psalm, and requested the people to sing it with him; at the end thereof, fastening a cloth upon his own eyes, he was cast over the ladder. It was much noted that before his last breath, when he had hung a pretty space, he lifted up his hands a good height and clapped them together several times to the great wonder of all the beholders.

28th. Two days since M. Henry Hudson returned to Gravesend. He set out with 14 others on 20th May last purposing to find a passage to the East Indies by the Northeast. At Nova Zembla they found a cross standing and signs of fire that had been made there, also many morses; but because of the great plenty of ice his hope of a passage between Newland and Nova Zembla was taken away. Reporteth that Willoughby's Land as it is laid on our cards is but a conceit of card-makers, and seems no other than Newland or Greenland. Nor is there any passage by way of Pechora, Russia, Greenland and Lappia because of the ice. Noteth that from 19th May till 27th July it was always day, with no use at all of candle in the betacle (which is the name seamen use for the little close place where the compass is kept).

On the morning of 15th June in latitude of 75° on a clear day, two of the company (their names Thomas Hills and Robert Rayner) saw a *mermaid*. She came close to the ship's side, looking earnestly on the men. A little after a sea came and overturned her. From the navel upward her back and breasts were like a woman's; her body as big as ours; her skin very white; and long hair hanging down behind, of colour black. In her going down they saw her tail, which was like the tail of a porpoise and speckled like a mackerel.

29th. A young morse living hath been brought to the Court where the King and others beheld it with much admiration, the like never having been seen alive in England. Although this beast is very strange in shape yet is it of strange docility and apt to be taught. The bringer is Capt. Jonas Poole who this summer past made a voyage to Lapland and Cherry Isle whence he brought back 31 tuns of oil and more than a hogshead of morses' teeth; they slew near a thousand of the beasts.

30th. The silver mine in Scotland still promises well. According to the assay each ton yields £120. They have taken out 150 tons, and the farther they delve, the wider the vein broadens and widens. They are digging in two places, and each yields 14 tons a week; so the quantity increases daily, but since many things needed for refining are not to be had in Scotland, the King has ordered the earth to be sent into England.

31st. The Treaty in the Low Countries is dissolved. The States declare they will not relinquish the Indian navigation nor will they agree to a free exercise of the Catholic religion. Spinola hath begun a fresh negotiation through the French commissioners for a 12 years' truce.

The plague again groweth this year. In the last week of July 50 died of it; and this month 45, 70, 79 and 73.

3rd September. From Madrid came a report that Sir Anthony Shirley was dead in Rome, but immediately afterward he passed through the city with 20 followers to speak with the King at Lerma. Many *pasquinados* were put upon the gate and walls of the King's palace, tending to a mislike of the government, as of the King's play, losing 700,000 ducats to the Duke of Lerma and his sons while his household servants in Madrid remain without any pay for 18 months past; of the misspending of thousands paid by Castile to the King; and the like. These libels were set up in Madrid, Lerma and Vallodolid and other places all in one night. Sir Edward Baynham pretendeth to spend the rest of his days in a monastery where he shall have time enough to repent his misgoverned time spent at home.

4th. Because of the plague in the City, Parliament is again prorogued till 9th February next.

5th. One William Dence a seaman (who was taken at sea by Capt. Jennings the pirate) being examined at Bristol, declares that Jennings told him as a friend that he should beware of Ward who is at sea with three Marseilles ships. When they take Christians they either cast them overboard or sell them into Barbary as captives. Ward is now turned Turk. Jennings said that if the King will grant them a lease of their lives for certain years, they will come back, but never for any pardon, for they may be hanged with their pardons round their necks. Also he will not wear the King's colours any longer, but the young Prince's and honour him, hoping in time he will have wars. Jennings has as his consorts Capt. Roofe of Dartmouth, Bishop and Sackwell, with their ships.

14th. Upon an assay of the ore from Scotland privately taken in the Tower it is now found to hold not above 8 ozs. of silver in the hundredweight by reason of abundance of spar and filth in the ore which should have been removed by the miners. This (after the charges of melting and fining deducted) is no more than £30 the ton.

15th. The States have declared that they will wait no longer than the end of this present month for a conclusion of the treaty.

17th. The gentleman employed by the Duke of Wirtenberg at his departure from Dover embarked 8 horses. Whereupon the searcher's servant demanded 2*s.* each, viz., 12*d.* for himself and 12*d.* for my L. of Worcester's minister, being the ordinary fee. The gentleman refused to pay, asking whether the searcher would stay him for the fees. The searcher told him no; he would rather give him the fees than intercept his passage if he came by the King's licence: which courtesy the gentleman took as an affront. Moreover this gentleman gave protection to 7 persons. When he was desired sight of his pass, he refused to show it. Hereupon M. Mayor sent for the master of the ship and wished him to be well advised what passages he carried over, binding him in £20 not to transport any without warrant. The gentleman, much discontented, returned into the town and showed his pass, which was but for himself and two servants; but no cause of staying being found, pass was given to the other persons and they departed.

Some days since my L. of Pembroke played at cards with Sir George Wharton and others, where Sir George showed such choler that my L. told him, 'Sir George, I have loved you long and desire still to do so, but by your manner in playing, you lay it upon me either to leave to love you, or to leave to play with you. Wherefore choosing to love you still, I will never play with you more.' The next day they hunted with the King, and my L. of Pembroke's page galloping after his Lordship, Sir George came up to him and lashed him over the face with his rod. The boy told his Lordship, who finding by strict examination that the boy had not deserved it, demanded of Sir George why he did strike his boy. Sir George answered he meant nothing towards his Lordship. 'I did not strike him,' answered Sir George. 'Then I am satisfied,' said the Earl. 'God's blood!' said Sir George, 'I say it not to satisfy you.' 'But, sir,' said the Earl, 'whoso striketh my boy without cause shall give me account of it, and therefore I tell you it was foolishly done of you.' 'You are a fool,' said Sir George. 'You lie in your throat,' said the Earl. The Duke of Lenox, the Earl of Marr and others coming up, the matter rested for a while, and everyone began to gallop away on the hunting.

The Earl being gone some minutes, Sir George spurred his horse

with all speed upon him, which was observed by the Earl of Montgomery who cried out, 'Brother, you will be stricken.' The Earl
instantly thereupon received Sir George with a sound backward
blow over the face which drove almost back upon his horse's croop.
But company being present, they galloped again till in the end the
stag died in Bagshot town, where Sir George comes up to the Earl
offering him a paper, protesting there was nothing in it unfit for his
Lordship to read. The Earl said, 'Sir George, give me no papers here
where all they may see us who know what hath passed; but tell me,
is not the purport of it a challenge to me.' 'Yes,' said Sir George.
'Well,' said the Earl, 'this night you shall have answer.'

Having come home, my L. of Pembroke sends privily for Sir John
Lee, to whom he delivers the sword that my L. of Devonshire gave
him; which Sir John receiving goes to Sir George and tells him that
it is the Earl's sword, and the next morning, being Sunday (16th)
the time when they should fight; and therefore willed him to withdraw himself and take the measure of the sword, for the Earl would
not take one hair's breadth of advantage at his hands.

Upon this, first Sir George and afterwards the Earl were sent
for upon the King's commandment and ordered not to stir in the
matter; after which Sir George comes to Sir John Lee and says that
if my Lord would break the King's commandment he would do the
like. Sir John said he knew that the Earl was very scrupulous of
breaking the King's commandment, but yet he would undertake to
bring Sir George where the Earl should be, all alone, with that
sword by his side. Nevertheless upon another command being given
out, both were convented before the Lords, and last before the King,
and the matter there ended.

19th. The L. Deputy held sessions at Liffer on 12th where Phelim
Reagh, with all the rest of them, as well relievers and abettors
as actors in the rebellion, were tried and executed as traitors to
the number of 20 or thereabouts. The £500 set upon the head of
O'Dogherty and £200 for the body or head of Phelim have been
paid to the parties who did the service out of the booties taken from
the rebels, so that the King's charge did not exceed £100; all other
rewards for the killing or apprehending the chief rebels are levied on
the country.

20th. The City ditch is now being cleansed out. The King is much
troubled about an answer to his Book which is lately come over and
is thought the most part the work of Parsons, though some of it by
others as may be seen by the difference of the style. The Earl of

Dunbar is returned from Scotland with a new legion of Scots, worser than the former. Sir William Godolphin hath lately been sent by the King to survey the mines, of which he speaks great wonders.

Capt. Edmund Whitlock is dead, and he is lamented by all his boon companions as if the world had not been worthy of him. His death was sudden as were all the actions of his life.

This Whitlock in his young years was a hopeful student of Christ's College in Cambridge and came thence to Lincoln's Inn where he misspent his time with good companions. He therefore betook himself to foreign travels about 1587 and having studied in the Universities of Rostock, Witenberg, Prague, Rome and other places he was at length put in charge of a company of foot in France until the wars ceased. Then he returned to England after an absence of almost a dozen years. And now because of his experience of foreign affairs, his knowledge in the tongues, pleasant behaviour and the great liberty of his wit in his conversation, he fell into good liking with many English noblemen and gentlemen, and especially with the Earl of Rutland, whereby he had the mischance to be led by that nobleman into the mutiny of the Earl of Essex. For this reason he was had in much suspicion (as he was known to be pragmatical and martial) and was clapped up in Newgate and brought to the King's Bench Bar to be indicted of high treason; but in the end he was committed to the care of his brother and friends until he was quite discharged. He was again in misfortune over the Powder Plot, for by ill hap he dined with my L. of Northumberland and Thomas Percy the day before that conspiracy should have been executed. He was again imprisoned, but at last delivered as nothing appeared by any examination that he was acquainted with that business. After his delivery he lived with most dependency upon the Earl of Northumberland and had licence to resort to him in the Tower. At the time of his death he was at Newhall in Essex with the Earl of Sussex, and fell into a distemper of body by the unseasonable heat and his own overcarelessness that he was taken with an extraordinary looseness which weakened him much, upon which he was let blood, and not long after went away quietly as in a slumber. He was exceedingly pleasant in his conceit and so good a companion that he was much esteemed by divers great men; he was extreme prodigal and wasteful, and very valiant. In that great quarrel between Sir Francis Vere and the Earl of Northumberland he carried the challenge from my Lord and afterwards even challenged Sir Francis himself, for which a warrant was sent after him by the Council so that he was fain for a good while to hide himself.

A few days before Whitlock, being in want when M. Holland's company broke by reason of the plague, sought to be at Mrs. Jones's house, who in her husband's absence declining it, he went in the night, his boy carrying his cloak bag, on foot to my L. of Sussex, who going the next day to hunt, the Capt. not then sick told him he would see him no more. A chaplain came to him, to whom he delivered his understanding, and soon after died; and my L. hath buried him with his own ancestors.

21st. Gervase Markham hath translated into English Ludovico Ariosto's *Satires*, in 7 discourses, *videlicet*: Of the Court and courtiers; of liberty and the clergy in general; of the Roman clergy; of marriage; of soldiers, musicians and lovers; of schoolmasters and scholars; of honour and the happiest life. Addeth an Argument to show the reasons and occasions why Ariosto wrote these satires.

24th. Sir Henry Wotton, the Ambassador in Venice, complaineth greatly that there be many English gentlemen in Florence, drawn thither by the beauty and security of the place and the purity of the language; among them a knot of English Catholics, partly banished, partly voluntary residents, whereof Toby Mathew is principal. These men with pleasantness of conversation and force of example greatly endanger the faith of any Englishman that shall go thither.

27th. The Queen lately dined with Sir Henry Lee at his house of Lee's Rest near Woodstock, and gave great countenance and had long and large discourse with Mrs. Vavasour (whom Sir Henry took as his mistress soon after he left his office as Champion to Queen Elizabeth in 1590); and within a day or two she sent a very fair jewel valued above £100. This favour put such new life into the old man to see his sweetheart so graced that he swears he will have one more fling to the Court before he die, though he thought to have taken his leave this summer when he went to present the Prince with an armour that cost him £200, and within a year or two will serve his turn neither for jest nor earnest.

29th. There has now reached the King's hands an answer to his book on the Pope's Breves and also the Cardinal Bellarmine's own letters against the Oath of Allegiance. In both are many passages which touch the King nearly, and he is preparing to answer. To this end he departs for Royston with his theologians. The King is very ready to undertake this work and shows a kind of rivalry with the Cardinal who is reputed the most learned on the Pope's side.

The new book is entitled *Responsio Matthaei Torti et Theologi Papiensis, ad Librum Inscriptum Triplici Nodo Triplex Cuneus*. This

Tortus is chaplain to the Cardinal Bellarmine (who is reputed the real author). On the point that the Oath is concerned only with the obedience of the subject and not of religion, replieth that the Oath was not a thing by itself but parcel of an Act detecting and repressing of popish recusants. And as for the King's declaration of his great clemency towards Catholics, shown in his proclamation that all priests who are not in prison may go freely into exile: if exile is mercy, what sweet names will he give to the rack and the rope? Addeth moreover that the two Briefs which Pope Clement VIII sent to the English Catholics shortly before Queen Elizabeth died, these were written in favour of his Majesty (and not against him as he allegeth) for they exhorted Catholics to promote the succession of an upright and orthodox Monarch; and that the King's own envoys had given good reasons for believing that he was such, and not at all averse from embracing the Catholic Faith. Which hope was confirmed when the King himself addressed kindly letters to the Pope and to the Cardinals Aldobrandino and Bellarmine, in which he begged, amongst other things, that there might be some Scotsman made Cardinal to be his representative at the Court of Rome.

The *Ark Royal* which is being rebuilt at Woolwich dock was today launched in a blustering day, with the wind at southwest, but with little difficulty, and brought to her moorings. Her name is altered to the *Anne Royal*.

30th. This past month there have died weekly of the plague 123, 136, 104, 143 and 147.

3rd October. Tom Coryat is come back from his travels wherein in 4½ months he journeyed 1,975 miles, and visited 45 cities in France, Savoy, Italy, Rhetia, Helvetia, Germany and the Netherlands; and hath much to say of all of them, but above all of Venice where he remained 6 weeks. Their music (saith he) is exquisite but their playhouses very beggarly compared with ours. He saw a woman act with as good grace and gestures as any masculine actor. Also one tormented with the strappado: the offender, his hands bound behind him, is conveyed into a rope that hangeth in a pulley, and hoisted up in the rope to a great height with two several swings, where he sustaineth so great torments that his joints are for the time loosed and pulled asunder. Of his own observation reporteth much of the famous Venetian courtesans, for he visited one in her house, not (saith he) for sport but to convert her by persuasive speeches and to learn of the manner of her life.

Barnaby Rich hath a second part to his book of Faults, called

Room for a Gentleman in praise of war and gentlemen, and dispraising the women and lawyers of our age. Declareth gentlemen to be of three kinds: in respect of blood, of virtue, and of both. Yet some would also have of riches and wealth; but riches can never add degree to a gentleman, though a ready instrument to put in practice certain virtues belonging to gentry, namely bounty and liberality. Noteth also that there are comprised under the title of gentry all ecclesiastical persons professing religion; martial men that have borne office and have had command in the field; all students of arts and sciences; and by our English custom all Inns of Court men professing the Law. It skills not what their fathers were, whether farmers, shoemakers, tailors or tinkers, if their names be entered in any of the Inns of Court they are all gentlemen.

10th. Sir George More is at last reconciled with M. Donne his son-in-law, and will pay him as portion for his wife £800, or £20 quarterly for their maintenance till it be paid.

12th. This Sunday the King before he went to Newmarket called the L. Coke and all the other Judges of the Common Law before him to answer complaints made by the Civil Lawyers for the general granting of prohibitions. The L. Coke amongst other offensive speech said to the King that his Majesty was defended by his laws; at which saying the King was very much offended and told him he spake foolishly for he was not defended by his laws but by God, and so gave Coke a very sharp reprehension for that and other speeches; and said that Sir Thomas Crompton (the Vicar General to the Archbishop) was as good a man as he, Coke having used some speech against Crompton. The King would have been much more offended had not the L. Treasurer most humbly on his knee used many good words to pacify his Majesty. But in the end he gave a gracious countenance to all the other Judges and said he would maintain the Common Law.

14th. Our statesmen and soldiers show too small regard for degree. Sir Thomas Edmonds, the Ambassador in Brussels, hath lately played the part of a tall gentleman rather than of a grave Ambassador in drawing upon Sir Edward Baynham for the little respect he used towards him. Likewise Sir Thomas Studder, one of the Colonels in the Low Countries, was standing at the backdoor of his house when it fortuned that Capt. Bruce passed by him and looked him in the face but did not salute him, whereupon Studder gave him a blurt with his mouth. At that Bruce turned back and Sir Thomas asked him whether he had no better manners: whereunto Bruce answered that he was as good a man as Studder and had no cap for any men but those he liked. At that the Colonel replied that the Ambassador was angry with Sir Edward Baynham because he put not off his hat to him and there was as much difference between the Ambassador and Baynham as between Bruce and himself, and thereupon lifting up his leg, let a fart at him, and bid him carry that in his teeth to his companions.

16th. Of all the matters in the book that came from Rome, none disturbs the King more than to find himself reproached for having written to Pope Clement VIII and the Cardinals Aldobrandino and Bellarmine that he was kindly disposed towards the Catholic religion and desired a Scottish Cardinal to be appointed by whose means he could more safely and easily treat with the Pope in Rome. When the King read these words and considered their importance, he remembered that Sir James Elphinstone, L. Balmerinoch, who is now President of the Court of Sessions in Scotland was his Secretary at that time. It so falls out that L. Balmerinoch is at Royston, with the Earl of Dunfermline, to beg the King not to lay fresh burdens upon the Catholics in Scotland. L. Balmerinoch was thereon summoned to the King's presence and by him questioned. He is said to have declared that he wrote the letters to the Pope and the Cardinals by order of the King; nor can he remember their contents except that they were written in support of a Bishop, a kinsman of his, who was aspiring to the purple and wished the King's intercession. This matter is much talked of and may do great harm, for the King is exceedingly wroth at such an attack on himself. He has forbidden the sale of the book until his own reply is ready.

17th. The Deputies for both sides have left the Hague, each man to his own home. Before departing the Marquis Spinola and the rest of the Deputies for Spain were entertained by the Prince Maurice. They have now returned to Brussels. After the departure a paper was found in the dwelling of Richardot, which was his instructions from the Archduke, to the effect that he should insinuate a union between Flanders and Holland, and rely more on the French than the English Commissioners. It is variously conjectured whether this paper was left by intent or casually.

M. Daniel Tuvil who last April set forth a book of *Essays Politic and Moral* (treating of such matters as persuasion, opinion, affection, reputation and observation) now hath a second called *Essays Moral and Theological*, of learning and knowledge, respect, temptation, poverty.

18th. The King being greatly disturbed that he is charged with

110

having written letters to the Pope and certain Cardinals hath written to the Council declaring his innocence, and demanding of them how he may make his innocency manifest. They are to call the L. Balmerinoch before them to be examined. To this letter the King added in his own hand: 'Though ye were strangers to the country where this was done, yet are ye no strangers to the King thereof, and ye know if the King of Scotland prove a knave, the King of England can never be.'

20th. The Council have answered the King's letter, but in their reply they made no mention of the ways whereby the King's reputation can be freed; at which the King is indignant, as also at the reports that are being spread abroad, especially since the L. Hay and two or three others were witnesses of his speeches with Balmerinoch. At first (saith his Majesty) Balmerinoch made no stick to confess that he himself was the maker of the letter despatched to the Pope and the Cardinals; and that he had often solicited the King for it, which was as often refused; but at the last (he declared) through his importunity the King granted it. But this the King denieth.

This conference was held in the King's withdrawing room at Newmarket, where he purposely left the bed-chamber door open that two or three might hear what passed between them. In the afternoon Balmerinoch confessed his own guilt in the presence of his fellow Secretary, and on his knees craved pardon of the King. As for the L. Hay, he speaks very bitterly against L. Balmerinoch, saying that he never saw man look as he did that Sunday; and if rigour is spared in his punishment, the King's honour can never be cleared, for the least sparing will ever be thought collusion betwixt the King and him.

21st. L. Balmerinoch hath now confessed that in the year 1598, at the earnest desire of the late Archbishop of Glasgow (then Ambassador in France) and others who were anxious to have had some correspondence between the King and the Pope, he presumed divers times to move the King, and offered the frame of such a letter as he would have him sign; but the King ever refused. Hereupon, relying on the assured hopes of greater statesmen than himself of the benefits that would come of the Pope's friendship, he caused Sir Edward Drummond to draw up a letter to the Pope, commending the late Bishop of Vaizon to be made a Cardinal. This letter, and others to the same effect to the Dukes of Florence and Savoy and certain Cardinals, he presented one morning when the King was going on hunting in haste. The King finding the letters to be in Latin signed them, not suspecting that one was to the Pope. Thereafter Sir Edward added the Pope's style both in the beginning and above the King's sub-scription in the end. Now Balmerinoch protesteth before God and His angels that this confession is true. He asketh no pardon but that the King take such a course as will make known to the world the King's innocency and his own offence.

The L. Roos, grandson of the Earl of Exeter, has been travelling in Italy with my L. S. John, and M. John Mole as their tutor, but coming to Rome M. Mole is taken by the Inquisition, and there is small hope of his recovery for he had on him certain translations of Plessis' books that talked of Babylon and Antichrist. Nevertheless there is great means being made for his release.

The weekly bill is but little abated, for last week died 247, and of the sickness 124. On Sunday there was a nest of Brownists discovered about Finsbury, whereof five and thirty were apprehended with their preacher, one Trundle, that used to exercise at Christ-church. The Bishop of Chichester is appointed to answer Bellarmine about the oath of Allegiance, which is very contrary to his disposition not to meddle with controversies. The Bishop of London is to search for and take such books as are to be found written against the Book published not long since against the justification of the Oath.

22nd. The King is now well contented with the zeal shown by the Council in the trial of the L. Balmerinoch and hath written in his own hand to the L. Treasurer saying: 'The name given me of James included a prophetical mystery of my fortune, for as Jacob I wrestled with my enemy upon the 5 of August for my life and overcame; on the 5 of November I wrestled with my wit; and now in a case ten times dearer to me than my life, I mean my reputation, I have wrestled and overcome with my memory.'

24th. Although the King has appointed the Bishops of Bath and Wells and of Chichester to answer Bellarmine's book, yet he himself is very busy writing in his own hand and hath written 10 or 12 sheets, for proceed in this business he will. Now he seeks of my L. of Salisbury certain particulars of the examinations of Garnet and Fawkes and other matters of the late conspiracies.

The L. Deputy declareth that since this great territory of Ulster is escheated to the King who is now sole proprietor of the most part of it, he may retain it for ever by a firm establishment of his Crown. Because the disparity of estates in Ulster has been that which over-swayed their chieftains and troubled the whole land, the Deputy would have the escheated lands divided among many, that the principal gentlemen and the honester and best sort may be satisfied without envyings. Further, it is better for them to be assigned their

portions in the plains where (besides that they may be better overlooked) they shall be encouraged to labour; for in the woods and
places of strength they will be given to running up and down the
country with their cattle (which they call 'creaghting'), or in idleness,
and so retain their ancient pride and fierceness; and also be able
continually to steal out of these dens and annoy the civil inhabitants
that should otherwise be settled in the plains. If this Province of
Ulster could be once settled, then were all the occasions of great
revolts gone; the land would be peopled and improved; the King's
revenues increased and those of his other dominions more converted
and spent upon themselves.

25th. The Bellman of London (which Dekker wrote this last spring)
now taketh a second walk, entitled *Lanthorn and Candlelight*, dis-
closing the divers ways of cheating used towards gentlemen of
worship, as of a rogue that feigneth to be an author who comes up to
a knight with a little book fairly apparelled in vellum, with gilt fillets
and fourpenny silk ribbon having dandling at the four corners. The
title being superficially surveyed, the knight sees the book carries his
name, and under it stands an epistle, just the length of a henchman's
grace before dinner. So the knight, surveying this little sunbeam of
Phoebus shining thus briskly in print, thanks him for his love and
labour, and to cherish his young and tender muse gives him 4 or 6
angels, inviting him either to stay breakfast, or if the sundial of the
house points towards eleven, then to tarry dinner. In this way many
knights are cheated, for the falconer (as this kind of rogue calls
himself) deals with a herald for a note of all the knights' or gentlemen's
names of worth that dwell in their circuit, and prints off so many
epistles as they have names, the epistles dedicatory being all one, and
vary in nothing but the titles of their patrons.

28th. This last week the weekly bill was 240, of which 102 died of
the plague; in the previous weeks this month there died 103, 131, 124.

1st November. Sir Ralph Winwood, in the King's behalf, hath
made a remonstrance to the Assembly of the States, urging them to
accept the truce on the conditions offered. If they fail in the means of
fighting so powerful an enemy and must needs depend on the support
of their neighbours, our King is too just, religious and peaceful to
foment a war which howsoever just at the beginning would show as
unjust from the refusal of peace. As for subsidies, a small would be
useless, and a large would be ruinous to us; and either would throw
us into war, to which the King will only be driven to maintain the

honour of his Crown or the safety of his subjects. Those who are now treating with them are not the Archdukes or Kings of Spain, but the Kings of France and England and the Princes of Germany, all friends to the States. They are content with the Archduke's declaration of their freedom and recognizing them as a sovereign state, and they promise to guarantee the truce. The two Kings are too deeply pledged to let them fall at the end of a 10 years' truce; let them therefore embrace the truce for it is less dangerous than war.

Likewise the President Jeannin urges them to make peace with such fervour that he is suspected by the King of France to have been won over by presents from Spain. The States are divided, Zealand being desirous to continue the war, as is Count Maurice who declares roundly that the Kings of England and France are waging a worse war against the Provinces than the Spaniard. Barneveld and the other Provinces are for peace on any conditions; as are the poorer sort and those who live inland and have suffered the worse. Yet a peace will bring us many discommodities, for if an increase of trade be allowed the Netherlands, the revenues of this Kingdom will greatly diminish.

2nd. One Henry Alred, yeoman of the King's Chapel, was admonished by the Chapter for drunkenness, many great disorders, and threatening to spill the blood of the Sub-dean. A prick was set upon his head, as is used in the King's house in such cases, as a warning to his mending his ways. This same Alred caused great offence last March by his fearful blasphemies, execrations and threats uttered when the sacrament was being administered in the Chapel.

10th. The Bishop of Chichester hath little leisure these days, he is so spurred on by the King in his answer to Bellarmine, which he could perform very well if he might take his time and not be troubled with arguments obtruded upon him continually by the King. There is set forth a book of the examination, arraignment and conviction of George Sprot who was executed at Edinburgh in August; with a long preface by Dr. George Abbot, Dean of Winchester, against those who employ their wits and tongues to obscure that matter of the Earl of Gowry's conspiracy. This confession of Sprot makes Gowry's conspiracy hang more handsomely together and hath much pleased the King. The Indian fleet is now come home but without any noise of many millions.

11th. The truce goes on for certain in the Low Countries for 10 years, with all reasonable satisfaction to the States in matter of sovereignty, religion and traffic; but the men of war mightily oppose it.

20th. One J. W. a Catholic priest hath put together *The English Martyrology*, printed abroad, a summary of the lives of the Saints of the three Kingdoms of England, Ireland and Scotland, collected into months; and at the end a catalogue of those who have suffered death for the Catholic cause since King Henry VIII; of these 70 died in the reign of King Henry; 183 under Queen Elizabeth; and 12 since the coming of the King from Scotland.

27th. Today Capt. Roger Orme and Lieut. Ashpoole were called before the Council concerning a declaration made in Holland by Ashpoole that in his presence Orme wounded himself in three or four places to cast a slander on Sir William Windsor as if he had caused certain men to lie in wait to have killed Orme. Ashpoole now confesses that, his conscience being inwardly afflicted and terrified by a vision, Orme was indeed set upon and hurt by some of the rebels. For his slander Ashpoole is committed to the Fleet.

28th. The young Earl of Essex, who of late was in the Low Countries, is now returned from his travels.

30th. The King, taking to the quick the L. Treasurer's remonstrances concerning the dispensing of his benefits and favours to his servants, is now resolved to be less adventurous in his bounty. It is said that on a day the L. Treasurer having received a peremptory warrant for a grant of £20,000 for Carr, and apprehending that the King was as ignorant of the value of what he had granted as of the worth of him that was to receive it, caused the money to be laid upon the ground in a room through which the King was to pass. The King, amazed at such a sight, asked the Treasurer whose money it was, who answered, 'Yours, before you gave it away.' Whereupon the King fell into a passion, protesting he was abused, never intending such a gift. And casting himself upon the heap, scrabbled out the quantity of £200 or £300 and swore he should have no more.

The plague is somewhat abated, for this month past there died of it in all 322.

1st December. The young L. Cranborne was married today to the Lady Katherine, daughter of my L. of Suffolk, very privately at the Lady Walsingham's lodging by the Tiltyard; there were few at it, for his side only Sir Edward Cecil, Sir William Cooke, Sir Fr. Bacon and Sir Walter Cope; the bride's mother was not present. There are many rich presents of plate.

2nd. The King complaineth that no order is yet taken for a restraint of the buying and selling of venison in London, for never was venison so common both of hind and doe as this winter. He cannot endure that all his care to preserve his game is eluded in such manner, and common sale made of his does and hinds which all come out of his grounds. Further he will have order be taken to prevent the taking of partridges in nets and engines in all places of his resort.

Thomas Heywood has a long heroical poem in 17 cantos, called *Troia Britanica: or Great Britain's Troy*, with many pleasant poetical tales interspersed, and concluding with an universal chronicle from the Creation to this present time. Of the Puritan, saith—

> In our reformed Church too, a new man
> Is in few years crept up, in strange disguise,
> And call'd the self-opinion'd Puritan;
> A fellow that can bear himself precise;
> No church supremacy endure he can;
> No orders in the Bishop's diocese:
> He keeps a starch'd gait, wears a formal ruff,
> A nosegay, set face, and a poted cuff.
>
> He never bids 'God speed you' on the way,
> Because he knows not what your bosoms smother,
> His phrase is, 'Verily'; 'By yea and nay,'
> 'In faith,' 'In truth,' 'good neighbour,' or 'good brother.'
> And when he borrows money, ne'er will pay:
> One of th' elect must common with another;
> And when the poor his charity entreat,
> 'You labour not, and therefore must not eat.'

9th. The King is at Thetford where he was received by three cormorants that planted themselves upon the church and would not be removed by ringing of bells, the shouting of the people or shooting of pieces at them until after much levelling one of them was taken down with a bullet and then his fellows flew away. The young L. Cranborne set forward for France three days ago with three barges in very blustering weather accompanied with Sir Thomas and young Harry Howard his new brothers-in-law who are to part from him in Paris and to go for Italy. He went away two days earlier than was given out to avoid the multitude of followers that would have brought him on his way.

12th. M. Robert Harcourt who set out for Guiana with a ship of 80 tons, a pinnace of 36 tons, and a shallop of 9 tons and 97 persons whereof 60 were landsmen is now returned with many observations of that country. Noteth that the current of the great river of Amazons is so violent that 30 leagues from land they found the water in the sea as fresh as in a spring. He took with him an Indian who served Sir John Gilbert many years, also another Indian named Martin whom he had brought to England four years ago; with these two as interpreters he was most kindly treated by the Indians. At a place called Caripo in the River of Wiapoco they came aboard with good store of their country provisions, one or two arrayed in old clothes which they had gotten from an Englishman sent to trade there by Sir Walter Ralegh last year; but for the most part both men and women go stark belly naked, except that the better sort of the men wear a little piece of woven cotton cloth over their privities. This country had been taken possession of for Queen Elizabeth by Capt. Charles Lee, who lived among them divers years and is buried in Wiapoco. To these people M. Harcourt made an oration, telling them of King James and how he would permit his people to live among them and defend them against their enemies; which they accepted gladly and had expected long; Sir Walter Ralegh, said they, had promised the like but nothing hitherto performed. M. Harcourt noteth that the lowlands of this country be unhealthful by reason of the many swamps but in some places in the mountains it is healthful, and here are many minerals and mines full of metals. The middle sort of land aboundeth in meadows, pastures and pleasant streams. Of the commodities the principal is sugar canes, also cotton wool; many drugs and simples for physic; and a little green apple so violent in its operation that one bite will cause a man to sleep to death, of which apple his cousin took a bite and though he spit it out again yet for 2 days space he had an extraordinary sleepiness and purged him 60 seats. Tobacco also is another commodity. They came away from Guiana in September and anchored at the Isle of Trinidado, where they found 3 English ships. Here is a pitch gotten in the earth in very great abundance, most excellent for trimming ships for it melteth not in the sun. Thence they came to an island called Meves where is a hot bath that in 24 hours cured a man's hand that had been burnt with gunpowder and other diseases. In this voyage there died but three.

15th. The Commissioners inquiring into the abuses in the Navy have met several times these past months, examining many witnesses. Today they heard the testimony of M. Matthew Baker, master shipwright, who uttered many things against M. Pett, and especially of the great ship now building, declaring that Pett is very insufficient for the work; that the timber is ill chosen; and the cost will far exceed the estimate.

16th. In Paris, one Borghese, a young fellow, was lately executed for giving himself out to be the Pope's bastard. The sentence was not given by any Court of Parliament but by a Master of Requests. Upon examination he confessed that he never knew father or mother, but that his nurse ever told him he was such a man's son; that he had always been well maintained, but especially since this man came to the place he had received great sums by unknown means, with a caveat not to come to Rome.

17th. The Prince complaining to the King that his lodging was too far distant, the King replied that he could take such course as he would to remedy it. Hereupon the Prince sent to the Earls of Southampton and Pembroke to move their households and horse as he wished to occupy their lodging. When they refused, he sent his own people to remove them perforce, at which these Lords were in great indignation. This action is regarded as a great proof of spirit in a Prince who though only fifteen years old gives the highest promise in all he does.

20th. The Venetian Ambassador at Paris coming to visit the Spanish Ambassador gave him the title of *Excellencia*, who in return saluted the Venetian as *Illustrissimo Signoria*, of which he complained to the Pope's Nuncio who told the Spanish Ambassador of his complaint. Learning of this, the Spanish Ambassador sends his secretary to the Venetian, who tells him that his State is not to be compared with that which belongeth to so mighty a King as the King of Spain. 'Why,' saith the Venetian, 'our State hath ever been respected as a kingdom, and the Ambassador thereof so accepted of and entertained'; and added that the State of Venice had also a kingdom under them; for they are King of Candia. 'You,' quoth the Spaniard, 'Kings? You are a State and Head of a company of factions, mutinous and rebellious' and on such terms parted.

23rd. The executing of Borghese is generally ill taken in France as savouring of too much severity, for the sentence read out at his death was only for usurping the name and arms of the family of the Borghesi; and the Nuncio himself says that if he had thought they would have used such rigour he would not have prosecuted it so far. There are many jests and epigrams made of it.

28th. Dr. John Dee the noted astrologer is lately dead at Mortlake, and is buried in the chancel of the church there. He was born in 1527, and while a Fellow at Trinity College in Cambridge was reputed a conjurer, because at a play of Aristophanes he devised a great scarabaeus to fly up to the heavens with a man and with his basket of victuals on his back. He was greatly favoured by Queen Elizabeth who employed him often, though her rewards were less than her promises. In his middle years much given to alchemical experiments and intercourse with spirits, wherein he was greatly cozened by his assistant one Edward Kelly with whom he travelled into Poland. Kelly on a time propounded that they two should have their wives in common, which he declared had been commanded by an angel. After his return into England, Dr. Dee was made Warden of Manchester College, but most unhappily, and of late years hath lived very poorly in his house at Mortlake, being forced to sell his books and plate. He hath written many books, of which most still lie unprinted.

OTHER BOOKS AND PLAYS PRINTED IN 1608

i. From Cambridge, *A Discourse of the damnable art of Witchcraft* by William Perkins, declaring that they grossly err who deny that there be witches; that witches truly convicted should be punished with death; that the miracles of the Popish Church are but Satanical wonders. Discourseth of the nature of witchcraft in general; the practices thereof; of divination; of working witchcraft; of witches and their punishment; the application of the doctrine of witches to the present times. The signs denoting a witch be these: if a person be notoriously defamed for a witch; if a fellow witch or magician give testimony of such a person; if after cursing there follow death or some mischief; if after quarrelling or threatening, a present mischief doth ensue; if the party suspected be a child, servant or near neighbour of a known and convicted witch; if the party suspected do have the Devil's mark upon his body; if being examined, he be unconstant or contrary to himself in his deliberate answers.

ii. A vast work by Edward Grimestone called *A General History of the Netherlands*, from the earliest times to this present year 1608, with many engraved pictures of the great ones of those parts.

iii. *An Apology for John Wicliffe* by Dr. Thomas James, keeper of the books in Sir Thomas Bodley's Library at Oxford, to answer the objections against his doctrines made by Father Parsons and others. These answers are taken from divers works of Wicliffe in his own hand in the Library.

iv. *The Customer's Alphabet and Primer* by Thomas Milles, containing their creed or belief in the true doctrines of the Christian religion, with an answer to all such as would persuade others that the bringing home of traffic must needs decay our shipping. The true motive of this work is a natural defence of poor despised and contemned customers by whose disgrace the King receives such loss and the State much wrong. Noteth that a steady standard of money and store of coin in the Prince's treasury makes all things cheap, holds trades in request, shows Kings to be powerful, and subjects wealthy; so as the standard falls into uncertainy the contrary ensueth whilst coin itself by usury in merchandising exchange casts out industry and trade.

v. Of the plays printed this past year, three are by Shakespeare, *videlicet, A Yorkshire Tragedy, Pericles*, and *Antony and Cleopatra*; and of others, *Your Five Gallants, Law Tricks, Humour out of Breath, The Second Part of the Honest Whore, The Rape of Lucrece, A Mad World My Masters, The Dumb Knight*, and the two parts of that troublesome play of Byron written by Chapman, dedicated to Sir Thomas Walsingham and his son, but with the offending act omitted.

BYRON'S SPEECH OF DEATH

Horror of death, let me alone in peace,
And leave my soul to me, whom it concerns;
You have no charge of it; I feel her free.
How she doth rouse, and like a falcon stretch
Her silver wings; as threatening Death with death;
At whom I joyfully will cast her off.
I know this body but a sink of folly,
The ground-work and raised frame of woe and frailty;
The bond and bundle of corruption;
A quick corse, only sensible of grief,
A walking sepulchre, or household thief;
A glass of air, broken with less than breath,
A slave bound face to face with death till death—
And what said all you more? I know besides
That life is but a Dark and stormy night
Of senseless dreams, terrors and broken sleeps;
A tyranny, devising pains to plague
And make man long in dying, racks his death;
And death is nothing; what can you say more?
I bring a long globe and a little earth,
Am seated like Earth, betwixt both the heavens,
That if I rise, to heaven I rise; if fall,
I likewise fall to heaven; what stronger faith

120

Hath any of your souls? What say you more?
Why lose I time in these things? Talk of knowledge,
It serves for inward use. I will not die
Like a clergyman; but like the Captain
That pray'd on horseback, and with sword in hand,
Threaten'd the sun, commanding it to stand;
These are but ropes of sand.

1609

4th January. Parliament is again prorogued till 9th November by reason of the dearth and scarcity of all kinds of victual, lest by drawing such a concourse of people hither the prices of all things (already very high) be increased, and also draw gentlemen out of their counties where their hospitality would give relief to their poor neighbours. The King hath rewarded his players £40 for their private practice in this time of infection that they might be enabled to perform their service before him in these Christmas holidays.

10th. Sir Walter Ralegh's estate of Sherborne that hath long been in dispute is at last fallen into the hands of the King, who hath bestowed it upon Sir Robert Carr. Ralegh had formerly conveyed it to his son upon his death, but after his attainder a flaw was found in the conveyance by reason that a necessary clause had been omitted, so that the King might take it when he would. Nevertheless it was the King's first intention to establish the estate upon the Lady Ralegh and her children, but wishing to provide handsomely for his new favourite he proceeded no further. All these holidays Lady Ralegh hath been an importunate suitor on her husband's behalf, and Ralegh himself wrote to Carr very piteously; but now it is past recall, for said the King, 'I maun ha' the land, I maun ha' it for Carr.' This error or oversight is so gross that men ascribe it to God's Own Hand that blinded him and his counsel.

12th. The King's reply to the Cardinal Bellarmine is now ready to come out. It is said that there are many matters in the book which may move the Pope to some step as excommunicating or deposing the King, or declaring him heretic, or absolving his subjects from the Oath of Allegiance. The French Ambassador has twice urged his Majesty not to answer in his own person, and received a kind of assent, for the King said that there would not be wanting others to answer for him. The Council also consider that it would be of greater dignity to reply by another hand.

16th. There is printing *A True Historical Discourse* of Muly Hamet's rising to the three Kingdoms of Morocco, Fez, and Sus, with the disunion of those kingdoms by civil war kindled amongst his three ambitious sons, which happened these 7 years past; together with the adventures of Sir Anthony Shirley who with Sir Edwin Rich went to those parts in 1605 on embassage from the Emperor of Germany; concluding with a large account of the religion and policy of the Moor or Barbarian. Noteth that on 26th November 1607 Muly Sidam, one of the aforesaid sons, was aided by Capt. John Giffard and 6 other English captains and 200 Englishmen, who were slain all but 30 through the treachery of the Sidamians who deserted to the enemy.

17th. The King has lately attended in person two meetings of the Council for the further consideration of the plantation in Ulster. The project for the settlement of Tyrone is so highly approved of that it is resolved to follow the same in the other escheated lands. Sir Arthur Chichester is directed to make an estimate of the number of all servitors to be provided for, whom he thinks most worthy, but sparingly, since many suitors will be attracted to a place so large and fertile.

21st. Capt. Christopher Newport is again returned from Virginia, with much news of the colony and of Capt. John Smith, the new President. In June last Smith, Scrivener and 14 others took the barge to seek the head of the River of Patawomek, but after 12 days some of our gallants tired of that voyage and would have returned, but Smith would not. They endured many dangers from the savages, and a mine which the savages reported proved of no value. At one time Smith was in great danger of his life in strange manner, for spying many fishes lurking among the weeds, he sported himself to catch them by nailing them to the ground with his sword. It chanced that taking off his sword a fish in fashion of a thornback with a longer tail wherein is a most poisoned sting, she struck him an inch and a half into his wrist; and in four hours his hand, shoulder and part of his body had so extremely swollen that by his own appointment they prepared his grave in an isle which they then called Stingray Isle; yet by the help of an oil which Dr. Russell applied, ere night his tormenting pain was so well assuaged that he ate the fish to his supper. They returned to Jamestown on 20th July where they found the last supply of men all sick, and of the rest none able to do anything, but all complaining of the pride and cruelty of Ratcliffe the President that had riotously consumed the store and set them to build an unnecessary palace for himself in the woods. The news of Smith's discovery appeased their fury, but conditionally that Ratcliffe should be deposed and Capt. Smith would take on the government. Their request being affected, he substituted M. Scrivener his dearest friend in the Presidency, equally distributed the private provisions which

Ratcliffe had engrossed, appointed more honest officers to assist Scrivener (who at that time lay sick of a calenture), and in regard of the weakness of the company went off again to finish his discoveries. He set out in the barge on 29th July with 12 men.

On this journey they spent 3 days at Kecoughtan where the weroans, or chief men, feasted them with much mirth. Then they went forward to the country of the Massawonecks, and here 7 or 8 canoas prepared to assault them; yet they made ready to encounter although but 5 men with Smith could stand, for the rest (being newcomers) were sick almost to death. These sick men were laid under the tarpaulin, and their hats put up on sticks to make them seem many. The savages fled away from the barge till our men anchored right against them, and at length they sent two unarmed in a canoa. These being given a bell brought aboard their fellows, presenting the Captain with venison, bear's flesh, bows, arrows, clubs and targets. Next morning they were all gone.

Then they entered the River of Tockwogh, and here when the savages saw them furnished with the Massawonecks' weapons, our men pretended to have taken them perforce. So the savages conducted them to their palisadoed town and entertained them kindly. It was the daily order of our men to have a prayer and a psalm, at which solemnity the savages much wondered, and began themselves in a most passionate manner to hold up their hands to the sun; and then embracing Smith they adored him in like manner and treated him very honourably. Thence they came among the people of the Tapohonecks and here they fell almost into an ambush. Thus after many dangers they returned to Jamestown on 7th September, where they found Scrivener and divers recovered, but many dead and some sick. The harvest had been gathered in but much of the provision spoiled with rain.

Three days later by the election of the Council and the request of the company Smith received the letters patent and took upon him the office of President. And now Ratcliffe's palace was stayed as needless; the church repaired; the storehouse recovered and building prepared for the expected supply. The fort was reduced to good form; the order of watch renewed; and the whole company every Saturday exercised in a field prepared for that purpose. The boats were then trimmed for trade, and on their journey encountered Newport with the second supply from England.

At the coming of Newport with his orders to bring back pitch, tar, wainscot, clapboard, glass and soap ashes, Smith objected that these were hard to obtain when they had no provision to live in the country. To which Newport replied that he would undertake to fraught the pinnace with 20 tons of corn in his discovery and to re-fraught her again from Powhatan; and besides he would leave a great proportion of the victuals from the ship, inferring that Smith's propositions were but a device to hinder him, and that the cruelties he had used on the savages might well hinder these designs. So all the works were left, and 120 men appointed as a guard to Newport.

But Smith to show that the savages were not so desperate as New-port pretended, and because the coronation of Powhatan would consume much time, undertook himself to intreat Powhatan to come to Jamestown to receive his presents; and whereas Newport would not go without a guard of 120, he himself went to Werowocomoco with but 4 men. He found Powhatan absent, but Pocohantas and her women entertained him, and presented him with a Virginian masque. Thirty young women came naked out of the woods, only covered with a few leaves before and behind, their bodies painted, but all differing. Their leader had a fair pair of buck's horns on her head. With shouts and cries, they cast themselves in a ring about the fire, dancing and singing for nearly an hour. Then they solemnly invited him into their lodgings, where he was no sooner in than these nymphs pressed and hung about him crying out 'Love you not me? Love you not me?' This salutation ended, the feast was set, and the mirth ended they conducted him with firebrands to his lodging.

Next day Powhatan came; but he would not go to Jamestown, for said he, 'If your King have sent me presents, I also am a King. Your father' (for so Smith had called Newport) 'is to come to me, not I to him.' And with this answer Smith returned. So Newport with 50 men went to Werowocomoco with his presents of a crown, ewer and basin, scarlet cloak and apparel. Much ado they had to persuade Powhatan to kneel to receive his crown, he not knowing the meaning of a crown nor the bending of the knee. At last by leaning hard on his shoulders, he stooped a little and three having the crown in their hands put it on his head, when by the warning of a pistol the boats let off a volley of shot, at which the King started up in a horrible fear till he saw all was well. In requital for this kindness he gave his old shoes and cloak to Newport. He also gave him a heap of wheats' ears containing about 8 bushels of corn; and with this and what they bought in the town they returned to the fort.

The ship having now disburdened herself of 70 persons, with the first gentlewoman and woman servant that arrived in the colony, Newport with 120 men set forward on his discovery, leaving Smith the President at the fort with 80 or 90 men, such as they were, to relade the ship. Newport and his company marched some 40 miles, and discovered two towns of the Monacans; and on their return searched many places for mines, from one of which their refiner persuaded them that he extracted a small quantity of silver; but the savages would not trade with them and they found no corn. So the company returned to Jamestown, all complaining and tired with toil, famine and discontent at such fruitless certainties as Smith had foretold them.

As soon as they were landed, the President dispersed as many as were able, some for glass, some for tar, pitch and soap ashes; but 30 of them he himself conducted 5 miles down river from Jamestown to make clapboard, cut down trees and lay in the woods. Among the rest were two proper gallants of the last supply to whom such work was strange pleasure; yet within a week they became masters, making it their delight to hear the trees thunder as they fell; but the axes so blistered their tender fingers that many times at every third blow an oath would drown the echo. For remedy of this sin the President devised to have every man's oaths numbered, and at night for every oath to have a can of water poured down his sleeve, with which every offender (himself and all) were so washed that a man could scarce hear an oath in a week.

When the President returned to the fort, seeing the time consumed and no provision gathered, himself embarked in the discovery barge and went to Chickahamania where he so wrought with the savages that notwithstanding the corn was bad that year he returned with 100 bushels. At this some of the company so envied his good success that there was talk of Newport and Ratcliffe deposing him.

All this time (which was 14 weeks) that the ship was at Jamestown there was such trading underhand between the soldiers, the sailors and the savages that within 7 weeks of 200 or 300 axes, chisels, hoes and pickaxes, scarce 20 could be found; pikeheads, shot, powder or anything they could steal from their fellows was vendible. And likewise the sailors would trade the provisions from the ship. In this way the officers, gentlemen and careless governors are sold, the adventurers cozened, and the action overthrown. Nevertheless Newport and the mariners still report that there is plenty in Virginia, which so moved Capt. Smith the President that had not Newport cried *peccavi* he would have discharged the ship and caused him stay a year in Virginia to learn to speak of his own experience.

At his return to England, Newport brings with him divers sorts of wood for wainscot, the trials of the pitch and the rest, soap, ashes, as well as four hogsheads of a red root called *pocones*, which is esteemed an excellent dye.

23rd. The King is looked for in London at the end of the week. He hath erected a new office and made Sir Richard Wigmore Marshal of the Field, who is to take order he be not attended by any but his own followers, nor interrupted and hindered in his sports by strangers and idle lookers on. The Council are very busy in plotting how to plant Ireland with English and Scots; the whole project is likely to come forth shortly in print. We are like enough to fall out with the Duke of Florence if we knew how to hurt him; our merchants are forbidden to trade any more to Leghorn and are minded to translate that traffic to Genoa. The least of our East Indian ships is arrived at Dartmouth with 100 ton of cloves, without seeing or hearing anything of her consorts since they parted from the coast of England.

24th. There is come a very straight letter from Capt. John Smith, the President in Virginia, answering the complaints of the Treasurer and Council of the Virginian Company which were taken out by Capt. Argall. For the charge of the voyage of £2,000 or £3,000, they in Virginia have not received the value of £100; nor can the Company expect much, for the planters are ignorant miserable souls that are scarce able to get wherewith to live. For the coronation of Powhatan, it will be the ruin of them all. From the Company's ship they have not received provision in victuals worth £20 for more than 200 to live on. When they send again, he would rather but 30 carpenters, husbandmen, gardeners, fishermen, blacksmiths, masons, diggers up of roots, well provided, than a thousand of such as they have. Nor can the Company yet look for profitable returns.

29th. The pirates increase in Ireland, where Capt. Jennings lately entered the river of Limerick after a great fight and the loss of 60 men with a great freight and a ship of Amsterdam. It is very doubtful whether they can be subdued by the King's ships which are driven to revictual or repair every three months to England where the contrary winds and the mariners' affection to their own homes long detain them.

2nd February. At Whitehall was enacted a masque of Ben Jonson's devising which he names *The Masque of Queens*, being a celebration of honourable and true Fame bred out of Virtue. The masque was preceded by a foil or anti-masque of 12 women in the habits of hags or witches, sustaining the persons of Ignorance, Suspicion, Credulity and the like. The King being set and the whole company in full expectation the scene which first presented itself was an ugly Hell, flaming beneath and smoking to the top of the roof. Then to hollow and infernal music came forth sundry witches, all differently attired, some with rats on their heads or shoulders, others with ointment pots at their girdles, all with spindles, timbrels, rattles or other venefical instruments. The device of their attire and the invention of the scene and the machine was M. Inigo Jones's. The witches thus making their charms, Ate their Dame enters to them and they fall into a magical dance, full of preposterous change and gesticulation (for they do all things contrary to the custom of men, dancing back to back and hip to hip, making their circles backward and the like). In the heat of their dance was heard a sudden loud blast of many instruments, with which not only the hags but the whole scene also vanished, and in place of it appeared a glorious building, figuring the House of Fame, on top of which were discovered the twelve Masquers, sitting upon a triumphant throne made pyramid-wise. Hereupon comes forward a person, dressed like Perseus, expressing Masculine Virtue, to enumerate the eleven Queens, who were such as Penthesilea, Camilla, Candace, Boadicea etc., and lastly Bel-Anna, Queen of the Ocean. So the Masquers, having descended, mounted in three triumphal chariots wherein they rode about the stage. Then they descended from their chariots and danced two curious dances, after which they took out the men and danced the measures for a full hour. In their third dance they disposed themselves into letters honouring the name of Prince Charles; and after that they fell to galliards and corantos, and so taking their chariots again returned to the House of Fame. The dancers in this masque were the Queen, the Countesses of Arundel, Derby, Huntingdon, Bedford, Essex, Montgomery, the Viscountess Cranborne, and the Ladies Elizabeth Guildford, Anne Winter, Windsor and Anne Clifford.

12th. The Council has ordered that every suitor that hath preferred a petition to the Council Table shall upon Mondays and Saturdays attend upon M. Secretary Herbert, who together with a Master of Requests and a Clerk of the Council shall give them an answer indorsed upon the petition, or otherwise, to prepare their suits against the next sitting of the Lords. And in case the petitioners do not rest satisfied with such answer as they receive but shall prefer another petition of the same matters, they are to be forbidden entrance into the Court by the porter, and the keeper of the Council Chamber is not to suffer them to come into the Chamber.

14th. John Donne now seeks to be preferred to be secretary to the

Virginia Company. The Pope hath written to the French King complaining that our King misuseth him continually in table talk and calls him Antichrist at every word; which doth so incense his Holiness that some papists fear it may drive him to thunder and lightning with excommunication.

15th. The L. Deputy reports that Ireland at this present is in good quiet. By reason of a fine of 1,000 marks upon the northern counties, and the effectual levying of a small part of it (with intimation to levy the whole arrear if they shall neglect to perform their duties) the principal rebels are driven to great necessities, for which they lie close. But the treasury is empty long since and they have tried every lawful means to supply their wants. Now at length the soldiers of necessity are forced to cess upon the counties adjoining or by violence to borrow of them, with incredible bitterness and grudging on both sides. He begs therefore that the King will make even with them for what is past, and send their portion in the beginning of every quarter, for nothing is saved by this protraction of time and the subject is much damnified and discontented.

17th. The negotiations for the truce in the Low Countries continue and most of the matters in dispute have now been resolved.

19th. This Sunday it should have been dead low water at London Bridge at 12 o'clock in the forenoon; but quite contrary to course, it was then high water. And then it ebbed almost half an hour, and suddenly if flowed again almost 2 foot higher than it did before and then ebbed again until it came to the right course.

20th. In the session of Parliament which ended in November 1606 an Act was made whereby the L. Mayor, Communalty and citizens of London were enabled to bring to the City fresh water from the springs at Chadwell near Ware and Amwell near Hertford by a trench or cut of 10 feet wide, for which satisfaction or recompense was to be made to the owners of the ground by mutual assent or through the Courts at Westminster. This Act was further extended in the session ending in July 1607 to allow the use of trunks or vaults of brick or stone. Nevertheless nothing was done until M. Hugh Middleton, goldsmith, obtained from the City those powers granted by the Act. Hereupon he set surveyors to work and now at length the work is begun.

21st. There passed foul words betwixt the Spanish Ambassador to France and the Venetian at a ball at Queen Margaret's, wherein the French King took such pleasure that he could not forbear to say,

'This farce is better than the comedy.' On Sunday one Richard Taverner going into the field with one Bird (of his own feather) about some swaggering quarrel left him dead in the place in Theobald's Park, himself hurt in the thigh and not yet heard of.

27th. There is news of a bloody battle between Sir Edmund Baynham and Sir Griffin Markham in the Low Countries, who fell out in a discourse about the Powder Plot, and fought with short sword and pistol upon horseback. Markham was left for dead on the field, and the other covered all over with cuts and gashes. It seems some angry planet reigns amongst these swaggering companions, but it is none of the calamities of these times.

3rd March. The King came back last Saturday and means not to stir far all this Lent, unless it be for 2 or 3 days in a week to Hampton Court or Oatlands. The new Earl of Dorset died on Monday night, leaving a heavy widow. His son the Saturday before seeing him past hope married the Lady Anne Clifford (with whom he had been in speech in his grandfather's time) and so prevented the Duke of Lenox and others that made earnest suit for his wardship. Barnabe Rich hath written a book called *A Short Survey of Ireland*, which is nothing but a treatise to prove the Pope Anti-Christ.

14th. The L. Balmerinoch was tried in Edinburgh 4 days ago before the Scottish Lords. Being come before them, he was desired to say whom he would have speak for him. He replied he had great necessity to speak, the cause being such as concerned his life and state; but, said he, he had greater need to hold his peace by reason of his offence, which was such as admitted no excuse; and his grief for it was so great that he would not extenuate his crime; nor would he have any friend or lawyer make that seem less which he would have the world to know to be such as it is.

As for the fact, firstly, he declared that he could never draw the King to hear with patience his motion, but he utterly and absolutely refused to take that course against his conscience. He himself had conceited that politic and unnatural course, and so applied himself to that crooked device which brought him into the estate where now he stood.

Secondly, that whereas some in malice to the King or friendship to himself might report this course to be too rigorous and cruel, his offence was such that the King could extend no favour to him without the damage of his own honour; and he would not be spared at such a rate as the King's honour. For himself, he had no aim at the alteration of religion or to bring in a toleration by the writing of that letter, but merely a politic course which he conceited for the King's right; and this he declared to be true as he shall answer God at the day of Judgement. Nor was it gain nor private advantage that drew him to it, for he never expected any reward.

So the jury was called and all the indictment was read which aggravated his crime; also there were shown the fruits of that letter. To all this Balmerinoch replied not one word. Then was read his confessions, and his speech to the Council at Whitehall of his sorrow, and his sin, and his desire to give the King satisfaction to the last drop of his blood; also a letter from the King to him. Then the jury went together, and after a time returned to find him guilty of all parts of the indictment. The Lords conferring on the bench, the L. Justice signified they would proceed no further till they know the King's pleasure; but in the meantime they advised L. Balmerinoch to fit himself for God.

24th. The King's Accession Day was passed with the ordinary solemnity of running and ringing. The tilters were the Duke of Lenox, the Earls of Arundel, Pembroke and Montgomery, the Lords Chandos, Compton, Waldon and Hay, Sir Thomas Somerset, Sir Richard Preston and the two Alexanders. The Duke of Lenox exceeded all in features, the L. Waldon in followers, and Sir Richard Preston in a pageant, which was an elephant with a castle on his back; and it proved a right *partus elephantis,* for it was long a-coming, till the running was well entered into, and then as long a-creeping about the tilt-yard, at which time the running was intermitted.

30th. The King's book in defence of his *Apology* (which he now avers to be his own) is in the press, and therein he little spares the Pope or his party, which others do as frankly imitate both in books and preachings, without straining courtesy or mincing the matter any longer. And this (some say) is the best effects that can be foreseen of the King's great pains which would better become a private man. The Bishop of Chichester's book, which is likewise finished and much hearkened after, comes out at more leisure.

31st. There be 26 pirates captured in Ireland and now held at Bristol, where the Mayor is bidden to deliver them to the Sheriff in safe custody, who shall hand them to the Sheriff of the next county, and so from Sheriff to Sheriff until they be brought safe to London for trial by the Court of Admiralty; and especial care to be taken lest they escape.

3rd April. The treaty for truce for 12 years in the Low Countries was at last signed on 29th March between the hours of 10 and 11 in the Townhouse at Antwerp. All the States' demands have been granted that carry either show of reason or colour of justice, which easiness in the Archduke's Deputies (whether proceeding from the extreme necessity of Spain or their desire for quiet) puffed up the States' Deputies into such a conceited humour that for days together, they thought nothing should be refused them though never so unjust or void of reason, and that the English and French Commissioners should support them in all their impertinent demands. When the treaty had been signed by both sides, the English and French Commissioners were importuned also to sign, which they did albeit reluctantly. Thus end the wars in the Netherlands which have continued for almost 50 years, longer than any great war of former times, to the great damage and division of all Christendom and the advantage of the irreconcilable enmity of the Turk.

7th. Some time since Jennings the pirate was taken in Ireland. He came to the River Shannon and there offered to submit himself to the King's mercy and to surrender the ships and goods. After conferring with the Earl of Thomond he came ashore without the privity of his company, except a few who were inclined as he was. In consideration of his submission and his contrition, the L. Deputy would have some favour shown him.

There is a proclamation calling in the King's Book of Apology for the Oath.

8th. The Duke of Cleves and Juliers (or Gulich) has suddenly left this world without a child. Had he died some months ago it might have broken off the Treaty, for his Dukedom lies between the United Provinces and the territory of the Archduke Albert. Cleves is held to be, without dispute, *foedum femininium*, and therefore the Elector of Brandenburg who married the eldest daughter of the eldest sister of the late Duke hath the most apparent claim; but the Duke of Neuburg also hath a claim. It is generally thought that the succession will lead to war.

9th. The old Lady Montague, that was so notable a friend to priests, died yesterday at her house at Battle in Sussex, having fallen into a palsy 2 months since during the great Frost. The day before she died five priests that were in the house offered Masses for her in honour of the Blessed Virgin Mary. She built a chapel with a fair altar of stone, a choir for singers, and a pulpit for priests where a sermon was made every week, and on great feasts the Mass was sung, sometimes even with deacon and subdeacon. So many Catholics resided in this house or repaired thither, sometimes as many as 120, that it was called 'Little Rome'. She had also another house on the Thames-side near the Bridge which is a common place of retirement for priests coming into England.

10th. The Treaty was ratified by the Archduke and the States at Antwerp on the 4th, and next day proclaimed with great solemnity before the Townhouse with sound of trumpet, in the presence of the English and French Commissioners and the Deputies of the States, who were entertained to a sumptuous feast; and in the evening bonfires were made in all the squares and streets of the city.

11th. Yesterday the shops in the new Bourse were richly furnished with wares; and today the King and the Queen with their royal children and many great Lords and Ladies came thither and were entertained with speeches, gifts and ingenious devices; and then the King gave it a name and called it 'Britain's Burse'.

12th. The answer made by the King to Bellarmine's chaplain in reply to his Majesty's *Apology* has been held in the printer's hands for many weeks during which it has been revised and corrected by his Majesty. A few days since the booksellers began to sell it but now it is recalled because of some grave errors made by the printer and the reader, and all who hold copies are commanded to bring them back, when they will be exchanged for the corrected edition without further cost. This new book comes out together with the *Apology*, which too has been revised, and is now openly acknowledged to be his Majesty's own work.

This new addition is called a *Premonition* to all most mighty Monarchs, Kings, Free Princes and States of Christendom, dedicated to Rudolph II, Elect Emperor of the Romans, and subscribed, 'James by the Grace of God, King of Great Britain, France and Ireland; Professor, Maintainer and Defender of the True, Christian, Catholic and Apostolic Faith, professed by the ancient and Primitive Church, and sealed by the blood of so many Holy Bishops, and other faithful crowned with the glory of Martyrdom.' Herein his Majesty declareth that he did not put his name to the first print, for he thought it not comely for one of his place to set his name in the refutation of Bellarmine's letter, for, saith he, 'I was never the man, I confess, that could think a Cardinal a meet match for a King; especially having many hundred thousand of my subjects of as good birth as he.' As for Father Parsons, whom he termeth the English Paragraphist or rather perverse pamphleteer, 'since all his description must run upon a *P*. hath truly observed that my Arms are affixed in the frontispiece thereof, which useth not to be in books of other men's doings; whereby his malice in pretending ignorance, that he might pay me the soundlier, is the more inexcusable'. Bitterly rejecteth those words of reproach applied to himself as *nugae, temeritas, vanitas, impudentia, blasphemiae, applicatio inepta,* and the like; utterly denying that he is heretic or apostate, which causeth him to give an account of his own faith in matters controversial. Thence to the primacy of Peter, wherein he digresseth many pages to show that the Pope is that Antichrist of the Apocalypse, and the Roman Church the Whore of Babylon. Writeth much of Garnet's case. Maintaineth 'that no man, either in my time or in the late Queen's, ever died here for his conscience. For let him be never so devout a Papist, nay, though he profess the same never so constantly, his life is in no danger by the Law, if he break not out into some outward act expressly against the words of the Law.' Concludeth by exhorting all Kings and Princes, his loving Brethren and Cousins, to defend the ancient liberties of the crowns and commonwealths against the ambition of the Pope. Addeth thereto a confutation of sundry passages in the Cardinal's book.

21st. The Easter holidays were spent at Court with accustomed solemnities. On Sunday (16th) the Bishop of Bath, Dr. James Montague, preached to the household, and the Bishop of Chichester before the King. The Tuesday was well fitted with a chaplain, Dr. Smith, Head of a House in Cambridge, who so well baited all the great ones, terming them *suffragatores aulicos* for abusing the King's ear in preferring of suits, judges for prohibitions, patrons for impropriations and selling of benefices, and all sort of officers for corruption in their places, and that in so plain and broad terms, he scarce escaped baiting himself. The King is now at Theobalds, having in hand the translation of his Book into Latin, wherein he useth Sir Henry Saville and others, and it will yet be a fortnight's work. Meantime the English book will come out again, well purged of some oversights.

25th. The Adventurers for Virginia today heard a sermon at Whitechapel preached by M. William Symonds on Genesis 12: 1-3, applying to the Colony the promises made to Abraham; and answering the objections commonly used, as that in entering another country there must be effusion of blood.

26th. Some days since my L. of Northampton brought in Capt. George Weymouth to deliver his opinion of the work upon the great ship that is building, who reports Pett to be no artist and altogether inexperienced; that his Majesty is cozened; and the frame of the ship unfit for any use but as a dung boat. Since these matters touch Sir Robert Mansel Treasurer of the Navy, and Sir John Trevor a Surveyor, and the honour of the L. Admiral, Pett wrote a letter to the L. Admiral which my L. took to the King, who thereupon joining the Earls of Worcester and Suffolk commanded all three to repair to Woolwich to examine the ship and give a true report. Yesterday these Lords came to Woolwich and called before them the master shipwrights, Baker and Bright, and Capt. Weymouth. Having heard what they alleged, they reported to the King that the charges against Pett arose of inveterate malice. This morning Pett's accusers come to my L. of Northampton complaining bitterly of the favour shown to Pett. Whereupon my Lord goes to the King grievously complaining of the partiality of the three Lords, and beseeching that he might himself make another examination. The King now declares that he will himself hear the cause indifferently between the parties.

The King's Book is not yet on sale, for certain passages from the Fathers were found to be in error; and four Bishops are at work upon it. The King is angry because he hears that an answer has already been prepared in the Netherlands, and he declares that he has been betrayed as the book must have been shown before it was printed.

27th. The Council have commanded that Jennings the pirate be sent over from Ireland; but as for pardoning him, when the like favour was shown to Capt. Coward he then returned to his former courses. Those who were induced to give up their captain and ship on offer of pardon are also to be sent for examination.

1st May. Last autumn and again this spring many hundred thousand of young mulberry trees have been brought out of France and planted in many shires of this land; and divers persons begin to breed worms and to make silk since by trial and experiment it hath been found that silk-worms will live and breed in England, and their silk is fit for taffeta, stockings and sewing silk. Equal to the best that is made in Granada.

3rd. A sermon by M. Robert Gray called *A Goodspeed to Virginia* is being printed, showing the reasons for the plantation and answering sundry objections, as by what right or warrant we can take away the land from the savages; to which he answereth that those people are vanquished to their unspeakable profit and gain, for by conquest they are abridged of the liberty of sin and impiety and drawn to a Christian kind of life. As for the great charges which some allege, these will be nothing to the benefit which will grow hereafter.

8th. This morning the L. Admiral came betimes to Woolwich, attended by his party in the present dispute; and shortly afterwards my L. of Northampton with his witnesses who went up and down the shipyard declaring that Pett should be hanged. About 8 of the clock comes the King in his caroche, attended with Prince Henry and the LL. of the Council. After he had reposed a while the King desired the L. Admiral to bring him to a sight of the work, which was done, a stage for the purpose having been made at the stem of the ship. Then he returned back to his place and seated himself in a chair under the state at a little table, with the Prince and the Lords and the L. Admiral on his right side, and the L. Northampton on his left with his party.

Silence being commanded by the gentlemen ushers, the King made a speech how much it imported his royal care to take to his personal examination a business that concerned the strength and honour of his Kingdom and State, besides the expense of his treasury. Then he addressed the actors on both sides, that none should either accuse for malice, or excuse for love or particular respects, for that he in the seat of justice (presenting God's person) would not be deluded or led by any coloured pretences from understanding the very plain truth of that business. He exhorted all whose consciences accused them of malicious ends or partial favour to give over and depart before they took the oath, declaring what danger it was to be perjured before the Majesty of God and the King.

Then the names of those to be sworn on both sides were read, and the oath read to them by the L. Treasurer; and all were sworn. For the L. Northampton were 14 seamen (among them Sir Henry Middleton, Capt. Weymouth and Capt. Christopher Newport), 8 master shipwrights, and 8 carpenters. The King willed the L. Northampton to begin his accusations, Pett being called to answer personally, he being on his knees before the King, with the L. Admiral on his left side and Sir Robert Mansel, Sir John Trevor right behind him. The accusations against Pett were exhibited by the L. Northampton in writing and alleged many particularities of the defects of the great ship, as of her proportions and depth, and her workmanship very ill done, and much of her timber overgrown and cross-grained.

The King perceiving the articles to be many and intricate to answer, contracted them to three principal heads: the point of art, the point of sufficiency of materials, and the point of charge; to which heads Pett was commanded to answer. Much time was spent in dispute of proportions, comparing the present frame with former precedents and dimensions of the best ships; and because one side swore that the square of the ship's flat in the midships was full 13 foot, and Pett's party that it was but 11 foot 8 inches, the King trusted to neither of their oaths but sent to have the measurement made by expert and impartial witnesses. As for the point of charge, it was maintained that it would not exceed the charge of other ships that were built in Queen Elizabeth's time, allowing proportion for proportion. It being now almost one of the clock, the King called for his dinner, referring the other points to be handled after dinner. All this time Pett had remained upon his knees, attacked by the L. Northampton and his witnesses, and frowned upon by the King, albeit Prince Henry encouraged him as far as he might, labouring to have him eased by standing up, but the King would not permit it.

So soon as he had dined, the King and the Lords went into the body of the ship to make trial of the goodness of the materials, and where the accusers had chalked with a mark the lower futtocks for red (or overgrown) wood, cross-grained, or unserviceable, the King caused them to be dubbed by the workmen; and being thus tried they were found sound; whereat the King said that the cross-grain was in the men and not in the timber. The King now began to give encouragement to Pett, and so came without board to survey the planks and workmanship, which gave him great satisfaction. Meanwhile those who were making trial of the measurements found them to be indeed as Pett had declared; at which there was a great shout, and the Prince called in a high voice, 'Where be now these perjured persons that dare thus abuse his Majesty with these false informations? Do they not worthily deserve hanging?'

So the King returned to the hall; and being placed in his seat and the room filled as full as it could be packed, he began a speech for the conclusion of the business, showing his satisfaction, and giving thanks to the L. Northampton for his great care and diligence to search out errors, notwithstanding he had been misinformed. Next he directed his speech to M. Baker, Bright and the other informers, bitterly reprehending them and willing them to beware how they did abuse the Majesty of God and himself, His substitute, with malicious informations. Then he showed Pett a very pleasing countenance, being now persuaded of his honesty and ability; and further he commended the great wisdom and impartial carriage of the L. Admiral. To this the L. Admiral replied in the praise of the King's justice, great wisdom and princely care in that day's work, which was of such intricacy as his Majesty was never accustomed to, and yet so clearly did he examine in so short place as if he had been only bred to such elements. The King having replied briefly, rose and passed through the hall; but before he took his caroche, at the motion of the L. Thomas

Howard, the L. Chamberlain, he called Pett before him and charged him on his allegiance and life that he should not quarrel or challenge any person whatsoever that had given information against him; and so gave Pett his hand to kiss.

The L. Admiral attended the King to Whitehall with the rest of the company, it being almost 8 of the clock before they went from Woolwich; but my L. of Northampton, seeing that all things had sorted out clean contrary to his expectations, took his way back to his coach and would not so much as take any leave of the King but posted away with no little expression of discontent, railing bitterly against his own instruments.

There is a Proclamation forbidding all foreign nations after August next from fishing upon any of the coasts of England, Scotland or Ireland without special licence from the Commissioners for Fisheries.

10th. The King has finished with the revising of his Book, and yesterday set out for Greenwich. He has again returned to his hunting, and four days ago he with the Prince hunted so hard that some of the horses died, one under the Prince himself; and they themselves were so weary that they were forced to sleep in a cottage in a village. The Queen and the Court were greatly perturbed, for the gentleman sent by the King to tell her of it, rested on the way being as weary as the others; for which he is now in prison.

15th. Sir Thomas Overbury is returned from his travels through the United Provinces, the Archduke's country and France. Noteth that had the treaty not been on foot last year during the great frost (which rendered their ditches and marshes firm ground) the Provinces would have been defeated by the enemy. Saith that the States have 20,000 ships of all sorts, and if the Spaniard is entirely beaten out of those parts, the Kings of France and England will take as much pains to suppress them as ever they did to raise them; for as our enemy they could give us the law at sea and eat us out of all trade.

18th. The King's Book is not yet come out, for it is being translated into Latin and French, and all are to appear together. It is said he will send it to all Princes in Christendom to be presented by the hands of his Ambassadors. The Court are very ill affected to this child-birth of the King, fearing that it may not prove acceptable to the world, and some about his Majesty say that he himself is in doubt lest by some Princes it be not received, or by others not esteemed.

20th. It is said in Venice that when the Pope was told that Fr. Fulgentio did preach but the gospel and the Word of God, he replied in great passion, 'Do you not know that to preach the pure Scripture

138

and the pure Gospel is to go about to ruin and destroy the Catholic Faith?'

22nd. The King's Book came forth again today in Latin and in English; it is further to be translated into French and Italian, but he is not satisfied with the translation. The changes made in the new impression are little more than quotations from the Scriptures, and a declaration that when he speaks against the Puritans, it is only of his own subjects, for he holds that all Princes may order the outward form of worship as they please. Many copies have been bound in velvet with the coat of arms and the corner pieces of gold, stamped with the rose and thistle, the lion and lilies. These will be sent to all the English Ambassadors to be presented to foreign Princes.

25th. There is a report from Spain that the Turk is preparing 200 galleys and 50 ships to put to sea; and that our pirates Ward, Bishop and Danseker will this summer gather a greater head than ever. Some say they will have at least 20 ships. Their conjunction with the Turk, in whose country they have their rendezvous, is much feared. Sir Anthony Shirley gave out much hope of reducing these rovers to his service by means of certain Flemings who pretend much influence with Danseker, and to that end drew money out of the Spanish treasury; but his hopes are much quenched. The pirates are reported to be hovering upon the coasts between S. Vincent and Malaga;Danseker's own ship is manned with at least 1,000 men. They have lately taken spoil of 11 or 12 ships, English, French and Spanish, and the Spaniard are neither able nor willing to meddle with them.

28th. Many motives and reasons are being alleged that the City of London shall undertake plantation in the north of Ireland, and especially of the late ruined city of Derry. This city, also Coleraine, may with little charges be made impregnable. The King offers to grant to these two charters of incorporation, and the whole territory between them (out of which 3,000 acres may be allotted to each town for commons) to be planted with such undertakers as the City of London shall think fit, paying only for the same the easy rent of undertakers. These towns would also have the benefit of all the customs on goods imported or exported, also tonnage and poundage, for 21 years. This country is well watered and supplied with fuel of trees and turf; it supplies such abundance of provision as may not only sustain the plantation but also furnish provisions yearly to the City of London, and especially for their fleets, as beeves, pork, fish, rye, beer, peas and beans, and in some years will help the dearth of the City. It is fit for the breeding of mares and cattle and sheep. It grows hemp and flax better than elsewhere and thus might furnish materials for canvas, cables, cordage and suchlike requisites for shipping; also for threads, linen cloths and stuffs made of linen yarn which is far finer there, and more plentiful than in all the rest of the Kingdom. The Harbour of Derry is very good, and the roads at Portrush and Lough Swilly tolerable. The sea-fishing is plentiful of all manner of fish, and especially herrings and eels. There be good store of pearls upon the coast, especially upon the river of Lough Foyle. If multitudes of men were set to work proportionately to these commodities, it would ease the City of an insupportable burden of persons who can be spared, all parts of the City being so surcharged that one tradesman is scarce able to live by another. Moreover these colonies may be a means to utter infinite commodities from London to furnish the whole north of Ireland.

29th. There is printing a book called *The Philosopher's Banquet*, drawing into one small volume many diversities of knowledge, pertaining to a man's body and health, ranks, trades, professions, diets, birds and beasts and many more; and answering questions; the whole enabling a man to discourse wisely and wittily at the table of his superiors, written first by Michael Scott in Latin, and now done into English. Noteth of the strange nature of the cock, that whereas all other creatures after the act of venery are dull and melancholy, only the cock (the country horologe) is otherwise, as appeareth by the flapping of his wings, spritely rousing of himself and sending forth of his note. Yet in his age it is observed, as at 5, 8, 12, 14 years, sooner or later in some instances than in others, he layeth a round and small egg in some hole or hedge, which by sitting upon, he bringeth forth some venomous serpent or other thing, but most commonly the basilisk, a serpent that poisoneth by his breath or sight.

2nd June. There is another book about Ward and Danseker, showing their pitiless courses, together with a list of the English ships taken by them to 6th April last, being 6 by Ward and 4 by Danseker, as well as others not yet known.

3rd. Today for the third day the King heard the differences touching the prohibitions made in the King's Bench and Common Pleas between the Judges of the Ecclesiastical and Temporal Courts argued.

5th. The new fleet for Virginia set forth from Plymouth on the 2nd, being the *Sea Adventure* as Admiral (wherein are Sir Thomas Gates the new Governor, Sir George Somers and Capt. Newport), the *Diamond* vice-admiral with Capt. Ratcliffe and Capt. King, the *Falcon* rear-admiral with Capt. Martin, the *Blessing*, the *Unity*, the *Lion*, and the *Swallow*, together with a catch and a boat called the *Virginia*.

8th. The King's Book is now seconded with a reply of the Bishop of Lincoln (Dr. William Barton) upon Parsons, dealing with him at his own weapons, but striking freely upon the other side when he terms deposing Princes, surprising their persons and renouncing allegiance to be either Jesuited or Genevated divinity, which will scandalize the Puritans. The Bishop of Chichester's book is in the press. Dr. Morton follows with a large volume and Sir Edward Hoby comes in with a work dedicated to the relapsed Ladies. So Paul's churchyard is like to be well furnished. The town is at present very empty and solitary, there being nothing thought on but flight and fear. In Oxford they are suddenly affrighted, and most of the scholars fled, the plague being broken out at Brazenose and S. John's College, and in two places in the town in two days. Sir Charles Cornwallis the Ambassador Resident at the Court of Spain is recalled to England, and bidden when he takes his leave of his Spanish Majesty to present him with the King's Book.

10th. This day and for two days past the King has heard the general cause of the abuses in the Navy in the Presence Chamber at Greenwich. At the entrance of the business on the first day my L. of Northampton made a great complaint of the dishonour he had reaped by the hearing at Woolwich, declaring that Pett and his associates had traduced him in every tavern and ale-bench to his great dishonour, and alleging the truth of his informers. The King took it ill that my L. should dare to question his just proceedings which he had taken such pains personally to hear and determine, and cut him off with a sharp reprehension. On that day sundry charges were made against Sir Robert Mansel, Sir John Trevor and the rest. Today Pett was called last to answer an accusation that in his voyage with the L. Admiral in 1604 he had sold to the Spaniards divers tons of brass ordnance and other provisions of shot and powder, which was fully answered; and the great inquiry concluded.

15th. The King is now occupied with nothing else but how his Book will be received. Those who are to carry it to foreign Princes leave within two days. Barclay the French poet who had the greatest hand in the Latin translation goeth to Lorraine, Savoy, Switzerland, Bavaria, Vienna and Prague; he is to apologize for those passages which touch upon dogma, and to declare that they are not intended to shake anyone in his own belief. On Saturday last (8th) the Book was sent to the Spanish Ambassador to be forwarded by him to the

King of Spain, but in spite of many entreaties he would not receive it, though the Earl of Northampton before it was brought besought him to burn it rather than reject it. The King has now sent the Book in post to his Ambassador in Spain. He was so angry that on Sunday he recalled an audience that he had granted to the Spanish Ambassador. The Ambassador of France declares that his master will certainly refuse to receive the Book; he had often urged the King to leave his design, so now at the receipt of the Book he will show his displeasure.

19th. The Prince's great ship is now almost ready at Woolwich. Yesterday the Prince came to see it, and again this afternoon with the King and great company. The King spent almost two hours surveying the ship within and without. Then he went into Pett's house where Mrs. Pett had prepared a banquet of sweetmeats, whereof he tasted plentifully, and at his departure gave special commandment not to launch the ship till his progress is ended. Shakespeare's Sonnets (of which some were long ago known among his private friends) have been imprinted by Thomas Thorpe, with an enigmatical dedication 'To the only begetter of these ensuing Sonnets, Mr. W. H.' To these Sonnets is added a poem of *A Lover's Complaint*.

20th. This May past at Hereford divers sports were held, as horse racing, cock fighting and the like, and among them a morris dance, wherein the dancers were all ancients, of whom several more than a hundred years old; in all 18 persons whose years together came to 1,837. The foreman was one James Tomkins, who at 98 years of age married a wife of 52, who brought him a child, yet living, and now 7 years of age. Their Maid Marian was old Meg Goodwin, aged 120, who was at Ludlow at the time of Prince Arthur's death (which was in 1502) and had her part in the dole.

23rd. Today the King, the Queen, the Prince, the Lady Elizabeth and the Duke of York with divers great Lords and many others came to the Tower to see a trial of the lions' valour against a great fierce bear which had killed a child that was negligently left in the bear house. This bear was brought into the open yard behind the lions' den, and the great lion put forth, who gazed a while but never offered to approach the bear. Then were two mastiff dogs put in, who passed by the bear and boldly seized upon the lion. Then was a stone horse put into the yard who suddenly scented both lion and bear but very carelessly began to graze in the yard between them. So six dogs were put in; most of them seized upon the lion, but suddenly they left him and seized upon the horse and would have worried him to death but three stout bearwards came in and took off the dogs one by one while the lion and the bear stared upon them. The lion was then suffered to go to his den again which he had endeavoured to do before. After that divers lions were put into the place, one after another, but they showed no more sport than the first, and everyone as soon as he espied the trap door open ran hastily back into his den. Lastly there were put forth the lusty young lions which were bred in that yard and are now grown great. These at first marched proudly towards the bear who perceiving them came hastily out of a corner to meet them and offered to fight, but both lion and lioness skipped up and down and fearfully fled from him, not willing to endure any fight, and seeking the next way to their den.

3rd July. Some weeks since the King, learning of the custom prevailing among the clergy in Ireland of alienating at pleasure the temporalities of their benefices, commanded the L. Deputy to call together the principal clergy and to point out the impiety of such courses and his grievous reprobation thereof, and also to notify them that if anyone hereafter be guilty of such contempt of his authority, that offender shall be marked as unworthy of preferment and shall be punished by civil punishment. Now a proclamation is come forth forbidding any ecclesiastical person from making any lease or grant out of the possessions of their churches or spiritual possessions other than during their incumbency, or for 21 years; and that such leases shall not be of the Bishop's seat or principal mansion; and further the felling of timber is prohibited except for the repairing and rebuilding of houses belonging to ecclesiastical possessions.

5th. There has lately appeared a little book in Latin, seemingly printed in France, which in words of the Scriptures answers sundry ridiculous questions. It touches upon the most secret affections of our Princes, and especially Queen Elizabeth and Henry VIII, who is drawn as Antichrist for he usurped the authority of the Pope. It came first into the hands of the Archbishop, and the King was little pleased that his Grace showed small diligence in finding out whence it came. Now it has been reprinted with an Apology against the King's Book, from which it seems likely that it has been printed in England; which greatly increaseth the King's indignation. Many copies are spread abroad in spite of the danger of those who sell it. This book is called *Pruritanus*, alluding to the Puritans. Of Queen Elizabeth, allegeth that though she styled herself Head of the Anglican Church and a Virgin, yet was she an immodest woman who gave birth to sons and daughters, prostituting herself with men of different nations, even with blackamoors. Of Henry VIII that he gave out Anne Boleyn was his wife, whereas she was his daughter. Mocketh our present King as a stranger from a barbarous land, of whom it is said *In exitu Israel de Aegypto Domus Jacob de populo barbaro*. Calleth the Scots 'locusts'.

Dr. Andrewes' answer to Bellarmine's book, written under the name of Matthew Tortus, is now come from the press in a great volume in Latin called *Tortura Torti*, wherein he examineth point by point all those objections to the King's Book, also the two Breves of Pope Paul the Fifth, and the Cardinal's letter to Blackwell, and many other matters that lie in dispute between the Romish and Anglican Churches. This book is dedicated to his Majesty by Dr. Andrewes who declares that he doubted of his ability for the work but he was moved to it when he saw the King himself standing in the forefront of the battle, and how unworthy a thing it had been not to lend his name to such honourable warfare in which battle was joined with Christ the Lord as *auspex*, and Christ the Captain of our Lord.

That bear which lately killed a child was today baited to death upon a stage by the King's commandment, and of the money which the people paid to see the bear killed, £20 is given to the mother of the child.

11th. From Oxford comes a book about honey bees by Charles Butler of Magdalen, called *The Feminine Monarchy*, with instructions for their due ordering. Herein are ten chapters of all such matters as may concern bee-keepers from the nature of bees to the managing of hives and the preparing of honey and beeswax.

12th. M. Albert Morton, nephew of Sir Henry Wotton, the Ambassador in Venice, hath brought to the King a strange relic, which Sir Robert Douglas found in Padua. Sir Robert heard that the Earl of Gowry, who was a student in Padua 11 or 12 years since, had left a certain emblem or *impresa* in the Signiory; and upon inquiring was all unexpected directed to the school of a dancer, where it hung somewhat obscured and blemished with dust among divers remembrances of such as had been his scholars. Sir Robert therefore caused a copy to be made which with the agreement of the dancing master he changed for the original. The device of the *impresa* appears as a shadow of Gowry's detestable treason, for what other sense (saith the Ambassador) can the reaching out at a crown with a sword in a stretched posture and the impersonating of his device in a blackamoor yield any honest beholder?

14th. The French King has received our King's Book kindly. When

144

the Pope's Nuncio in moderate terms complained against his accepting a book that contained passages contrary to Catholic teaching and the Pope's authority, the King replied that he could not but accept the Book politely but he had not read it, nor was he capable of understanding matters of theology. In private he was heard to say that the Book exhorts all Princes to open their eyes to the Pope's claim to release subjects from their oath of allegiance, but those who hold their tongues know better how to preserve their authority, meaning himself.

My L. of Hertford being aggrieved because of a judgement that the Earl of Salisbury gave as an arbitrator in a matter between him and the L. Mounteagle, words followed, and my L. of Hertford gave the lie to the L. Treasurer, who within an hour sent a direct challenge by his servant M. Knightley. My L. of Hertford required only an hour's leisure of consideration ('twas said but to inform himself of the special danger of so dealing with a Councillor) and returned his acceptation. They were both upon their way from their lodgings to have met in S. James's when they were interrupted by those sent by the King to prevent it.

24th. Last night about 10 or 11 o'clock the Kings' stable at Farnham fell on fire by negligence of a candle set on a post which fell into the litter and burnt the stable. Of 25 or 30 horses in the stable, all but four were conveyed safely. Two were burnt to death and two unlikely to recover. If the coach horses had miscarried the progress would have been short. The King lost a pad horse and a hunting horse, likewise the Earl of Worcester; all the saddles are burnt and the Queen's coach harness. While this tragedy was acting, it was a world to hear the reports which were set going. Some said it was a new Powder Treason; an Englishman said a Scotchman was seen there with a link and fired the stable; others said it was a device to set the stable on fire and draw all the guard and Court thither that they might work some practice on the King. Nevertheless neither the King, Queen nor Prince slept the worse or ever waked until the morning in due time.

27th. The Venetian Ambassador hath been cozened by a Flemish priest whom he took into his household on the departure of the French Ambassador. This priest was allowed to leave certain parcels of books in the Ambassador's house, which were taken out one by one for sale among Catholics without the privity of the Ambassador until it was reported to him that these books were that itchy pamphlet called *Pruritanus*. Hereupon he caused the priest to be shut up

145

in a little chamber, but he escaped by a window. The Ambassador has sent the rest of the books to the Council, expressing great indignation that he should have been used in this way.

31st. It is so long since any general musters or survey of the armed forces were taken that the Lords Lieutenant are summoned to cause a general view to be made of all the forces in their counties, both horse and foot, and to observe the numbers trained and untrained; and especially to supply the room of such officers as are dead or insufficient or moved out of the county; and to amend the defects of armour, weapons and furniture. The musters may be taken in several divisions to save charge, but all to be in one day lest those who are unprovided shall borrow arms from other parts of the county. Certificates shall be returned by the last of November.

3rd August. The plague hath continued all this year, seldom less than 50 in each week. This past week 100 died of it. Sir Thomas Parry (the Chancellor of the Duchy) hath been shrewdly frighted; for first he was driven from the Duchy house to Lambeth by the plague which knocked at his door and took away his porter; and now he is driven back again from his house at Lambeth, his secretary dying suddenly of the plague and another sick in the house. The sickness increaseth, but as yet less than was feared.

4th. The King is resolved to send 1,000 Irish, swordmen and disaffected, to serve in Sweden, as well for the state of the Kingdom as for the plantation, that as many Irish as possible may be vented out of the land. Some of the gentlemen of better sort are to be their commanders, and the King will be at the charge of their transportation, and the Deputy may disburse small sums to put them into such clothing as may cover their nakedness and take away the mark of their miserable and barbarous condition; to be made of English fashion but of country stuff, which is cheaper, for upon reaching Sweden they shall receive new apparel and arms. No English, whether as commander or otherwise, shall be permitted to transport him with the rest, for this would deprive the Kingdom of its best defence.

7th. On 11th April last died the L. John Lumley leaving no heir. He was a notable collector of books and rarities which he added to those gathered by his father-in-law the late Earl of Arundel, who at the time of the dissolving of the monasteries collected many manuscripts which were then scattered abroad. The King hath now purchased this library and sent it to be kept at S. James's, with the rest of the library of his predecessors.

146

10th. That play of *Troylus and Cressida* which was printed early this year by Richard Bonian and Henry Walley as acted by the King's Servants at the Globe and written by William Shakespeare is now issued with a new title and an Epistle declaring it to be a new play never staled with the stage, never clapper-clawed with the palms of the vulgar. Moreover, say they, 'when he is gone and his comedies out of sale, you will scramble for them and set up a new English Inquisition'. Nor would the possessors of it ever willingly have allowed it to be printed.

16th. The Austrian Archduke Leopold, who is cousin to the Archduke Albertus, at the instigation of the King of Spain hath occupied the town of Juliers, thereby despoiling the Princes of Brandenburg and Neuburg of their rights. His pretext is that he will hold the country until the true heirs of Cleves are determined.

20th. My L. of Northumberland busieth himself in the Tower with learned men, as Harington the mathematician, Hughes and Warner who are his constant companions and are called 'the Earl of Northumberland's Three Magi'. They have a table at his charge and constantly converse with him either singly or together; as also doth Sir Walter Ralegh. My Lord hath written a little discourse of advice to his son, how a nobleman should govern his household and manage his servants, fetched from his own experience and misfortune, full of bitter jests and observation. Noteth that he was so poorly left at his father's death that nothing remained but wainscots and things rivetted with nails, for wives commonly are great scratchers after their husbands' deaths if things be loose. It is but a small pain to let an unreasonable woman sit still and be angry without a cause, for the trouble rests only in the strength of their tongues; though nowadays a woman is called a 'lady of spirit' who in former times was but plain 'scold'. Hath little good to say of women, but if, saith he to his son, 'you must needs love, love a mistress for her flesh and a wife for her virtue'.

26th. One who knew the Chauss in his own country declares that he was no true Ambassador but a garboilious fellow of the French Ambassador's; and 'tis a deadly sport to mock at a great Prince. This Mustapha has enriched our English tongue with a new word, viz., to *chauss* or *chouse*, meaning to cozen, for though a mean man with no authority yet was he very handsomely entertained in London for several months in 1607.

29th. Yesterday died somewhat suddenly Sir Francis Vere, the most famous soldier of our time, who was today buried in the Abbey

Church at Westminster. He was born in 1560, and first saw service in 1580. Then he made a voyage to Polonia. He received his first company in 1586, and sithence has been busied in all the wars of the Low Countries, as well as the Cadiz Voyage and the Islands Voyage. His greatest fame was at the battle of Nieuport and then at Ostend. He left the Low Countries in June 1606, and these past months has written his commentaries on his wars and experiences military.

30th. Capt. Jonas Poole is returned from his seventh voyage to Cherry Island, bringing with him many morses' teeth and the skins of bears, of which one is 13 foot long. In June they set up a pike with a white cloth on it and a letter signifying their possession for the Muscovy Company. They were in great peril by the ice which stove in the planks of their ships, but at the last all got away safe. On one day Poole and his cooper slew about five and forty morses in two hours with two lances and took their teeth. They also slew many seals.

31st. It hath rained these 40 days together besides many grievous nights, and the crops are rotting in the fields. Moreover the drought in the early part of the summer caused the hay crop to be poor so that there is great dearth of everything.

2nd September. There are two young white bears at Paris Garden brought back from Cherry Isle by Capt. Poole after they had slain the mother.

4th. From Venice it is reported that the Pope with his own hands delivered a censure to the Secretary of the Venetian Ambassador (the Ambassador himself being sick) to be sent immediately to forebar that State from receiving the King's Book. He seemeth to have despatched the like to all other Princes of his own colour with incredible celerity. Divers at Venice have asked our Ambassador for copies, insomuch that he would have the King send one of his best ships laden with them. From Tuscany it is said that the Grand Duke having received his copy consigned it to his confessor who by order of the Inquisition there hath burnt it. Likewise it hath been refused by the Duke of Savoy. In Rome the Pope hath forbidden it by public edict, and for greater defamation couples it with Beza's *Confessions*; at which those in Venice say: 'the more opposition, the more curiosity'.

8th. Three priests are said to have come to Rome from England to beg the Pope to order the Jesuits not to meddle with the affairs of the Catholics in England because they are a cause of great mischiefs to the faithful and do more harm than good.

The Jesuits who for some time have been trying to have Ignatius canonized have at last persuaded the Congregation of Rites to declare him *Beatus*, with Masses in his honour. To make the celebration splendid they invited many Cardinals and the Ambassadors of Spain and France. The Spanish Ambassador came first and took the higher place. When the French Ambassador came he was much put out, and calling for a chair to be set upon the high altar, he sat down in it; for which he is much blamed; but the General of the Jesuits is also reproved for his imprudence.

10th. The French King is determined to meddle in the affairs of Cleves. Whereupon the Archduke Leopold sent to persuade him otherwise, alleging that it would be an impossible blow to the Catholic Church if the Dukedom fell into the possession of a heretic. To which the King answered that he was a lover of justice, but, said he, he holds the two Princes of Brandenburg and Neuburg the lawful heirs of the Dukedom of Cleves and Juliers; and so he disposes himself to maintain their right. As for their religion, however contrary it may be, yet it must not be a pretext to do injustice, and he will oppose any Prince of Austria as an unlawful intruder. Nevertheless Richardot persuaded the King to agree to a cessation of arms for a year on all sides, and meanwhile judges to be appointed to determine the succession. But on his way back from France, Richardot himself fell sick at Arras and there died.

16th. Because of the continuing sickness in the City, Parliament is again prorogued till 9th February next.

17th. There is some great trouble in Venice concerning the King's Book and certain hot speeches uttered by Sir Henry Wotton, insomuch that a special post (who left Venice but 9 days ago) has come to the Venetian Ambassador here. The Ambassador immediately set out for Theobalds to ask for an audience with the King, but then learnt he was hunting and would sleep at Wanstead, whither his Majesty came at sundown after the death of the deer. Nevertheless, although weary after the hunt and a day of continual rain, and half dressed, yet he received the Ambassador, who spoke for about an hour very warmly of the conduct of Sir Henry Wotton and of the affection of the Venetian Republic. The King asked certain questions concerning the inhibiting of his book by the Inquisition, and then said that we all seek salvation by the road that seems best to each. One takes one road and one another; let each follow his own; but for his part, he confessed, that if the Republic were to send to England a book attacking his religion, he would not tolerate it but would certainly prohibit it; but in the meanwhile he must await the report of his own Ambassador. When the Ambassador had departed, the same night the King with his own hand straightway wrote to my L. of Salisbury to warn him of the complaint, and concluding, 'I only wryte this unto you nou, that incace this pantalone come unto you, you maye give him the lyke deferring ansoure, albeit if I shoulde tell you my conscience, if this mannis tale be trewe, my ambassadoure hath usid this matter with a littel more fervent zeale then temperate wisdome.'

27th. The Lords have been much troubled at their last sitting about the dissension between Sir John Kennedy and his Lady, who having expelled her husband from her house was afterwards thrown out of it herself by him who came at midnight with eighteen or twenty men; and being refused entry, broke open the doors and scarce gave her leisure to save herself by a back door in her petticoat, with a doctor who was then with her. Both of them were wandering all night almost naked through hedges and ditches till they came to a friend's house where they shifted and sheltered themselves. The Lady complained to the Lords as if she had been put in danger of her life.

29th. The account of Sir Henry Wotton's troubles at Venice is now come. On S. James's day, he presented the King's Book, together with a letter signed by the King and addressed to the Doge. In his speech he set forth the reason why the King had written the book which he now acknowledges to be his; which is not to impeach other Princes or to spread a novel doctrine, but to arouse them to consider the question of temporal authority that the Pope goeth about to violate. The Doge having kissed both letter and Book returned thanks, declaring that he received the Book as a sign of his Majesty's kindly disposition towards the Republic. But as soon as the Ambassador had gone, he handed the Book to the Grand Chancellor who carried it off to the secret chancery to be locked away.

Soon afterwards the Pope's Nuncio came to the Cabinet to complain that the Book contained many doctrines contrary to the Catholic Faith and that it should be prohibited. They were very unwilling to send orders in writing to the booksellers (as is done in the case of ordinary books) but they instructed the Prior of the Guild by word of mouth to command the booksellers neither to receive nor to sell the book. Further, the Chancellor of the Inquisition was warned not to record in writing any report of the proceedings.

When the Ambassador heard of it, he came again on 10th September to the Doge to complain that it was a graver injury to his master to prohibit his Book after it had been received; for acceptance was an act of ceremonious affection, whereas prohibition was an overt offence. He complained very bitterly that for an Inquisitor Friar to prohibit the Book written by the King of Great Britain, this was indeed a matter of the gravest, and a mortal wound to his Majesty's honour. He complained also of that libel which was put abroad in England, although the good name of the Venetian Ambassador was not touched therein. The Senate then considered the matter and agreed upon their answer, which was that the orders concerning the Book had not been issued by the Inquisitor but by the Inquisition, whereon three Senators do sit as assessors, and that they had acted in the most discreet manner, which showed what care they took to avoid any prejudice to his Majesty's reputation.

Next day the Ambassador was summoned to hear their resolution read out; which put him in great indignation, so that he spoke with choler and unadvisedly to this effect: 'It seems strange to me, and will seem strange to his Majesty, that without having read or considered the Book in the Senate, they have resolved to destroy it. How can you know that there are dogmas in it contrary to religion? You could not have known before the Book was presented: nor after, unless it was read.' Then, after other words had passed, he said, 'Further I must say that if there is a State which has little need of alliances, it is England, which has no interest in the provinces of Italy. For my part I will not represent the affair to his Majesty with exaggeration, for it is indeed so gross that it needs no emphasis. It stands clear enough in its nakedness.' To which he added that they should not in this matter regard him as an accredited Envoy but as a poor private gentleman until his Majesty's pleasure was further known.

The Senate was greatly moved by these words of the Ambassador, and agreed forthwith to send in post to the Venetian Ambassador in London to complain to the King. Further they resolved to send a special Ambassador of most honourable rank. Four days later Sir Henry Wotton came again to the Cabinet in milder mood, declaring that since an Ambassador Extraordinary was to be sent, his honour was restored and he could again return to his position as an accredited Ambassador, adding that if he had seemed too jealous, servants ought to show more zeal than their Masters where honour was at the stake. Finally, he justified himself against the charge that in his office as the King's Ambassador he had sought to separate the Republic from the Catholic Faith, concluding, 'Although it is the wish and desire of every Christian to see all others of his way of believing, still what the

Devil (pardon me) does it matter to my King that some draw to the Pope's side rather than to his? Clouds come and clouds go. I trust that the amity between the two Powers will endure to the end of the world.'

30th. This past month the weekly deaths from the sickness were 141, 158, 210 and 144.

4th October. An English ship is come into Plymouth from the East Indies with 700 tons of pepper.

5th. Sir William Paddy lately escaped a great danger at Barnelms, where the house was assaulted by Sir John Kennedy by night with a band of furious Scots, who besides their warlike weapons came furnished with certain snippers and searing irons, purposing to have used him worse than a Jew, with much more ceremony than circumcision. Sir William having the alarum given him fled like a valiant knight out at a back door, leaving his breeches behind him, and the Lady by his sweet side in a smock with her petticoat in her hands till they recovered the next castle. And now he walks London streets with three or four men in defence of his dimissaries. The matter betwixt Sir John and his Lady is in hearing before the Lords, who are told a different tale which is so carried that Sir William is not so much as mentioned.

There is one Coe, a poor pelting lawyer, who for a petition against my L. Chancellor is committed to the Gatehouse by the Lords; and upon his censure he gave himself a light hurt in the breast with his knife as if he would have stabbed himself, but obtained no more by it than to be kept a close prisoner. The Court is full of Dutchmen who come to treat about the several pretensions to the Duchy of Cleves, which is thought in the end will come to partages, though as yet there is arming on all hands. Sir Anthony Shirley hath received a sound box of the ear in the Court of Spain by a nobleman, which they say he is content to pocket up with some verbal satisfaction.

16th. Capt. Cyril Tourneur, himself a soldier, hath written *A Funeral Poem* upon Sir Francis Vere, setting forth the many attributes of that famous commander.

> His praise may justly then extend thus far;
> He was a Man, fit both for Peace and War.
> Whose monument, while History doth last,
> Shall never be forgotten, or defaced.

19th. Although the plague diminishes, yet it has spread to Hampton Court where two of the Queen's grooms of the chamber are dead of it; and it has also reached Royston and the King's household. His Majesty has left Royston and returns to Hampton Court next week.

20th. Sir Charles Cornwallis is on his way home from Spain. He received his recall in July but could not take his leave of the King of Spain earlier, for when the King is away from Madrid no Ambassadors may be received without some special notion or allowance. At length upon his solicitation, he was summoned to kiss the hands of the King and the Queen; but before he went in, the Duke of Lerma sent for him and advised him plainly that in taking leave he should give no cause for discontent to his Majesty, especially by presenting the King's Book. The King his master, said he, is so entire and sincere in his faith and obedience to the Church of Rome (from whence upon pain of excommunication the receiving or reading of such books is directly forbidden) that he begged the Ambassador not to present the Book whereby might be avoided a refusal that would be so unpleasing to the one to give and so distasteful to the other to receive. From the Duke the Ambassador went to the King and the Queen, whom he found attended with many Grandees and Nobles. He delivered his letter of revocation and said that he had been commanded to deal in another matter, but he had been prevented since he had heard from the Duke of Lerma of his Majesty's pleasure to the contrary. The King gave him a very gracious farewell but would say nothing of the Book.

23rd. The four agents sent by the City of London to view the proposed plantation of Ulster are now in Ireland where they are conducted by Sir Thomas Phillips as their host and guide (and privily instructed to show them the commodities of best advantage, but to keep from them all matter of distaste, as fear of the Irish or of the soldiers). They are said to have found all things far better than they expected, yet the Deputy prays God they prove not like their London women, who long today and loathe tomorrow.

Amongst others who would be an undertaker is the L. Audley, who would plant 100,000 acres in Tyrone, on which he would build thirty-three castles and towns each of which shall consist of at least 30 families. For these acres he would pay a rent of £533. 0s. 8d. When Sir Arthur Chichester heard of it, he wrote to the Earl of Salisbury that 100,000 acres in Tyrone is more than the whole county is found at by the book of survey. As for L. Audley, he is an ancient nobleman apt to undertake much, but his manner of life in Munster, and the small cost he has bestowed to make his house fit, does not promise

153

the building of substantial castles nor a convenient plantation in Ulster. Besides which he is near to himself and no lover of hospitality. Such a one would be unwelcome to that people and will soon make himself contemptible; and if the natives be not better provided for, they will kindle many a fire in his buildings before they be half finished.

26th. The deaths from the plague this week were but 55, but in the weeks previous 154, 177 and 131.

29th. The Irishmen intended for the wars in Sweden have sailed from Lough Foyle in four ships, but they were collected with much ado, for the priests gave out that this was but a pretence of the English to have the swordmen out of the country, and when they were put out to sea they would be cast overboard and so drowned, every mother's son of them. On the other side the priests in Leinster and Connaught persuaded the people that it was altogether unlawful to go to such a war where they should fight for a heretic and usurper against a Catholic and the rightful King. Notwithstanding, Sir Arthur Chichester, with his wonted diligence, gathered the men and went himself to Carlingford to see them embarked.

On one of the ships was a mutiny raised in which they took prisoner the gentleman appointed to oversee them, captured the ship, slipped the cables and let her run upon a shelf with intention to land and escape away; but a contrary wind set which held them in harbour until the forces of the next garrison came up with boats and they were forced to yield. The Deputy ordered that the chief actors should receive exemplary punishment, and gave money to the master of the ship to provide new compasses and other necessaries which in their drunken fury they had spoiled. Nine hundred of these men are natives of Ulster, such as troubled the quiet, wild, cruel malefactors and thieves.

2nd November. Signor Francesco Contarini, who was the first Ambassador sent to the Pope after the Interdict, is being sent as Ambassador Extraordinary from Venice to satisfy the King of the late trouble with our Ambassador.

3rd. Sir Robert Shirley, who accompanied his brother Sir Anthony on that notable expedition to the Sophy of Persia some 12 years since, thereafter remained in the country as a General to the King. He has now been made Ambassador Extraordinary for the Sophy and comes to do business for his Master in the Courts of Europe. In May he was reported to be in Prague, whence in September he travelled to the Court of the Grand Duke at Florence where he had a solemn meeting with the Great Turk's brother. He is now in Rome where he was most honourably received. He is dressed in the Persian attire with a cloak of black velvet trimmed with gold, and he wears a turbant with a cross on the top to show he is a Catholic. He has had an audience with the Pope in presence of some Cardinals, and after presenting his letters he made a long oration setting forth the esteem in which the King held the Pope and the good treatment of Christians in Persia, the wars with the Turks and the victories gained, hoping the Pope would unite all Christian Princes against the common enemy. When the Turk is beaten, saith he, his Master will become a Christian and obey the Pope.

7th. From Spain comes news that the great levies made of late were all to be employed for destroying the Moriscos in the Kingdom of Valencia. To this end the King assembled 80 galleys and 20 sail, and in divers parts of the country above 70,000 soldiers. They in one instant seized on all the towns and villages of the Kingdom, and at the same time proclaimed in them all that within three days upon pain of death all the Moors should repair to the seaside to be embarked. Many attempted to have fled and were immediately executed. The rest (who are said to number at least 80,000 households) have daily their hands bound and so put aboard. What they will do with them is yet kept very secret. Some say there is a commission to put them all ashore in Barbary; and others that it is to cast them all into the sea.

9th. The King is troubled with a pain in his foot which has kept him in London. The doctors say it is the gout but they dare not tell him so. He departs for Royston in two days, and the Prince goes with him. The plague has again broken out at Court where two pastry cooks have died of it, to the alarm of all, so that the Queen may go to Hampton Court. It is said that two great Ladies of the Court have become Catholics, and one of them persuaded some gentlemen from hearing the first sermon of the Italian Ascanio Spinola who has been presented to the church intended for the Italians. This man, who was formerly a Catholic, committed many crimes and came to England hoping to live upon the Catholics, but being disappointed he was forced to lurk in taverns. He was arrested and then changed his religion. Four ships are to be sent out by the Levant Company, accompanied by a ship of war, and with them three other ships well armed against the pirates to whom of late Sir Francis Verney has joined himself.

The King's Book, together with his letter, hath now been offered or presented to divers Princes. The Archduke in the Netherlands said he could not receive such a book with a free conscience since he himself had been a churchman. The Emperor refused audience to Barclay, as did the King of Bavaria; but the King of Hungary and the Duke of Savoy, though they refused the Book, accepted the letter.

10th. Sir George Wharton and Sir James Stuart, both young men about the King, being at cards in my L. of Essex's chamber in Whitehall came to blows with daggers, but were then parted. Yesterday Sir George challenged the other, and they have killed each other in Islington Fields. One coach carried them alive to the field and brought them home dead. Their friends discourse strangely of the humours of those that might have stopped youth's fury. Both are much lamented, being of good disposition and having lived in very good friendship. They are both buried in one grave in the church at Islington. Sir George was a son to the L. Wharton and brother-in-law of Sir Henry Wotton; Sir James, who married the Lady Dorothy Hastings, was a great minion of the King, and of his own family. The smallest trifle breeds quarrels between the Scots and our English. The King thought it prudent to remove at once from London to Royston with the Scots who usually follow the Court. The pain in his foot has ceased.

15th. These past months a certain Frenchman, by name Francis de Verton, has gone up and down the country for the distribution of mulberry trees, to the number of 100,000. He hath visited 15 counties and divers great Lords.

22nd. Five days since M. Hudson and his company, who left Amsterdam on 25th March, came into Dartmouth. They set forth towards Nova Zembla, but thence passed to Newfound Land and along southward to 44° of latitude and thence to Cape Cod and so to 33°. In all this while they were much troubled with the currents which continually bore them out of their reckoning. They report much of the coast, and of their dealings with the savages who for the most part were friendly, but some treacherous, from whom they lost one man, shot through the throat with an arrow. They left the coast of Virginia in October. Noteth that one night when there was a great storm of wind their cat ran crying from one side of the ship to the other looking overboard, which made them wonder, but they saw nothing.

23rd. The Puritans have presented a book in the form of a request to the King to be reintegrated into their livings, for which they are much blamed. The commissioners sent to view the lands in Ulster for the City of London have returned, and confirm the King and the City in their resolution to build another London there. The news that Sir Francis Verney hath seized the portion of wine coming to the King from Marseilles is confirmed; and he is said to have taken a much richer prize. The work of translating the Bible goes forward, the Old Testament being already done.

25th. Our Catholics in Brussels report that the Pope, to manifest his dislike of that profane libel called *Pruritanus*, hath forbidden the reading of it to all his obedient children upon pain of excommunication, and being also much displeased with Cardinal Bellarmine for provoking the King to write by his *Tortus*, hath enjoined him upon pain of his indignation not to publish any answer to the King's Book without the knowledge and special direction of the See Apostolical.

28th. The general opinion is that milder courses will be held with the Catholics, for not only did the elected Bishop of Ely (Dr. Andrewes) advise the same in his sermon before the King on the 5th, a day used in time past to exasperate, but my L. Treasurer upon Thursday last, commending the quiet behaviour of recusants and acquitting them from being culpable of that monstrous Gunpowder Treason, thought it was expedient they should more mildly be dealt with. Some of the pursuivants that violently behaved themselves in Oxfordshire this summer his Lordship hath commanded upon their return they shall be apprehended, committed to Newgate and punished.

A great part of Constantinople hath been consumed with fire, and among other houses the Serraglis wherein the Grand Signor kept his women; so as the fair creatures were inforced to lodge abroad. Twenty-three pirate ships were this summer consumed by fire by the Spanish fleet, whereof not Sir Anthony Shirley but a Spaniard commanded. And yet the pirates are in great strength. The principal of the Turkoman fleet are gone over to them, and among others Sir Fr. Verney, who renouncing his faith, is circumcised and become Turk. They deal most barbarously against the King's subjects, but especially against the Scots of whom they spare none.

30th. The King is at Royston with the gout, although he doth call those traitors who say it is the gout, and cannot get one day free to go to his sport. This may hinder his return. From Ireland there is shameful news of one of the King's ships there and Bishop, lieutenant to Ward the pirate. Sir William S. John the captain of the King's ship (which is a pinnace) heard that Bishop was at Ardmore and made after him, anchoring before the haven where he was. Which Bishop perceiving sent one of his men for liberty to go out, professing that he was not there for mischief but only for victuals, and that for his part he loathed that course of life and would leave it but he would not be brought thereto by force and would rather die there than be hanged at Wapping. Sir William having made answer that he was there to entrap him, Bishop came out desperately upon him, and both ships being grappled together, it was Sir William's ill chance that after a long and lusty fight, his ship was entered and himself and the Master with some others killed, and the pinnace carried away by Bishop, but of this the reports differ, some saying that he sent back the ship, and another that he hath not possessed her at all, but only saved some of his men from her. Some of the ships that went for Virginia are lately returned with word that their Admiral wherein was Sir Thomas Gates was so scattered by a tempest from the rest of the company that hereunto they can hear nothing of her. The rest having landed their company in Virginia report that there is dissension among them by reason of their minister being somewhat a Puritan, and the most part refuse to hear his sermons.

The men from Ireland, some 1,000 or 2,000 strong, that were shipped to go to the wars of Sweden, being taken with a tempest their ships were forced to put back and came into the Thames. There the men are landed to refresh themselves in Kent, and cannot be gotten on board again, but spread all over the country, which is now pestered with them. The Masters of the ships are much blamed for suffering them to land.

Dansecer the pirate has now turned against the Turks and has slain a hundred of them and freed 300 slaves. Then as the Spanish *flotta* was entering Seville with 8 galleons and 2 galeottas he took from the Spaniards a great galleon and two ships and withal half a million of gold in booty. Having by this action received pardon from the French King if he would quit piracy, he has now come to Marseilles, bringing with him booty worth 400,000 crowns. He was met by the Duke of Guise with every sign of joy. This action of Dansecer is expected to bring ruin to Ward.

This past month the plague diminisheth, the weekly deaths being 84, 69, 67, 59 and 51.

1st December. Of the proceedings in Virginia during the past months they report that when Capt. Newport last departed for England with so little accomplished for replenishing the store, the company (which now numbered 200) was so affrighted with famine that

Smith the President went to Nansamund and there forced the savages to load his three boats. Then, being invited by Powhatan to come to him with the promise that he would load the ship with corn if he would send men to build him a house and give him a grindstone, 50 swords, some pieces, a cock and a hen and some copper, the President sent him three of the Dutchmen and two English, and himself followed with Capt. Waldo, leaving Scrivener as his deputy at Jamestown. He took with him in the barge twelve men, and in the pinnace went M. George Percy (brother to my L. of Northumberland), M. Francis West and others. On their way they were warned that Powhatan intended to seize their arms and cut their throats. They spent their Christmas at Kecoughtan among the savages in extreme severe weather, feasting in great plenty. On January 12th, they reached Werowocomoco where the river was half frozen, and next day came to Powhatan who pretended that he had not sent for them nor had he any corn; for (as afterwards appeared) the Dutchmen would have betrayed the President, for they had told Powhatan of the wants of our men at Jamestown, and preferred Powhatan's plenty, since they little expected that Jamestown would escape both Powhatan and famine. Many speeches passed between Smith and Powhatan, who three times sought to betray him unarmed, and once he was secretly warned by Pocahontas who came to them in the dark night alone through the woods. Moreover Powhatan sent two of the Dutchmen (who were named Adam and Francis) to Jamestown feigning that the President had sent for arms, which they gave to the savages.

The President was also in great danger from a savage King called Opechancanough who promised trade. Here the President was warned in his lodging that they were beset with 700 savages. Opechancanough pretended to appease Smith's suspicion of unkindness and tried to draw him out of the door alone by a great present, which bait was guarded by 200 men, each with his arrow nocked to shoot. In a great rage Smith caught the King by his long lock of hair and bent his pistol at his breast. Then he led the trembling King through his own people, who cast away their weapons little dreaming that any durst use their King in that manner. So they thronged about him, bringing their presents and so wearied him that he retired to rest. When some of the savages saw him asleep, and his guard carelessly dispersed, 40 or 50 each with a club or an English sword began to enter the house, but they made such a noise that he awoke and betook himself to his sword and target, and others of his company charging in like manner the house was quickly cleared.

In the meanwhile at Jamestown, Scrivener (who had begun to decline in his friendship for the President) thought to cross his designs and would needs visit the Isle called the Isle of Hogs in the skiff. He took with him Capt. Waldo and M. Anthony Gosnol and eight others; but she was so overloaded that in a violent tempest she sank and all perished. Their bodies were found by the savages who were thereby the more emboldened. This heavy news was brought to the President by M. Richard Wiffin who came alone through the woods to Powhatan, and there not finding the President and seeing the preparation for war assured himself that mischief was intended. For three days he was hidden by Pocahontas and by her means sent to the President who was in his turmoils with Opechancanough. The President swore him to conceal the unhappy news, and himself dissembling his sorrow, went on board with his men, leaving Opechancanough at liberty as he had promised.

And now he returned to Powhatan, who again tried to betray him by poison which made the President and M. West sick but expelled itself. At length they came back to Jamestown, having in return for 25lbs. of copper and 50lbs. of iron 220 lbs. of deer suet and 479 bushels of corn. They now cast up the store and finding sufficient till the next harvest the fear of starving was abandoned. The company was divided into tens or fifteens, and as business required, four hours was spent every day in work and the rest in pastimes. The treacherous Dutchmen with the aid of their consorts in Jamestown still closely purveyed powder, shot, swords and tools to Powhatan and instructed the savages in their use.

The President also had another escape. On a time returning from the glasshouse alone armed only with his falchion, he encountered the King of Paspaleigh, a most stout strong savage who attempted to have shot him, but he prevented that shot by grappling with him, when the savage perforce bore him into the river to have drowned him. Long they struggled in the water until two of the Poles came up, and they took the savage as a prisoner to the fort, where his wives and people came daily to visit him, until finding the guard negligent he escaped. Capt. Winn with 50 chosen men attempted that night to have regained him, and so had done if he had followed his directions; but he trifling away that night, next morning the savages braved him to come ashore and fight. A good time both sides let fly at each other and our men took two canoas and burnt the King's house.

The President fearing that these bravadoes would but encourage the savage began himself to try conclusions, whereby several savages were slain and others taken prisoners. He burnt their houses, took their boats with all their fishing weirs and planted them at Jamestown for his own use, and he resolved not to cease till he had revenged himself on all that had injured him. The savages did their best to draw him to their ambuscado but as soon as he landed, they threw down their arms and desired a peace, upon which a young savage made a notable peace speech justifying the escape of their King, and declaring that they desired his friendship; saying moreover that if he would promise them peace they would relieve him, but if not they would themselves remove. 'We know', quoth he, 'you cannot live if you want our harvest and that relief we bring you; if you promise us peace we will believe you; if you proceed in revenge, we will abandon the country.' Upon these terms the President promised them peace, and so all departed good friends.

At this time also two savages who were brothers were taken. One was kept prisoner in the dungeon, the other sent to recover a stolen pistol or his brother would be hanged. The President pitying the prisoner sent him victual and charcoal for a fire. His brother returning and finding the prisoner so smothered in smoke and so piteously burnt that he seemed dead, broke out into such bitter agonies that the President (to quiet him) said if hereafter they would not steal, he would make him alive again; and by *aqua vitae* and vinegar they did restore him again but so drunk and frantic that his brother was as much grieved as before; of which malady, upon promise of good behaviour hereafter, the President promised to recover him; and so caused him to be laid by a fire to sleep, and next morning he recovered his perfect senses. Then being dressed for his burning, each was given a piece of copper, and they went away so well contented that it spread among the savages for a miracle that Capt. Smith could make alive one that was dead. This and many other such accidents so amazed and affrighted Powhatan and all his people that with presents they desired peace, returning many stolen things. After that those that were taken stealing, both Powhatan and his people sent back to receive their punishment and the country became quieter.

For the three months following Newport's second departure from Virginia, that is until April, the company made three or four last of tar, pitch and soap ashes, dug a well of sweet water in the fort, built twenty houses, recovered the church, provided nets and weirs for fishing, and (to stop the disorders of their thieves within) built a blockhouse in the neck of the island with a garrison to oversea trade with the savages. Also they digged and planted 30 or 40 acres of ground. Their three sows in eighteen months had increased to 60 and odd pigs; and near 500 chickens brought themselves up without food given. The hogs were transported to Hog Isle where also a blockhouse was built with a garrison to bring notice of any shipping. These labours were brought to a sudden stop when in searching their casked corn they found it half rotten and the rest consumed by rats, which drove them to their wit's end. The country people brought squirrels, turkeys, deer and other wild beasts; and they had also great plenty of sturgeon, but lack of corn caused the end of all. Eighty men were sent down the river to live upon oysters; and 20 with Lieutenant Percy to fish at Point Comfort; and many were billeted among the savages. Yet such was the strange condition of some 150, that had they not been forced to gather and prepare food they would all have starved, for they preferred to sell everything they had, not only kettles and tools but even the ordnance, rather than work; and they tried to force the President to abandon the country, until he found out the author of these complaints, one Dyer, whom he worthily punished, and to the rest declared that if he found any more runners with the pinnace to Newfound Land he would hang them; and, said he, 'he that gathereth not every day as much as I do, the next day shall be set beyond the river and be banished from the fort as a drone till he amend his conditions or starve'. This order, though many murmured, caused the most part so to bestir themselves that of 200 (except they were drowned) there did not perish beyond seven.

Meantime the President tried in vain to recover the Dutchmen with Powhatan, using one William Valdy a Switzer as his messenger, little suspecting that he was a double villain in league with the Dutchmen, who importuned Powhatan to lend them forces and they would kill the hogs, fire the town and betray the pinnace. With this plot they acquainted many discontents in the Fort, but it was revealed to the President who sent to have killed them. While this business was in hand, there arrived on 10th July Capt. Argall, sent to truck with the colony and to fish for sturgeon. He brought news of the great supply and preparation in England, and letters to the President much taxing him with hard dealing with the savages and not returning the ships fraughted. This ship the President retained until the fleet arrived.

Seven of the ships sent out from England in May arrived dispersedly in the middle of August, with Capt. Ratcliffe (alias Sicklemore), Capt. Martin and Capt. Archer (all of whom had previously been sent back from the colony), five other captains, and sundry gentlemen. Ratcliffe, Archer and Martin had so exclaimed against Smith that all mortally hated him ere even they saw him. Nevertheless in a short while the best of the new come captains, hearing the general good report of the old soldiers, when they understood the malice of Ratcliffe, Archer and divers others, became the President's faithful friends.

Jamestown being now thronged with an unruly company, Smith the President seeing his own authority so unexpectedly changed would willingly have left all and returned to England; but since there was small hope of the coming of the new commission (being with the Admiral that was supposed cast away), he would not suffer those unruly spirits to proceed. He therefore sent M. West to the Falls with 120 men, and Capt. Martin with as many to Nandsamund. Moreover since the President's year was near expired, he made Capt. Martin President, but he knowing his own insufficiency and the company's untowardness in three hours resigned it again to Capt. Smith and proceeded to Nandsamund. Here the savages used him kindly; yet such was his jealous fear that in the midst of their mirth he surprised their King and occupied his island; whereat seeing him so distraught with fear, the savages were emboldened to assault, release their King and carry away 1,000 bushels of corn, he not offering to intercept them; only he sent to Jamestown for 30 good shot, which were sent, with whom he did nothing but came away with them to Jamestown leaving his company to their fortunes.

As for the company with M. West, the President went to see them and found them planted in a place not only subject to the river's inundation but environed with intolerable inconveniences; for remedy thereof he traded with Powhatan for a convenent piece of land, called also Powhatan, but the company refused that place. The worst misfortune was that when the savages brought in their contributions to M. West, these newcomers took their corn, robbed their gardens, beat them, broke open their houses and kept some prisoners, so that they daily complained to the President that those whom he had brought them for protectors were worse enemies than the Monacans. For nine days the President sought to restrain them. Then seeing that nothing would prevail, he set forth for Jamestown, No sooner was the ship under sail than twelve savages assaulted them and slew many. But within half a league the President's ship grounded so that a parley was held, and now they were so amazed that they submitted themselves to him under any terms. He put by the heels the chief offenders and the rest he seated at Powhatan, which was a strong savage fort with dry houses and near 200 acres already planted; and so delightful that the old planters called it Non-such. Nevertheless when Capt. West returned to them, they went back again to the open air at West's fort.

On this journey back to Jamestown, as the President was sleeping in his boat, one fired his powder bag, which tore the flesh from his body and thigh 9 or 10 inches square in most pitiful manner; and to quench the tormenting fire he leapt overboard and was near drowned. In this state without chirurgeon he was conveyed 100 miles to Jamestown, where Ratcliffe, Archer and the rest of their confederates were near to their trials. They, seeing the President unable to stand and near bereft of his senses by his torment, plotted to murder him in his bed, but his heart failed who should have given fire to the merciless pistol. They plotted therefore to usurp the government. The President had notice of their project, and his soldiers importuned him but to take away their heads that would resist his command; yet he would not suffer them.

And now seeing there was no chirurgeon to cure his wound, his commission to be suppressed, and that in his disabled state he could no longer subdue those factions and range the country for provision, he went on board ship and took order for his return for England, resolving to appoint for governor one who could take order for the mutineers; but found none. In the meantime, seeing him gone, the company persuaded M. George Percy (who was to have gone sick to England) to stay with them and be their governor.

Divers searches have been made for those who were left in Virginia by Sir Walter Ralegh in 1586, but the savages declare that they are all dead, and Powhatan himself confessed to Smith that he had been present at the murder of that colony, in proof whereof he showed a musket barrel, a brass mortar and certain pieces of iron that had been theirs.

6th. Dansecer has now come to Paris in company with the Duke of Guise who has received a great sum. Dansecer sold 60,000 crowns' worth of goods in Marseilles, and is said to be worth at least half a million. Of late the Spanish Ambassador demanded from the French King that the galleon taken by Dansecer should be given back, but the King replied that he had done good service to Spain and to the other nations by ridding the sea of so famous a pirate.

7th. Cardinal Bellarmine in his own name hath written an *Apology* to the King's Book with its *Premonition*, defending himself and those doctrines which his Majesty so mocked in his Book. As for the arguments to prove the Pope Antichrist, declares that the King has brought forward nothing new, and such arguments as he did use were taken directly from the books of others (whom he names). To the King's declaration that no one ever suffered death in England for conscience's sake unless he first transgressed the Law, the Cardinal answereth that since the Law forbids anyone to receive a Catholic priest into his house, or be reconciled to the Church, or to hear Mass, or to do many things plainly appertaining to religion, one who dies for transgressing such a Law may rightly be said to have died for his religion. It matters little whether he dies because he professes the Catholic Faith or because he broke that Law which commanded him to renounce his Faith. Defendeth Garnet against the charge that he had known of the Powder Plot otherwise than in confession; nor if Garnet had warned the King that his life was in danger from traitors, would the King out of respect for the seal of confession have forborne to demand their names, even causing Garnet to be tortured until he revealed everything. And so for the King's appealing for a unity of the Churches outside the Catholic Faith, he is but baying the moon; for how can disputes be ended when the disputers have no umpire but the Scriptures which each man can interpret as he pleases?

A copy of the book has come into the hands of the L. Treasurer who has sent it to Royston for the King.

The plague is much abated, for this past week but 18 died of it.

10th. Sir Thomas Lake writes to the L. Treasurer from the King (who is now at Newmarket) that he is much troubled because the Colleges in Cambridge and Oxford are backward in receiving Scottishmen, alleging their ancient statutes made heretofore when the hostile laws were made. He would have the L. Treasurer (as Chancellor of Cambridge) and the Archbishop for Oxford have a visitation made of the Universities that these statutes may be taken away, for it is an indignity which the King will not endure, especially as he hath been so good and gracious a patron; but if they persist he will make them see he can be otherwise than he hath been.

11th. The Churchmen would draw the King into writing against the late book, though he himself would have it answered by some mean person and in scorn only. The book is sent to the Bishop of Ely to be considered before the King's coming.

The Prince of Condé fearing some bad measure in France, where the King has long made love to his Lady, hath withdrawn himself with her into the Archduke's dominions, whither the King sent his Captain of his Guard to bring him back. The Princess is received most honourably by the Archduchess in Brussels. This Prince is the heir of France next after the King's own young children.

Sir Robert Shirley is now in Milan having been at Loretto, and about to go for Spain either by sea from Genoa, or by land through a skirt of France. His habit and half of his train and most of his language is still Persian, except for the jewelled crucifix (given him by the Pope) which he carrieth upon the top of his turban. He was made welcome to the Pope, rather for the glory of his long journey than for any fruit of his errand which tendeth to keeping on foot the war between the Emperor and the Turk; at which the wise men mock, seeing that the Emperor is not now able to oppose himself to the burghers of Prague. Toby Mathew goes with him into Spain upon a familiarity woven between them at Florence.

14th. The Prince now begins to take a great authority upon him and expecteth his creation at Candlemas at which time he will have accomplished the age of 16. He maketh himself already very much respected, and even by our greatest men in authority, and out of the pregnancy of his spirit men make many descants of things that may hereafter ensure.

The Irish who were put back from their journey to Sweden have been collected, some from their ships, some straggling about the country, to be penned up and kept here till the spring, for by this the Sound is frozen. They are 1,200 and are kept together by 400's in several places. The great ship which the East India Company's merchants are building at Deptford is finished, being at least of 1,000 or 1,200 tons.

There is a learned work called *The Trial of Tobacco* by an ancient physician named Edmund Gardiner, taken from 75 authors and learned men, on the nature and qualities of this herb, its use in physic, with many receipts for the cure of sundry disorders. But he would have tobacco regarded as an herb of rare quality for healing, and not drunk (as it is termed) for wantonness; for it is a fantastical attracter and glutton feeder of the appetite, taken of many when they have nothing else to do, than of any absolute or necessary use; which is much to be discommended. To such, it is a great empairer of bodily health, accelerating their deaths before either Nature urge, malady enforce or Age require it.

16th. The L. of Howth hath long had a grudge against the Archbishop of Dublin who is Chancellor of Ireland, whom he hath sundry times accused and maligned. Lately he assaulted the Chancellor's son in Dublin in very gross sort. On a Sunday, while the L. Deputy was at the sermon and Sir Roger Jones at tennis in a court in S. Thomas's Street, thither comes the L. of Howth with some dozen men, carrying a cudgel in his hand. Sir Roger, having left off play, looking around him and seeing my Lord's approach, called earnestly to his man for his sword. Meanwhile a gentleman there at play caught the L. of

Howth in his arms and held him in the entrance so that his followers could not easily enter; but they leapt over the rail and one of them lighted a blow on Sir Roger's sword before it was fully out of the scabbard and others plied him until it brake. So he was driven back to the other end of the court, defending himself with his broken sword till he was gotten past one Simon Barnwell, who endeavoured all he could to prevent them, but he was thrust through and soon died. Sir Roger, finding himself in that desperate strait, cried out aloud, 'Fie, my Lord, will you suffer me to be murdered?' Then the L. of Howth willed them not to kill him; and thereupon two held him up until his Lordship took him by the bosom, asking if he would now say he was a coward? Sir Roger answered that he neither would nor never did: what he had said he would not deny, that he was a valiant man among cowards. 'That's all one,' said the Lord; and with threats willed him to kneel down and ask his forgiveness, which Sir Roger refused; but at last was pressed to acknowledge that his life was in his Lordship's hands; and that, said Sir Roger, he could not deny. 'Then go thy ways,' said the L. of Howth, striking him over the side of the face with the hilt of his rapier, 'like a boy as thou art.' And so they parted.

The report of the fray was brought to the L. Deputy while he was at the sermon. He directed the Mayor of Dublin (who was in the church with him) to apprehend the offenders. So the L. of Howth and six of his followers were carried to the Castle where Sir Arthur Chichester found them on his return to dinner. After debating of the matter with his Council, he committed the L. of Howth until the coroners had inquired upon the body of Barnwell; but the jury found it manslaughter; as indeed, complaineth the Deputy, would they if Sir Roger himself had been slain. So the Lord was released on bonds.

21st. Last week Dr. Thomas Ravis the Bishop of London died and is privately buried in Paul's without any ceremony. Two of the Turkey Merchants' ships are returned, laden to the value of £70,000.

22nd. Nineteen pirates were this day indicted at S. Margaret's Hill in Southwark and all found guilty and condemned, among them Jennings and Harris.

29th. A few days since word was brought to the King that the Lady Arbella had a purpose to cross the seas with a Scottish gentleman, Sir George Douglas, that she might marry him. The King therefore sent my L. Fenton (who is Captain of the Guard) and his Lady to fetch the Lady Arbella from the house of one of the Seymours where she remaineth, pretending friendship and an invitation to supper. They then conveyed her to the Palace where for some days she remained guarded, Sir George Douglas also is under arrest, and some of her servants and waiting gentlewomen. The Lady Arbella was brought before the King and the Council, and answered well. For a long while she has been living away from the Court and in great melancholy, both because of the little esteem that is had of her and because her means are so slight.

Seventeen of the pirates condemned yesterday, in the forenoon were brought from the Marshalsea to Wapping and there executed; Jennings was the first, who died very penitent. This afternoon between 4 and 5 of the clock almost at high tide the two remaining, Downs and Halse, were also executed, who had confidently expected their lives. Downs was very stubborn, scarce making any outward show of a mortified man, and two hours before his death, he was heard boastingly to report of the wealth of his robberies.

30th. Today the King with the Prince and divers Lords came to Deptford to the launching of the great ship. They were entertained by the Merchants of the Company to a sumptuous banquet. The King graced Sir Thomas Smith the Governor with a chain in the manner of a collar better than £200, with his picture hanging at it, and put it about his neck with his own hands. Then he named the great ship *Trade's Increase*; and a pinnace of 250 tons, made to wait upon her, is by the Prince named the *Peppercorn*. But the tide was so bad that the great ship could not be launched out of the dock, and the smaller (which was built upon the wharf) was so ill struck upon the launching ways that she could by no means be put off, which did somewhat discontent his Majesty.

31st. Now that his investment in the Principality of Wales and Cornwall is at hand, the Prince is eager to show forth his own skill in arms, and for such exercises hath chosen the name of Moeliades (which in anagram signifieth *Miles a Deo*). This day there appeared in presence certain men strangely attired, accompanied with drums and trumpets, before the King and the Queen and in presence of the whole Court, to deliver a challenge to all Knights of Great Britain to the effect that Moeliades, their noble Master, burning to try the valour of his young years now sent to present the first fruits of his chivalry at his Majesty's feet. After a short speech to the Queen, to the Earls, Lords and Knights, and lastly to the Ladies, they delivered their chartel concerning time, place, conditions, number of weapons and assailants, and took their leaves, departing solemnly as they had entered.

OTHER BOOKS AND PLAYS PRINTED IN 1609

i. *The Gull's Hornbook* by Dekker, being a guide to gulls about Paul's declaring how a gull ought to behave himself, and especially in Paul's Walk, an ordinary, a playhouse, a tavern, and in night walking.

ii. From Oxford, a book by William Heale of Exeter College called *An Apology for Women*, in opposition to that Act made last year wherein it was maintained that it is lawful for a man to beat his wife; which this author denieth by all religious, moral and civil laws.

iii. *The Husbandman's Fruitful Orchard*, showing divers secrets for the true ordering of all sorts of fruit trees in their due seasons with the manner of gathering and storing their fruits.

iv. A merry poem of ale-drinking at Pimlico, entitled *Pimlico: or run mad-cap*, wherein is inserted that ancient rhyme of Skelton's called *The Tunning of Elinor Rumming*.

v. *A Defence of the judgement of the Reformed Churches:* that a man may lawfully not only put away his wife for adultery, but also marry another, a treatise left by Dr. John Rainolds, and now printed but without any printer's name; written very invectively against Cardinal Bellarmine and his contrary opinions hereon.

vi. But five or six plays were printed this past year, viz: *The Case is Altered, The Turk, Every Woman in Her Humour, Two Maids of Moreclack, The Faithful Shepherdess.*

1610

3rd January. The Council learning that Sir John Wentworth and M. Danvers intended to pass over the seas to determine a quarrel by single combat wrote to Sir Ralph Winwood at the Hague to use his utmost to prevent that meeting and if possible compose their quarrel. But M. Danvers not arriving, Sir John goes to Sir Ralph Winwood declaring that he was bound in honour to tender his person in the place agreed, and now having given that satisfaction he holds himself fully acquitted, and so doth purpose, after he hath seen some of the best towns in those parts, speedily to return.

5th. The Lady Arbella keeps to her apartment, for she neither leaves her chamber nor is visited except by a few. Sir George Douglas is also free, but one of her gentlewomen is still in prison, because of too bold an answer she gave to the Lords of the Council, for she said briefly and firmly that neither ought their Lordships to pry into Ladies' secrets nor was it her place to lay them bare; had she heard anything hostile to the King, she would have withdrawn from the house, but it was none of her business to tell tales. The Lady Arbella's replies were considered very prudent and wise. She would neither affirm nor deny that she had thought of leaving the Kingdom, but said merely that since she was ill treated of all, it was but natural that she should think of going. It is said that the King will increase her income.

6th. These past few days the Prince hath feasted the Earls, Barons, and Knights who are chosen Assailants and Defendants. This evening in the Palace at Whitehall in the great Banqueting House were assembled the King, the Queen, the Ambassadors of Spain and Venice and all the Peers and great Ladies, with a multitude of others. Beside the King's chair of state was a sumptuous pavilion for the Prince and his associates, namely, the Duke of Lenox, the Earls of Arundel and Southampton, the L. Hay, Sir Thomas Somerset and Sir Richard Preston. Before the barriers sundry poetical speeches were delivered by the Lady of the Lake, and then by King Arthur, whereupon Moeliades and his 6 assistants were discovered: and Merlin speaks at length of the glories of sundry British Kings and Princes, and of King James as a goal for all posterity to sweat in running at.

Against these 7 challengers came 56 defendants, Earls, Barons, Knights, and Esquires, who had erected a very delicate place in the lower end of the room where they remained concealed, and from whence they issued and ascended into the middle of the Hall where sat the King and the Queen and the Ambassadors. Each Challenger fought with eight several Defendants two combats at two weapons, *videlicet*, at push of pike and with single sword. The Prince performed this challenge with wondrous skill and courage to the great joy of the beholders. These feats of arms began at 10 o'clock and continued till Sunday morning. The three prizes are awarded to the Earl of Montgomery, Sir Thomas Darcy, and Sir Robert Gordon, a Scot, more in favour to that Nation than for any due desert. Instead of a *plaudite*, they had an exceeding peal of ordnance.

7th. Today the Prince and his Assistants all in a livery, and the Defendants in their best bravery rode in a great pomp to convey the King to S. James whither the Prince had invited him and all the Court to supper (the Queen only being absent). After supper the prizes were awarded to those adjudged best deserving of the Defendants.

12th. The Lady Arbella is at liberty and cometh every day to the Court where she is very welcome and much made of by the King and the Queen, and on New Year's day was presented by the King with plate valued £200, and requited the King with a rich pair of slippers. She was committed for entertaining marriage with the Duke of Moldavia. It is thought that she did this out of policy to value herself towards the King, and to make herself the better considered of, when he should see how she was sued unto by foreign Princes.

There is a marriage between the Scottish Earl of Argyle and Mistress Anne Cornwallis. They were bidden last week to a feast at my Lady Hatton's (the wife of Sir Edward Coke), where many other Lords and Ladies were invited, among them the Earls of Pembroke and Montgomery. There was like to fell out a chance between Pembroke and Argyle for the places of sitting. Argyle had taken his place amongst the Ladies above the other, who rose from the table at the second course and so disordered the feast and the company, who muttered much with him at the Scottish Earl's presumption, Pembroke saying that if he offered him any more such an affront he would run him through with his rapier. The other withdrew into another room, and for the time there grew no further inconvenience of it. They departed without satisfaction one of another. It is thought that the prosecuting of that matter hath been hitherto only hindered by the occupation which the parties have about the Prince's combat.

Dr. George Abbot, Bishop of Lichfield, hath been admitted in the late Bishop of London's place.

The Commissioners for the Irish causes and the London Deputies for the plantation of Ulster met for the first time on the 9th and again today.

13th. One Nicholas Coffeteau, a French friar preacher to the King, hath answered our King's book very moderately and modestly (they say) yet he is nothing satisfied with this fawning nor takes it in better part than if, as he says, 'he should bid a turd in his teeth and then cry sirreverence'. The Bishop of Ely, Dr. Andrewes, is set awork to reply to Cardinal Bellarmine's answer to the King's Book, of which he makes no great account but thinks that either he is much crazed from what he was or else he did it with a contemptuous negligence. Dr. Andrewes' sermon upon Galatians iv, 4th verse, preached on Christmas day with great applause, is printing. The King with much importunity had the copy delivered him before his going to Royston and says he will lay it continually under his pillow.

18th. The Lady Arbella hath been examined by the Lords, and had some of her servants restrained, but the naked truth appears that her private retiredness was for want of money to clothe herself according to her rank against Christmas. Her troubles are due to a certain sum of money which she would send to Constantinople by Sir George Douglas for that Moldavian Prince who was in England many months ago. At that time he sought to marry Lady Arbella but the King said he would have first to establish himself in his kingdom. After leaving England he went to Constantinople where the English Ambassador received him, to the great indignation of the Grand Vizier and the Poles. She confesses the fault of womanish credulity in the matter of love with the Prince of Moldavia, and in the people's opinion remains somewhat touched with the spot of Popery; the discourse of her nearest servants would make one believe that she is rather given to the discipline of Geneva. When she was asked about religion, she replied that she had never intended to become a Catholic but her troubles had prevented her from coming to church for some time. She complains much of her ill usage, and recalls the King's promises to her. Although her pension is to be increased, she declares publicly that she is not satisfied, and she demands to be married, or at least to be allowed to depart and choose a husband. These last days she has been at Court, both at the barriers and elsewhere.

For the compounding of the jar between the Earls of Pembroke and Argyle (who alone among the Scots doth stand for his place among the English) the King has sent a peremptory command to my L. of Argyle to yield it to my L. of Pembroke until the next assembly of Parliament. The King has a royal purpose of creating a College at Chelsea chiefly for the handling of controversies in Religion, designing to that effect a dozen Doctors taken out of both the Universities, whereof 8 to be divines and 4 historiographers, and to maintain them there for the reading and writing of history and controversies.

25th. Sir Robert Shirley is now in Spain (with his great turban on his head) with his Embassage from the Persian. Toby Mathew is with him as a gentleman of his train.

26th. The Council have directed that if any indictment shall be preferred against Dr. Thomas Lodge for recusancy it shall be detained until they have been acquainted therewith. Dr. Lodge has but recently returned to England from Brussels.

28th. The Privy Council and the Commissioners of the City of London have agreed on the articles for the plantation of Derry and Coleraine. The City will levy £20,000. At Derry 200 houses are to be built and room left for 300 more and 4,000 acres allotted to the city; at Coleraine 100 houses built, with room for 200 more, and 3,000 acres. The two towns to have the customs of all goods imported and exported, and the rights of fishing and fowling. The King will maintain sufficient forces for their protection for the time. Of the houses, 100 to be built before 1st November this year.

31st. The Prince of Condé, entertaining the Marquis of Coeuvre in Brussels, was desired to drink to the King: but his reply being doubtful whether he drank to the King of France or of Spain, the Marquis asked him to make himself clear. Whereupon he said he drank to the King on whose country they were. The Princess being likewise invited to drink to the Queen, declared she drank to the Queen of France; whereat the Prince said that he did not know there was a Queen of France: there were five or six. When the French King heard these words, he was so enraged that he went off to the Arsenal, taking the Queen with him, and there it is determined to crown the Queen. In the matter of Cleves he has also resolved to help the Possessioners (as they call the Dukes of Brandenburg and Neuburg). The King in his anger also has told the Archduke's Ambassador in Paris that if the Prince of Condé is not obliged to return to France, he will march with 50,000 French to take him; and if they are not sufficient, then he will bring 100,000.

1st February. Blackwell the Archpriest has now published his defence in English, declaring that the Oath may be taken with a clear conscience. This defence is now also printed in Latin by order of the Archbishop of Canterbury, whereat Blackwell is indignant, which causes some to say that the translation cannot be faithful. The King is greatly pleased with the work, which he laboured all he could to forward. Blackwell receives a stipend from the King for his maintenance, and except that he is named a prisoner, he can go out and converse with whom he would, and so shows no zeal for his discharge.

There is also published a long and learned book called *Pseudo-Martyr* by John Donne to show that Catholics ought to take the Oath, and alleging that those who suffer death for refusing the Oath are no true martyrs. This work is in 12 chapters, of such matters as martyrdom and the inordinate affectation therefor; the obedience due to Princes; the authority of the Pope and that he hath no authority over this Kingdom. Donne dedicateth it to the King, 'having observed how much your Majesty had vouchsafed to descend to a conversation with your subjects by way of your books, I also conceived an ambition of ascending to your presence by the same way, and of participating by this means their happiness of whom that saying of the Queen of Sheba may be usurped: "Happy are thy men, and happy those thy servants which stand before thee always, and hear thy wisdom'."

2nd. Today the Ambassador Extraordinary from Venice, Signor Francesco Contarini, together with the Ambassador Liegier, Signor Marc Antonio Corres, were received in public audience by his Majesty. At the door of the Great Chamber they were met by the L. Chamberlain who went before them with his rod of office through two ranks of Ladies and Gentlemen, all richly dressed and covered with jewels. As they drew near to the King with many congés and mounted the dais, the King stepped forward and embraced them with great courtesy and affection. By him stood the Queen and the Princess Elizabeth, and on the right hand of the King, Prince Henry and the Duke of York. All the officers of the Court, each in his rank, stood at the foot of the dais.

When the King had read the letter of credence, the Ambassador declared that the sole reason for his sending was the good understanding between the Crown of England and the Republic, and their good regard for the King's favour to the Republic during the late disturbances. All the while he was speaking the King held his hat in his hand, and until he had made reply, when he covered and bade the Ambassadors the like. The King replied in French, but some of his words were lost to the Ambassadors, partly by reason of his Majesty's accent, and partly because he spoke rapidly. He said that though this Embassy was superfluous as regarding his constant affection towards the Republic, yet he was glad to receive it, for among all Sovereign States none took greater place in his love.

Then the Ambassador presented his letter to the Queen who made a profound bow to the King before reading. She took off her glove and gave her hand for the Ambassador to kiss. After further compliments, the Ambassador went to the Prince and to the Duke of York, whereat the King said, 'This one is determined to draw a sword in the service of the Republic.' Then he turned to the Princess. While Signor Contarini was speaking to the Queen, the King said to Signor Corres that he was sorry that Signor Contarini should have had to endure such fatigue, to which Signor Corres replied that the journey had indeed been laborious, and Signor Contarini was fresh from the toil of his service in Rome. That labour, replied the King, was the harder, for travail of mind is heavier than bodily weariness, but he would find none of the former here.

Signor Corres also asked my L. of Salisbury to say to the Duke that since he had so often represented him as a champion of the Republic, he was sorry to see him now without a sword. To which the King replied, 'He does not want to be a soldier now; he wants to be a churchman.' When Signor Corres asked whether he did indeed wish to be a churchman, the King interpreted his words, to which the little Duke replied that he wanted to bear arms for the Republic. With that the Ambassadors took their leave.

5th. On New Year's day Sir Henry Wotton the Ambassador in Venice came to the Doge and the Senate to wish him a happy New Year, although since the Venetians use the New Style the day with them was the 10th of January. But, said he, if he was the last to offer his good wishes it was because he followed the Old Style and the custom of his country. The Doge replied that the New Style had been introduced when he was Ambassador in Rome (which was in 1582 in the time of Pope Gregory XIII). The new Calendar was propounded to the Ambassadors and some were against it. Nevertheless the Pope held to his course, but first asked whether France or Venice would accept it, for, said he, if they three held together, the rest of the world would follow. Venice to please the Pope accepted the new Calendar, but the other States held back, so that the Republic is thereby cut off, for most States hold by the Old Style. It seems also that since the reform nothing goes well and the peasants declare that they can no longer hit the right day for sowing their seed.

6th. As about this time last year, the Thames again shifted tides very strangely.

8th. The Lady Arbella seldom comes abroad and lies in greater melancholy than ever. She complains that in a comedy there was reference to her person and to the Prince of Moldavia. The play was inhibited. She is very ill pleased and declares that in this coming Parliament she will cause certain persons to be punished, but none knows who.

The Council of the Virginia Company have set forth a proclamation that the ship which carried Sir Thomas Gates, Sir George Somers and Captain Newport was caught by tempestuous winds and did not make Virginia. Condemneth those disordered youths who have been allowed to embark secretly and to return to England where they spread vile reports wherever they go about the nature of the country and the government of the colony to colour their own evil conduct and the ground of their return. In the past fathers rid themselves of sons, masters of troublesome servants, wives of wicked husbands to the damage of the expedition. It is now decreed that at the setting forth of the L. De la Warr, which will be shortly, only tried artificers shall be accepted, such as smiths, gardeners, ironworkers, gunsmiths, sawyers, caulkers, turners, brickmakers, fishermen, fowlers, surgeons, coopers, ironmasters, ploughmen, barbers, carpenters, salt-workers, bakers, brewers, and vine-dressers as well as doctors for the body and learned divines to convert the infidels.

10th. Parliament came together yesterday, and today Sir William Morris spoke concerning the Union, whereon M. Speaker said that he should prepare a Bill, which is agreed.

11th. M. de la Boderie has been sent over from the French King as Ambassador Extraordinary to consult about the help which our King will send to establish the Princes in Cleves. These shall be 4,000 foot, sent from the English garrisons in the Low Countries. Sir Edward Cecil is to be General of the English soldiers. Today M. de la Boderie and the two Venetian Ambassadors dined with the King in full state. The King was waited on by the great Lords who in bringing the water, the meat and the drink offer it him on their knees. There was also a great showing of plate upon the sideboard. The King himself wore on his hat a jewel of five great diamonds, and a diamond chain from which hung the George. All the while the King spoke to the Ambassadors most affably, declaring that his ships had taken some pirates and he hoped to root them out for he would never pardon them. One indeed had offered £40,000 to recover his favour but he would not. It is thought by some that these words were intended for the French King who has lately pardoned the pirate

Dansecer, not without some valuable consideration to someone. There was a great company of lookers on. The French Ambassador has proposed an alliance between the Kingdoms of England and France and the United Provinces.

14th. In the Commons it was shown that since the last session 24 members are dead or removed; and new writs are ordered for the places of Sir Toby Mathew banished, Sir George Somers now Governor of Virginia, M. Hassard an elderly man bedrid and incurable. The matter being debated, M. Fuller said that the end of Parliament was to have a man present who represents.

15th. The King has given the Lady Arbella £2,500 to pay her debts and greatly increased her pension. Nevertheless she is much suspected, partly because she is still unsatisfied and is a lady of high spirit, partly also lest the malcontents may some day make use of her. There is also a rumour of some design of marriage with the son of the Earl of Hertford, for my L. himself was summoned before the Council and interrogated. He himself was not ill satisfied, but it is highly distasteful to the King.

Today there was a conference with the Lords to which the Lower House sent Sir Henry Hobart the Attorney, Sir Fr. Bacon the Solicitor, and Sir Edwin Sandys. The L. Treasurer spoke at great length. He began with a benevolent introduction, declaring how necessary it was that both Houses should meet to consult upon any occasion. The causes of calling this Parliament are two: the creation of the Prince as Prince of Wales and Earl of Chester and of Flint, and to demand some supply of money.

Concerning the King's wants and estate, he said that Queen Elizabeth entered the Irish wars having £700,000 in her coffers. From the time that Sir Henry Bagnal was slain at the Blackwater until her death, the charge of Ireland cost £1,600,000. When the King came to the Crown, he could not possibly dissolve the army upon the sudden, so that the charge of Ireland in his time was £600,000. Besides which he hath redeemed the lands mortgaged by the late Queen (£63,000), hath taken away the copper money and paid divers debts of the Queen's, all amounting to £300,000. The Low Countries hath cost him £250,000, and other charges (as the Queen's obsequies, the King's entrance, the entrance of the Queen and her children, the entertainment of the King of Denmark, and embassages and gratulations sent and received) £500,000. At Michaelmas 1603 he owed *in toto* £400,000.

At the present time by reason of the last subsidy; sales of land and mills; copyholders, freed woods and assarts; and old debts to the

Crown the debt now remaining is £300,000. But the King's certain charge is £1,400 per diem, which is £511,000 per annum. He finished this part of his speech with the question: 'Will you see the Ship of State drive so near the port and suffer it to perish, considering that your own fortunes are embarked therein?'

Then he considered the objections: the precedent is rare; the King is not in wars; the King gives much. Next he spoke of the doubts and expectation of breach of treaties, and of the competition for the Duchy of Cleves.

The third and last part of his speech concerned the grace and retribution to proceed from the King, which is a general redress of all just grievances. Then he enlarged on the duty of the King, his power and prerogative, and his grace and goodness. As for the first, Kings though so great ought not to demand contributions and subsidies at their pleasures, neither ought subjects to deny them out of humour when there is just cause for the good of the State. As for the King's prerogative, in some things his power is inherent and inseparable, whereof he gave four instances. Imposition upon foreign commodities; but herein it is to be seen that the shopkeeper do not raise his wares 6d. for every 1d. that the King doth impose. Secondly, his prerogative doth extend to our freeholds as in tenures and wardships. He may likewise appoint at his pleasure the times and places of his Courts of Justice. Lastly, the execution of penal laws doth belong to him, which in numbers and in divers other respects are very burdensome to the subjects; whereof he gave one instance in that at this present there are divers informations preferred into the Exchequer against many of the best in London who lend upon interest, wherein though they may expect the King's favour, yet the pardon is a remission of the penalty which is not due but given by a wise King.

He concluded that reasonable demands are not to be answered with cold supplies for that were to put the King upon the rock of necessity, and we know that necessity is a hard weapon.

17th. From Spain it is reported that the Moriscoes who fled into the mountains are now come down, enforced thereto by famine. Their King was hanged in Valencia and the rest are embarked for Barbary. The Spaniards now begin to clear Castile, Estremadura, and Andalusia of Moriscoes also, and proclamation is made that they shall all be gone in 30 days. In all their towns the King puts great store of munition and soldiers for fear of what may happen, for their number is infinite.

19th. Today the Commons debated upon the demands of the

Upper House. It was generally conceived that a subsidy would not give satisfaction to the King, for though it might discharge his debts, it would do no good for the supply of his yearly deficit which is £46,000 more than his receipts; and besides, a subsidy is never spoken of until the end of the Parliament, and doth voluntarily proceed from the Commons who will not be deprived of the thanks for it by any motion from the Lords. So leaving the matter of subsidies, they entered into consideration of the yearly contribution required and of the retribution to proceed from the King to his subjects; which is referred to the General Committee of Grievances.

Divers means of supply were proposed. The first, by M. Nicholas Hyde, was the due execution of the laws against papists and recusants and the entailing of land to the Crown which should come by attainder. By the first great sums of money might speedily be raised, if the whole might come to the King's lands; and by the other, the yearly charge of the King might be supplied and maintained with great plenty.

M. Nicholas Fuller proposed a taking back of the patents and grants of the King's customs and imposts which are very profitable to the farmers, by which means the King might receive greater benefit without further hurt to his subjects, whose good (saith he) 'we in this House ought especially to respect and provide for'; and he alleged also the King's advice in his book to his son, that he should be careful not to impoverish his subjects, for the riches of the subject is the best treasure of the King.

Other things proposed are the taking away of the purveyance, and a course taken so that the King may be provided for by a market at the Court Gate at reasonable prices for ready money without troubling the country, for which the subjects would yield a great yearly allowance. Also the discharge of tenures and wardships whereby the subjects should receive great ease and contentment.

Lastly M. Thomas Wentworth declared that all these courses would be to no purpose unless the King granted his pensions to his courtiers out of his own exchequer and diminished his charge and expenses. For (says he) 'to what purpose is it for us to draw a silver stream out of the country into the royal cistern, if it shall daily run out thence by private cocks? Or to what end is it to bring daily sacrifices, if others (like Bel's priests) steal it away in the night? And for my part, I will never give my consent to take money from a poor frieze jacket to trap a courtier's horse withal.' He therefore wished them to join in humble petition to his Majesty that he would diminish his charge and live of his own, without exacting of his poor subjects, especially at this time when we have no wars, but gather the fruits of peace upon the stalks of war. Or otherwise that some law might be made to this purpose as was done in the time of Richard II and Henry IV. Concluded that some course should be taken, 'without which all we can do is to no purpose, for though we now make supply, yet there may be the like overreaches hereafter if they be not prevented'.

Unto this Sir Julius Caesar, the Chancellor of the Exchequer, replied that laws of King Richard II were not fit for these times, for he was a dissolute and profuse Prince who was deprived of his Crown and Kingdom; and King Henry IV an usurper, and therefore willing to give contentment to his subjects with show of good laws. And for the other motions of wardships and purveyances, they were very profitable to the King, worth £60,000 and £40,000; if these were taken away the want would be far greater. Whereupon he entered into further declaration of the King's estate, and offered to give full satisfaction to any of the House that would come to him.

It was agreed to send a message to the Lords for a conference, at which meeting they would desire to know more certainly what those things were which his Majesty intended to give his subjects by way of retribution.

Of these grievances, it is to be noted that Wardship was first founded by William the Conqueror who gave lands to his followers on the condition that if the heir should be a minor the revenues should revert to the Crown. The wardship of minors is farmed out to some of the great Lords who enrich themselves thereby, for if a father dies leaving his children minors, the whole income goes to the former and not to the payment of the debts, so that when the children come of age they are burdened with their father's debts. There is another evil, that on the death of the father, many seek to be made guardians, and if they are not relations then they ruin the whole estate of the unhappy ward. If the wards are of good estate and rich, their guardians marry them to a daughter or niece, assigning any dowry they please: and if the ward refuse to marry, he must pay from his estate the dower of the Lady he has refused.

As for purveyance, the King hath an ancient privilege of purveyance and carriage, both paid at a very low rate. If his officers were content with taking only what is needed for the use of the Court this abuse might be endured, but the mischief is that if the Court require 40 capons, the officers call for a 100, and sell the remainder to their great profit, and in this way some grow very rich.

20th. M. William Seymour hath declared to the Council that since
180

he conceived that the Lady Arbella might make choice of any subject within the Kingdom, and himself a younger brother, unknown to the world, of mean estate, not born to challenge anything by his birthright, and therefore his fortunes to be raised by his own endeavours, and she a Lady of great honour and virtue and (as he thought) of great means, he did plainly and honestly endeavour lawfully to gain her in marriage. He therefore boldly intruded himself in her Chamber in the Court on Candlemas day, and imparted his desire to her, but both of them resolved not to proceed to any final conclusion without his Majesty's liking first obtained; and after that they met twice. He declareth further that there never was any marriage, contract, or other engagement between them, or marriage intended unless his Majesty's favour was first gained.

The late and long tempests have caused such extraordinary inundations in the Netherlands that a third of Holland is overflown with water. The damage is inestimable which these people suffer by the breach of the dykes which in many parts are carried away by the violence of the water. Every province doth bear a part, only Zealand by God's providence and the diligence of those employed about these affairs is free.

21st. M. William Crashaw, Preacher at the Temple, preached before the L. De la Warr and the rest of the adventurers for Virginia, comparing their action to the entering in of the Israelites into the Promised Land. Answered certain doubts and objections, as of the lawfulness of the action: a Christian (saith he) may take nothing of a Heathen against his will but in fair and lawful bargain, but we will give them more: civility for their bodies and Christianity for their souls. This action hath three enemies: the Devil, the Papists and the players, which last mock everything that is good and holy. They are enemies to the plantation because they are so multiplied here that one cannot live by another; and they see we will send no players to Virginia because we will suffer no idle persons there.

23rd. Marston the poet is turned minister and hath preached at Oxford.

24th. In the conference between the Lords and the Commons, Sir Julius Caesar having delivered the message of the Lower House, the L. Treasurer said that it was strange that since his Majesty had made known his wants, his demand should be only answered with a question: 'What will the King give his subjects?'

Whereupon he said that the demand of the King was a supply of his wants; wants, not of wantonness but such as the honour of a King and the safety of a Kingdom had drawn upon him; expenses of necessity and magnificence. His demand was a double supply to discharge the King's debts and support to maintain his estate. For supply, £600,000, whereof £300,000 is to pay his debts, £150,000 to furnish the navy, and £150,000 to lie in his coffers for war or any just occasion. For yearly support they demand £200,000 per annum for maintenance of the King, the Queen, the Prince, the Duke and Lady Elizabeth, which would be little enough if any yearly benefit which the Crown now receiveth be taken from it.

To this demand Sir Julius Caesar said that the Lower House had entered into consideration of the King's wants and of the supply thereof; but for subsidies they conceived that the Lords did not intend them, for those proceed from the House of Commons. And of any yearly contribution or support, they could not determine before they knew the King's pleasure what he was willing to depart withal to the subjects.

Then Sir Henry Montague, the Recorder of London, entered into the second part of the message, which was whether the Lords would join with them in the question to his Majesty whether it might please him that they might treat concerning the discharge of tenures. To this the L. Treasurer answered that he would give them no answer until he had consulted with the rest of the Lords; but in the meantime, he said that in the King's power there were three sorts: matters of sovereignty inherent in him, as to call Parliament, his coin, to proclaim war; matters of justice and protection of his subjects and redress of all just grievances; and rights, but such as were burdensome to the subjects. Concerning the first sort, the King would never part with them for any money. The second sort they should have freely, for these his Majesty hath taken an oath to give freely to his subjects, so that they are already contracted for in Heaven. Of the third sort, he reckoned a great number, which, he said, the King might haply be persuaded upon good considerations to yield his subjects; and he spoke of ten, as of the right of purveyance, the taking away of informers, wardship and others.

But, said he, that for the main matter of tenures and wardships, the very name of wardship did put them in mind they were under tutelage, being but a Committee; and therefore he said he would acquaint the Upper House with their desire, and therefrom make choice of a committee to attend his Majesty and to know his pleasure; and so they would receive an answer.

25th. The King is very unwilling that the Lady Arbella should marry M. William Seymour, for such a marriage would unite the two houses that are nearest to the Crown. Having first been separately examined, they were both summoned before the King, the Prince and the Council and commanded to give up all negotiation for marriage. The Lady Arbella spoke at length, denying her guilt, insisting on her wretched plight, and complaining that the King had given her patrimony to others, so that she had been obliged even to sell two rings which he gave her. She was then required to beg for pardon, but she replied that seeing herself deserted she thought no harm if she sought a husband of her own rank. Nevertheless if fault had been committed, she begged pardon. This did not satisfy the King, who demanded absolute confession of wrong and an unconditional request for forgiveness. To this she yielded, and received fresh promises of money, and leave to marry, subject to the approval of the King.

2nd March. This afternoon there was another conference between both Houses of Parliament, concerning two matters. The first was that of Dr. Cowell's book, called *The Interpreter*, which contains scandalous and dangerous matter against the authority of the Parliament, under the titles of Subsidy, Parliament and Prerogative, as that the King might make laws of himself and demand subsidies *de iure*, without consent of Parliament.

They then attended to a message by the L. Treasurer of his Majesty's answer to the motion concerning tenures; wherein, said he, he was to proceed with great caution and wariness, and to cut between wind and water, neither to blow them up with hope, nor drown them with despair. The purport of his speech was that the King would deliberate, yet before the recess from Parliament he would give a resolute answer. In the meantime he gave them full liberty to treat of those things which the L. Treasurer had formerly proposed, which, said he, they should not disvalue because they were offered, but rather highly value because they were never offered before by any King of the Realm unto his subjects.

The passages in Dr. Cowell's book that cause offence are these: Of *Parliament*: 'Though it be a merciful policy, and also a politic mercy (not alterable without great peril) to make laws by the consent of the whole Realm, because so no one part shall have cause to complain of a partiality; yet singly to bind the Prince to or by these laws were repugnant to the nature and constitution of an absolute monarchy.' Of the King's *Prerogative*: it is that 'especial power, pre-eminence or privilege that the King hath in any kind over and above other persons, and above the course of the ordinary Law, in the right of his Crown'. 'Now for those regalities which are of the highest nature (all being within the compass of his prerogative and justly to be comprised under that title) there is not one that belonged to the most absolute Prince in the world which doth not also belong to our King.' 'Only by the custom of this Kingdom, he maketh no laws without the consent of the 3 estates though he may quash any law concluded by them. And whether his power of making laws be restrained *de necessitate* or of a godly and commendable policy, not to be altered without great peril, I leave to the judgement of wiser men. But I hold it incontrollable that the King of England is an absolute Monarch.' Of *Subsidy*: 'Some hold opinion that this subsidy is granted by the subject to the Prince in recompense or consideration that whereas the Prince of his absolute power might make laws of himself, he doth of favour admit the consent of the subject therein, that all things in their own confession may be done with the greater indifferency.'

3rd. Today died Sir John Spencer, the rich alderman, so that all his great wealth comes to my L. Compton, who married Sir John's only daughter, Elizabeth in 1599 or 1600. This marriage was much talked of by our gallants at the time for it was like to a comedy or stage play. Mistress Elizabeth, being so rich a prize, was much sought after by our courtiers, but she fell in love with L. William Compton although her father had made choice of another whom she refused, alleging a contract with my L. Sir John, her father, was so angry that he beat and misused her, and hid her away; but upon complaint of L. William, Sir John in his turn was committed to the Fleet for a contempt; and they were married in spite of him; for my L. disguising himself as a baker's man came to Sir John's house carrying in a great basket of loaves, but he went out with his lady in the basket on his back. Nevertheless Sir John's wrath still continued, and he would not bestow on them a penny, not even when his daugher was brought to bed of a son.

On hearing of this, Queen Elizabeth declared that she would reconcile them to Sir John and herself be Godmother to the child. So she sent to Sir John to summon him to be gossip with her at the christening of a child whom she greatly favoured. Sir John, much flattered at such an honour, comes to the Court, and when the Queen named the child Spencer after his Godfather, he declared that since he had disinherited his own child this Spencer should be his only heir, whereupon the father and mother came forward from behind the arras and all was forgiven.

4th. The Plantation in Ireland hath brought forth a new Corporation of Aldermen and Assistants; but the people grumble at the unequal assessing of them towards the payment of £20,000 for the plantation and building of the two cities of Derry and Coleraine. The committees sit every day 4 or 5 hours.

8th. At a conference between the two Houses the L. Treasurer first delivered a message from the King concerning the book of Dr. Cowell. He began with an acknowledgement of his own wants. 'At this time', said he, 'I am to walk in a dangerous path, for I speak of special things concerning which I may easily speak amiss—of Kings, of laws, and of prerogative. Kings in Scripture, they be called *Dei*, and by Plutarch *Dei Simulacra*. Laws when they were first given, the Earth did tremble, and when they are undermined the monarchy will shake. Prerogative of Princes is a thing which will admit of no disputation.'

He declared that the King had taken into his consideration that book written by Dr. Cowell called *The Interpreter*, and examined the party, and he doth hold that the book is too bold with the Common Law of the Land, holding it a great presumption in any subject to speak or write against those laws under which he must live. Secondly, in his ignorance Dr. Cowell hath utterly mistook the fundamental and original grounds and constitutions of the Parliament. Thirdly, in the point of prerogative he hath waded in further than is fit for a subject, so that he hath offended both against the King and the Parliament.

If this book had been known to his Majesty before the Parliament began, he would have taken order for its suppressing which now he is resolved to do by a public act, whereby he will make known to all his people what great dislike he doth conceive not only of this book but of all others of like nature.

The King said further that for his Kingdom he was beholden to no elective power, neither doth he depend upon any popular applause, yet he doth acknowledge that though he did derive his title from the loins of his ancestors, yet the Law did set the Crown upon his head, and he is a King by the Common Law of the Land. Further, that it was dangerous to submit the power of a King to definition. Yet he did acknowledge that he had no power to make laws of himself, or to exact subsidies *de iure* without the consent of his Three Estates. And so the L. Treasurer concluded with a repetition of certain words used not long before by his Majesty upon report of certain speeches in Parliament wherewith he was discontented, saying that if they had denied him subsidies or any other matter of profit which rested in their own power and free will to give, it would never have angered him, 'Whereby' (said my L.) 'it may appear unto us that we have a man to our King (and happy are we that our King is a man) so his justice and integrity is apparent to all.'

After this speech ended, Sir Fr. Bacon said that he had a message from the Commons, which (saith he) 'I will deliver very faithfully and plainly without any affective curiosity; for ornaments of speech, they are but *bona peritura*, and speech of high sentence I cannot attain unto'. The matter of his speech was an excuse and a petition. The excuse that in formerly making motion to his Majesty concerning the discharge of tenures, they conceived that it had not concerned his Majesty in matter of profit, honour and conscience so far as they now understood the King did apprehend it.

Concerning utility, as the King did set it aside in his answer, so they in their proposition, sith therein they never intended any diminution of his estate.

Concerning honour, those portions of the Civil Law *De feudis* are but additional to the first institutions so that of themselves they are not imperial. Further, this matter of wardships is not an incident inseparable to the Crown. Those who serve in war, serve without respect of tenure, holding themselves bound as subjects, and no man ever made question whose tenant he was or how he held his land.

Concerning the point of conscience, howsoever his Majesty by discharge of tenures shall forgo the protection of his wards, yet he shall transfer them unto the care of those who, as they are bound by law, so by nature are bound to provide for their good, that is the next of kin.

He concluded that as they were excusable in proposing these things to his Majesty, so he desired their Lordships to join in petition that in the King's due time they might obtain an acceleration of his gracious answer.

Some days since Sir Edwin Sandys reported in the House great grievances against Sir Stephen Proctor who under pretence of a commission for exacting penal laws grieves the subject. The matter was referred to the committee of grievances who now report that he came into many men's houses with warrants under seals and took bread, beer, and bedding, bargained for £100 out of every £1,000, gave a quietus with a seal with a rose and a crown, took a bond for a fee to the L. Treasurer's secretary, and under pretence of looking for libels against the King rifled men's coffers. He was brought into the House and kneeled at the bar.

11th. One Robert Eliot was brought before the Council by the Recorder of London for setting up a wharf for which he hath driven divers great piles in the river, which wrought great annoyance both to the Bridge and the passengers, taking away the use of two of the arches, and hindering the strength of the waters that should come to the water works; nor would he remove them when warned, but contemned the authority of the City. Eliot is committed to prison until he have taken up the posts.

12th. The Earl of Northampton delivered to the Commons the King's answer to their motion, whereby he gave leave to treat concerning the discharge of tenures. The King, said he, had yielded to this motion for divers reasons: he noted their humility in that they would not presume to deal therein without leave; their dutifulness in referring all to his serious judgement; their caution in propounding it not as a grievance; their discretion in not desiring it gratis but upon valuable consideration; their judgement in joining with them the Lords of the higher House. Then speaking for himself, my L. used divers reasons to persuade them to proceed with cheerfulness and alacrity to supply the King's wants, setting forth his Majesty's great deserts.

15th. By the middle of April there will be ready from France 50,000 French foot, 5,000 Swiss, 4,000 horse and 50 pieces of artillery, and the King himself intends to go in person to the aid of the two Princes of Cleves.

18th. This day were made the funerals of Sir John Spencer, where some thousand men did assist in mourning cloaks or gowns, amongst which were 320 poor men who had every one a basket stored with a black gown, 4 lb. of beef, 2 loaves of bread, a little bottle of wine, a candlestick, a lb. of candles, 2 saucers, 2 spoons, a black pudding, a pair of gloves, a dozen of points, 2 red herrings, 4 white herrings, 6 sprats and 2 eggs. The poor L. Compton is now in great danger to lose his wits, for at the first news of such great riches (either through vehement apprehension of joy for such a plentiful succession or of carefulness how to dispose of it) he became somewhat distracted, and though afterwards reasonably well restored is now of late fallen again (but far more deeply) with the same frenzy. It is given out abroad that he hath suppressed a will of the deceased whereby he did bequeath £20,000 to his poor kindred and as much in pious uses, for the which the people exclaim that this affliction is justly inflicted upon him by the hand of God for such an impious deed.

22nd. The King having called both Houses before him in the Great Banqueting House at Whitehall then made a speech which lasted two full hours; first to make known to them his mislike of Dr. Cowell's book, and his resolution to suppress it; and second to satisfy the Houses that he did not assume any such extravagant authority as was spoken of in that book. He delivered his own opinion at large of the greatness of the authority of a Monarch, yet declared that it was fit for him and all other Princes to rule themselves according to the proper fundamental laws of their countries. He had no such dislike of the Common Law as he understood was reported of him. He commended the Civil Law as being more universal for use, and declared what defects he wished to be reformed in the Common Law. He admonished the Lower House concerning the grievances which they are in hand to present that they should deal with none but such as shall directly concern the Commonwealth and may be well proved, and nothing to be spoken against laws which are established, but only against the abuses of them. He wished also the laws against recusants to be better executed, and a law to be made for repairing the decaying of woods and lastly for the preservation of corn. His speech was received with great contentment by all parties, only the most strictly religious could have wished that he had been more sparing with the name of God, comparing the Deity with Princes' sovereignty; yet withal the speech had this plausible conclusion, that howsoever the sovereignty of Kings was absolute in general, yet in particular the Kings of England were restrained by their oaths and the privileges of the people.

24th. Today being Coronation Day M. Speaker and the Lower House went to a sermon at Westminster Abbey preached by M. Grant, Chaplain to the L. Stanhope, upon the text, 'Render unto Caesar the things that are Caesar's'.

26th. The reading or publishing of Dr. Cowell's book *The Interpreter* (made against the honour and prerogative of the King and the dignity of the Common Law of this land) is prohibited by proclamation. All who hold this book are charged to deliver it to the Lord Mayor or the Sheriff. Condemneth also the unmeasurable itching boldness of those who nowadays leave nothing untouched, neither God's divine secrets nor the deepest mysteries that belong to Kings and Princes.

29th. The old Lady Spencer is dead, following close on the heels of her husband, who gave away among her kindred £13,000 of the £15,000 which she was to have of my L. Compton. My L. is now altogether distracted and so frantic that he is forced to be kept bound. The administration of his goods and lands is committed to the L. Chamberlain, Privy Seal and my L. of Worcester. They came last week into the City and took an inventory in the presence of the Sheriffs of the goods, amongst which, it is said, were bonds of £133,000.

Here is expected the young Prince of Brunswick who shall be lodged with the Prince at S. James's. The speech is that he cometh for a marriage with the Lady Elizabeth and that he will stay for some months in these parts.

31st. There is a retort to that book of *The Bellman of London* called *Martin Mark-all Beadle of Bridewell*, declaring it to be old stuff, printed forty years ago and then called *A Caveat for Cursetors.* Relates how in indignation the crackropes summon a jury before which the Bellman is cited. Addeth also many words used by the fraternity not in the former book, with a rhyme of Martin Mark-all, his apology; and sundry tales of rogues such as Jack Cade, Puffing Dick and Cock Lorell, and others.

1st April. From Italy comes a strange book called *Sidereus Nuncius,* written by one Galileo, a Mathematical Professor at Padua, who by the help of an optical instrument (which both enlargeth and approximateth the object) invented first in Flanders and bettered by himself, hath discovered four new planets rolling about the plane of Jupiter, besides many other unknown fixed stars; likewise the true cause of the *Via Lactea,* so long searched; and lastly, that the moon is not spherical but endued with many prominences, and (which is strangest of all) illuminated with the solar light by reflection from the body of the Earth, as he seemeth to say. So, as upon the whole subject, he hath first overthrown all former astronomy (for we must have a new sphere to save the appearances) and next all astrology; for the virtue of these new planets must needs vary the judicial part, and why may there not be more? This author runneth a fortune to be either exceeding famous or exceeding ridiculous.

4th. Sir Robert Carr hath sold the estate of Sherborne to the King for £20,000.

5th. The widow Countess of Dorset, mother-in-law to the L. Compton, was today convented before the Lords for having carried herself intemperately against the L. Chamberlain and other Lords when they went to take administration of Sir John Spencer's goods. They were not only repelled by the Countess herself, but railed upon, and some of them, it is said, scratched in the face with her nails. She is committed to the Fleet. L. Compton is now amended in his brain and may recover. The truth of his frenzy is that through long watching and overmuch musing on his new fortunes, he got an ague, the fits thereof generally are accompanied with a kind of frantic humour.

Upon Sir John Spencer's death, his porter fell mad and was taken to Bethlehem, for L. Compton desiring to have the deceased's picture after that the body was lapped up in sere cloth, they were forced to rip the upper part of the cloth from the head to the breast. The porter, being about this work, left a piece of candle burning near the corpse to go somewhere else in the house. The candle fell upon the unripped part of the cloth and set it afire. The porter returning and seeing his master's face in the middle of a flame, began to cry out that his master was burning in hell, and continued afterwards in that frenzy. It is now said that he is recovered and that charge is given the Masters of Bethlehem to keep him close so that he may be examined upon his master's death, which is supposed to have been a little hastened by him and one of his fellows, who only attended him at that hour and gave so diligent notice of it to the L. Compton that he was there almost as soon as the old Lady could know of her husband's death, which came upon him on a sudden.

7th. The *Trades Increase*, of which Sir Henry Middleton is General with Capt. Nicholas Downton under him, the *Peppercorn*, and the *Darling* set sail from the Downs three days ago on the sixth voyage set forth by the Company. Each ship's company is commanded to assemble morning and evening for prayers. Blasphemy, swearing, thieving, drunkenness and other disorders to be severely punished, and no gambling allowed, which leads generally to quarrelling and murders. No buying, selling, or exchanging on board, and no man to ship more goods than his chest will hold, and such goods to be registered in the purser's books, so that if a man die his friends may learn what goods he owned. If the General can come by any rare things, as live birds or beasts fit for a present for the King or the Lords, he shall send them home.

9th. Today the King, the Prince and the young Duke of Brunswick had a solemn running at the ring, which both the King and the Prince carried away at their first course. Amongst the runners was the L. Compton, who may now with a quiet mind offer, as the Papists say, two fair candles to God, the one for the enjoying his great succession, and the other for the recovering of his wits.

11th. A new College is shortly to be built in Oxford, one Wadham, a Western man, having left £7,000 for the building and £800 yearly towards the maintenance of 16 Fellows and 40 Scholars. Sir Edward Hext has the oversight of the will and the land whereon it is to be built is already purchased. The King hath passed his approbation and wishes his statue to be set over the gate. There is also a project in hand to have all the Fathers new printed, for that the Romish Index hath perverted them. They have gathered together all the manuscripts and editions of the Fathers which they will have compared by twelve men selected for that purpose, and according to the most authentical copy they will guide themselves. The allowance will be some £40 to each man yearly. The mover and promoter of all this is Dr. James, the Keeper of the University Library.

17th. M. Henry Hudson has again set forth on a voyage for the discovery of the Northwest passage.

19th. Lundy Island hath been taken by the pirate Sackwell and ransacked, but they have now forsaken it. Capt. Peter Lambert, a great swaggerer, who was committed a month since for killing a Low Country Lieutenant, one Hamden, in his own house, was hanged a few days ago, and died a Catholic. His friends carried him in a coach from the gallows and would have buried him next day in Christ Church but were forbidden by the Bishop. He is now reported to be alive in France, having cozened ('tis said) the rope with a false neck which his friend the hangman bestowed upon him. The mad Countess of Dorset is again committed to the Fleet, for contrary to command she insolently pressed into the Privy Chamber to importune his Majesty.

20th. Today Prince Henry, with the young Duke of Brunswick, accompanied by the Duke of Lenox, the Earl of Arundel and others, came privately to the Tower and caused the great lion to be put into the yard, and five dogs at a course set upon him. These dogs were so fierce that on first coming into the yard they fell upon each other, for they did not spy the lion which kept close to the trap door at the other end of the yard. But when they saw him they flew all at the lion's head whereat he became enraged and furiously bit divers dogs by the head and throat holding their heads and throats in his mouth as a cat doth hold a rat, and tearing their flesh extremely with his claws; notwithstanding many of them would not let go until they were utterly spoiled. After the spoil of divers dogs and likelihood of spoil of many more the bearwards set a lusty dog upon the mouth of the lion which got hold upon his tongue, pulled it out of his mouth and held on so fast that the lion could neither bite him nor any other. Thereupon the young lion and lioness were both put out together to see if they would rescue the other but they would not, but fearfully gazed upon the dogs. Then two or three of the worst dogs left the

191

first lion and ran upon them, and chased them up and down the yard as they sought by all means to avoid the dogs; and so soon as their trap-door was open, they both ran hastily into their den, and a dog that pursued them ran in with them, where they all three stood like good friends very peaceably together. Then the bearwards came boldly in again and took off all the dogs but one from the great lion. The lion having fought long and his tongue torn, lay staring and panting so that all the beholders thought he had been utterly spoiled and spent, but on a sudden he seized upon the dog that remained and as soon as he had spoiled him, spying the trap-door open, he ran hastily into his den, and then never ceased walking up and down until he had brought himself into his former temperature.

22nd. My L. Compton having recovered his wits, those who would have begged his movables of the King are disappointed, but 'tis to be feared that he is a spendthrift, and so that which Sir John Spencer inordinately, miserly and graspingly gained, by sudden lavishness will vanish. Meantime his Lady hath set down the allowance that she thinks fit for herself. She would have yearly £1,600 for her apparel, and £600 for charitable works, and to be accountable for neither. She would have 3 horses for her own use; 2 gentlewomen (and for each a horse); 6 or 8 gentlemen; and 2 coaches each with 4 horses; and 2 coachmen; and for travelling 2 caroches, separately for herself and her gentlewomen; and laundresses and chambermaids to go before with the grooms to have all ready when she travels; and a horse for her gentleman usher, for she holds it indecent to crowd herself up with another in her coach; and besides her yearly allowance for apparel, she would have 20 gowns of apparel, 6 excellent good, 8 for the country, and 6 very excellent good; and £2,200 for her purse; her debts to be paid; and £6,000 to buy her jewels, and £4,000 to buy a pearl chain. Moreover she would have all her houses furnished and suited with all furniture as is fit; as beds, stools, chairs, cushions, carpets, silver warming pans, cupboards of plate, fair hangings and the like; and her drawing chamber in all the houses to be most delicately furnished. Moreover she would have him lend no money to my L. Chamberlain. Further, when my Lord shall become an Earl all these to be doubled.

27th. On S. George's Day there were great celebrations at Chester in honour of the Prince at the charges of M. Robert Amery the Sheriff, with many devices, as of two green men who were pursued by an artificial dragon casting fire from his mouth and afterwards slain; and many on horseback, presenting S. George, Fame, Mercury,

Chester, Rumour and the rest, and much delivering of poetical speeches.

30th. Barnaby Rich hath *A New Description of Ireland and the Irish*, to be profitably read by the citizens of London who are to be undertakers in that country. Writeth out of 47 years' experience in that country against M. Stanihurst because he was a Catholic. Saith much of the customs and manners of the Irish, and of the policy to be used towards them. He is a great hater of popery, which, quoth he, 'is a malady not easy to be cured, and I think these lines of mine will sooner move choler than give contentment or produce amendment'.

2nd May. The L. Treasurer hath sent over his secretary to take order to furnish the L. Cranborne with all necessaries to follow the French King in this journey against Juliers and more of our Court gallants talk of taking the same course if the voyage hold. Indeed it were fitter they had some place abroad to vent their superfluous valour than to brabble so much here at home. In one week there have been three or four great quarrels, the first betwixt the Earls of Southampton and Montgomery that fell out at tennis, where the rackets flew about their ears, but the matter was instantly taken up by the L. Chamberlain who brought them away to the King, who himself made them friends; and that night they supped together. Last week young Egerton, Sir John's son, and a near kinsman to the L. Chancellor fought with one Morgan, a lawyer's son of good estate. Egerton was left dead in the field and Morgan escaped very narrowly with two grievous wounds; he lies in Newgate and cannot yet be bailed out or dispensed. The L. Norris likewise went into the field with Peregrine Willoughby upon an old reckoning, and hurt him dangerously in the shoulder. Upon Salisbury Plain 11 thieves robbed a company of 7 merchants on the highway and killed them all; the thieves are all taken.

Upon the rumour that Peter Lambert had been seen in France the King suspected that there might have been cunning and cautelous dealing in his execution and would not be satisfied till the Sheriffs of London in the presence of much people took him up where he was buried, and upon view find that he was sufficiently hanged.

5th. The English soldiers who go for Juliers with Sir Edward Cecil are his own regiment entire, 9 companies from Sir Horace Vere, 5 from Sir John Ogle, and a Scottish regiment. Sir Hatton Cheke is Colonel of the English and Sir Robert Henderson of the Scottish.

7th. News has come that the French King lies slain in Paris.

193

8th. On Thursday last, being the 3rd of the month, Henry the Fourth, King of France, having been married ten years unto Mary de Medicis, daughter to the Duke of Florence, with great and solemn triumphs caused her to be crowned in Paris and invested with the crown and title of Queen of France and Navarre. Next day, the King appointed to see his Arsenal and to visit Duke Sully his Treasurer who was ill at ease, albeit some skilful astronomers and others forewarned and besought him from going abroad that day as being ominous. Yet Caesar-like he thought it not consonant with the Christian religion to hearken unto wizards and so took his coach about 4 o'clock of the afternoon, accompanied with the Dukes of Espernon, Montchasson and others. Riding through a straight passage, his coach was stopped with carts and coaches, upon advantage whereof one Francis Ravilliac of Angolesme, who oft and long before had sought opportunity to kill the King, espying the King sitting at the head of his coach and leaning towards the boot to speak to Espernon whereby he discovered all his left side, thrust a knife of a foot long into the King's side, but made no mortal wound because it struck against a bone. Then this audacious traitor suddenly stabbed the King again under the short ribs, which deprived him of speech and life that instantly he fell dead in the coach, and was carried into the Louvre. Ravilliac attempted to have done this treason in the forenoon as the King was walking in his new gallery at the Tuilery, but he was put back amongst the people by those who attended the King and esteemed him a rude rascal. This Ravilliac in his youth was of the Order of the Falicians but misliking their strictness of life forsook their house and order. Then he married a wife and for some time was a kind of lawyer, and lastly a schoolmaster.

This famous King, being as happy in peace as victorious in war, made three pitched fields and encountered 35 strong armies of his enemies, and besieged 300 cities and castles, forts and sconces, and is thus at last slain by a villain, being the third Henry of France to die violently.

The L. Treasurer today spoke to the two Houses on the French King's death, who, said he, was killed by a villain whose hand was guided by the Devil; and here he related the fact. When the town of Paris was prepared only for joy and pleased with their security, by the hand of a dog this great, potent and magnanimous Prince was murdered. This King stood in the breach betwixt foreign enmity and our own King. He was a King, rich and powerful in arms; and ours in want and indigence. A King whom the Catholics love and the Protestants admire for their freedom and liberty. The killing of such a King is a design of state and fit to be consulted of statesmen. The Queen is like to be Regent; but our case is better because we have a Prince past that danger. This is no Church matter but some great design for the change of affairs in Europe. We must now give occasions for foreign despatches to advertise how careful we are of our King, and how we provide for him; and in money, our only antidote to future mischief. He said he was no prophet nor the son of a prophet, yet he advised them first to provide for the King, for they might think he had great matters in contemplation. They must not always be in consultation but bring forth some worthy effects.

One William Folkingham hath a book called *Feudigraphia*, or a synopsis or epitome of all matters pertaining to surveying, and very pertinent to those concerned with the occupation, and buying and selling, measuring of all manors, lands, edifices, woods, waters, titles, evidences, etc.

9th. There was much ado in the House about the New Cut undertaken by Hugh Middleton and now far advanced for the entry of a new river and bringing it to London through the grounds of many men, who for their particular interests strongly oppose themselves to it and are like to overthrow it all. In this business there are sometimes employed as many as 600 workmen at one time.

The day after the French King's death, the young Dolphin was received King in the Court of Parliament, and his mother Queen Regent, who hath governed herself with admirable constancy, giving satisfaction to everybody. Those of the Protestant religion are assured and all ancient ministers of state confirmed. These beginnings give good hopes. She hath also sent for the Marquise de Verneuil (the King's mistress) by letter and hath given assurance of her security and affection. The morning of his death, the King was advertised by one La Brosse that he should run an extreme hazard of his person that day, and if he could escape it he would live for five and twenty years after; of which the King made no account. This accident hath caused my L. of Cranborne suddenly to return.

That project put forward by the Archbishop of Canterbury for the erecting of a College in Chelsea for the studying and handling controversies in religion now goes forward. The King hath passed his grant of the place and the lands about it for the building, especially at the solicitation of Dr. Mathew Sutcliffe the Dean of Exeter who doth give £1,000 out of his purse, and £300 a year to the building and maintaining of it. There are to be entertained 20 Doctors, amongst which will be two for History, besides other students to be entertained and instructed for that function.

11th. M. Speaker told the House that he had a message from the King's Majesty, and desired to know their pleasures whether they would hear it. Then he delivered it, which was to command the House not to dispute upon the King's power and prerogative in imposing upon merchandises exported or imported. Hereupon Sir William Twisden noting that the King was absent, and so had been for a week before, pressed M. Speaker to tell how he came by this message; wherein he, excusing himself for a long time, in the end did confess that he received the message from the body of the Privy Council. Whereupon it was concluded: That the same message coming not immediately from his Majesty should not be received as a message; and that in all messages from his Majesty, the Speaker before he delivered them should first ask leave of the House as had been anciently accustomed.

12th. Two of the ships sent out by the East India Company under command of Capt. Keeling have returned, very richly laden with aloes, pepper, mace and nuts. On their way outward, they were much distressed by storms and calms, and there was talk of returning to England, but Keeling sent for M. Hakluyt's *Book of Voyages*, whereby they were persuaded to make for Sierra Leone; which, as Sir Thomas Smith affirms, saved the Company £20,000. And here to keep his people from idleness and unlawful games Keeling caused them to act plays, which were *Hamlet* and *Richard the Second*. At Bantam they left certain English merchants to traffic in those parts. They had some trouble from the Dutch in Banda and among the Javans, but the Dutch are hated by the natives because of their insolency, and while our men were there the natives slew the Dutch Admiral and all his chief followers and council. They spent some time at the Isle of Mauritius on their return.

14th. The King hath sent to the House of Commons another message, requiring an answer with all expedition either negatively or affirmatively: 'Whether have you any purpose to refuse, or will you refuse, any message sent unto you by the Speaker, upon declaration by him made unto you that it cometh by warrant from his Majesty by word or writing, or from the body of the Privy Council'?

Upon this message received, the House chose a committee to consider an answer, and it was long debated. Concerning the Council, the general resolution was to make answer that they would receive no messages sent from the Council as messages sent from the King. And as for messages to be sent from his Majesty immediately, they were unwilling to answer what they would do *in futuro*. It was agreed to set down in effect: 'We have no will or purpose to refuse to receive any message sent or to be sent unto us immediately by your Majesty by our Speaker, either in word or writing; but to receive the same being delivered unto us according to the ancient order of the House.'

To this it was objected that it was not full enough to answer all the parts of the question, and that it contained a negative pregnant, which is when something is conceived in the womb of the future which is not yet delivered.

A Lamentable Discourse on the assassination of the French King by one Pelletier, translated out of the French, is now being printed by Edward Blount.

15th. Yesterday and today there was much dispute about Proctor's case and what was to be done with him. M. Fr. Moore said that his offences in effect deserved death but were not offences in law; as the using a seal in the name of the King with a crown on was treason in effect but not in law. So the taking of a poor man's cattle out of his ground by his servants by his commandment (pretending that his name was in the schedule as a debtor to the King where indeed he was not) which he delivered back to the man for £11 which as he pretended was a debt due to the King; this was felony in effect but not in law. So also his binding of a cutpurse in Middlesex as a justice of peace where he was not a justice was *praemunire* in effect but not in law. By the order of the House, Proctor is sent to the Tower.

16th. This day the French Ambassador had audience and gave the King notice of the King of France's death. The Court against Sunday are to put on mourning till the Prince's installation. Yesterday came notice from the young King and Council that they purpose to prosecute their design for the war of Cleves which hath added not a little courage to our deliberations for that enterprise. The States' Ambassadors dined with the King last Monday (14th) who drank to the success of that war. This day they are departed, having done little or nothing in their business, the King excusing himself upon the great difficulties both domestical and foreign (through the King of France's death) wherein he is entangled. The new Spanish Ambassador had his first audience on Sunday when by his countenance he gave no great impression to the Court of his sufficiency.

19th. Yesterday in the House of Commons a committee was appointed to treat of a message to the King to give him satisfaction for the matter of Impositions, and likewise of a message of satisfaction touching his message concerning Messages. Today while the matter was still being discussed, there comes another message from the King that he was much disquieted in mind concerning the order, as he had sent word a few days ago; but it was found upon examination that the Clerk had not entered it. Whereupon the House thought fit to stay the entering, and to give satisfaction to his Majesty by a message to the effect that they did humbly desire him to receive their assurance that they had no intention to vary from that duty which our ancestors have performed to his most noble progenitors; neither had they any other purpose in their proceedings than to retain that due respect from the Speaker which appertaineth to the House, and which those that served in that place before him did carefully perform. The King is well satisfied with this message, and hath appointed them to be before him on Monday next.

21st. The King made a long speech to both Houses. After repeating the beginning of his last speech, he began with a grievance which is that in 14 weeks nothing is done in the principal errand for which the Parliament was called, and not half so many days spent on that business as weeks in others, so as that which is the principal errand is made but an accessory, which came purely by accident, but much of it by too much curiosity. He declared that he was well satisfied with their answer concerning messages; and he would again forewarn them of the principal errand, and foreseeing an incident which will breed longer delay he chose to speak himself without messages on Impositions. In his last speech he had declared that it was not lawful to dispute what a King may do, but what a good King should do. He had no intention that they should forbear to complain of the burden and inconvenience, for they may complain of any just grievance; but they must not dispute the King's power of imposing in general, which he hath both by judgement and law. Let them leave to the King what he may do in his power and talk of the inconveniency. If they found any one or two impositions grievous, they must offer somewhat for it; and because he may err in the form of laying impositions upon misinformation, he would never do it but in Parliament. If they find better means to supply his state, he will not proceed to Impositions. But (said he) he neither could nor would bind his posterity, and he commanded them not to call his power or his prerogative in that point in question or to debate them.

This speech of the King's hath bred generally much discomfort, for to see our monarchical power and royal prerogative strained so high and made so transcendent every way that if the practice should follow the position, we are not like to leave our successors that freedom we received from our forefathers, nor make account of anything we have longer than they list that govern. What issue this business will come to, God knows, for besides his Majesty some great persons are engaged in this matter of Impositions, and no doubt will maintain their doings, knowing that though men storm never so much yet *vanae sine viribus viae*.

More priests than ever have come over into Ireland this spring and Masses are said openly in some churches. They labour to draw the sons of the principal gentlemen to seminaries overseas. A priest who was O'Dogherty's chief counsellor in the betraying of Derry was lately apprehended, but as the officers were carrying him before a justice of the peace, the country rose upon them and rescued him, notwithstanding that the officers showed the L. Deputy's warrant and told them the priest was a proclaimed traitor.

22nd. The King's speech is so distasteful to the Commons that they appoint a Committee to devise some course to inform him how much the liberties of the subjects and the privileges of the Parliament are impeached by his inhibition to debate his prerogative. Hereupon divers speeches were made. M. Fuller declared that the special privilege of Parliament is to debate freely of all things that shall concern any of the subjects in particular, or the Commonwealth in general, without restraint or inhibition. M. Wentworth said that in all ages the King's prerogative hath been examined and debated in Parliament. Also that in all Courts of Justice in Westminster the King's prerogative is ordinarily disputed, and therefore may be much more debated in Parliament, being the highest Court of Justice in the Realm.

Sir Fr. Bacon, the Solicitor, took upon himself to answer these reasons. He said he had been a Parliament man ever since he was seventeen years old within which time he did observe that the Parliament had received divers inhibitions from the Queen to restrain them from debating the matter in question; wherein he took this difference, that if the matter debated concerned the right or interest of any subject or the Commonwealth, if an inhibition came, he would not advise the House to desist but to inform the King of the liberty of the House. But if the matter in question were an essential thing which concerned the prerogative and the power of the Crown, then the House did always desist from proceeding any further upon such inhibition received. And he gave divers instances of his time; as concerning the late Queen's marriage and the matter of Succession and the like. And therefore he persuaded the House to present these matters of Impositions as grievances (which the King had given leave to do), but not to question his power and prerogative to impose.

In answer to this speech divers stood up, and it was moved that as' the King had granted freedom of speech at the beginning of the

Parliament concerning all matters of the Commonwealth (which could not be taken from them without shaking the foundation of the Liberties of Parliament) so they should by a Petition of Right make known their liberties to his Majesty. This was agreed, and a petition accordingly drawn.

24th. The LL. of the Council have notified the L. Mayor that this` day week Prince Henry is to come from Richmond to Westminster to be created Prince of Wales. The Companies of the City are required to meet the Prince on the water at Chelsea, accompanying the L. Mayor in such sort as when the L. Mayor goes to Westminster to take his oath.

Upon this accident of the French King's death the young L. Cranborne came posting away which if there had been any stirring was not the means to avoid but rather to run into danger; but the world apprehends that he had another adamant to draw him hither, the desire to gather the first fruits of his young lady.

25th. Yesterday morning Sir Julius Caesar and 10 or 12 more with him went to Greenwich and there delivered the petition of the Commons to the King, who returned answer in the afternoon that this petition was grounded upon two matters: a mistaking of his message, and a jealous interpretation of his speech. His message did not absolutely forbid them from treating of the Impositions, but only until they heard his further pleasure, not with any intent for ever to restrain them, but he being 70 miles away, and hearing of their disputations thought fit to understand their intentions. He granted their petition but put them in mind to observe three things: not to impugn his prerogative; to seek his content and satisfaction; to endeavour to unite and conform his subjects' hearts unto him. Further he offered that if a convenient number of the House upon any doubt conceived would come unto him at any time, without using ceremonies and compliments, they should have access to him privately either in his gallery or elsewhere to debate familiarly of those things that might come in question.

When this answer was reported the House was well satisfied, and thereon entered into debate of three special things, which were the execution of the laws against the papists, impositions, and support to be given the King.

Concerning recusants it was agreed to petition the King that he should make order by proclamation or otherwise that all recusants in or near London depart forthwith to their houses and none come hither or within ten miles of the Court; that all be forbidden to repair to the houses of foreign Ambassadors to hear Mass. All Jesuits and Seminary priests remaining in prison and convicted to be committed to close prison and none to have access to them, and those that are at liberty on bonds to be committed. All recusants to be disarmed and their armour to be disposed according to the Statute.

From Rome comes news that on 15th April Father Robert Parsons died in the English College there, of which he has been Rector since 1597. When he felt the approach of death, he asked that the cords with which his dear friend Edmund Campion had been tortured should be wound round his neck. He kissed the cords very reverently, saying to those about him that they brought back a lively remembrance of those first days when he too had been so near to giving his life in the service of the Catholic Church; and thereat he fell a weeping that since God had not accepted his blood, He had at least accepted the sweat of these almost 30 years, for which he gave infinite thanks. And so amid the prayers and tears of his watching brethren and his sons (for so the young men of that seminary regarded him) he gave up his spirit in peace.

29th. On the 23rd of this month, Francis Ravilliac was arraigned and convicted for the murder of the French King. He pleaded guilty and would not reveal any other accomplice or confederate, whereupon a most terrible sentence of death was pronounced against him. On Friday last (25th) he was brought out of the prison naked in his shirt with a lighted torch of two pound weight in one hand, and the knife wherewith he killed the King chained to the other. He was placed standing upright in a tumbril or dung-cart, and so conducted with a guard of citizens to the capital church in Paris where he was adjudged to do penance. After this, being accompanied with two Doctors of Divinity who would persuade him to save his soul from everlasting punishment by revealing his associates (which he would not), he was carried to the Greve, a spacious street in the middle of Paris where was builded a very substantial scaffold. Du Vicquet, the King's Attorney-General, was appointed principal to the execution and to gather, if he could, some further light of this conspiracy.

At his coming upon the scaffold he crossed himself. Then he was bound by the executioners to an engine of iron and wood, made like a S. Andrew's cross; and then the hand with the knife chained to it and half the arm was put into a furnace flaming with fire and brimstone wherein the knife, his right hand and half the arm were in a terrible manner consumed; yet nothing would he confess but yelled out with horrible cries. After this with tongs and iron pincers made extreme hot in the furnace, the executioners pinched and seared the dugs of his breasts, the brawns of his arms and thighs, and other fleshly parts of his body, cutting out collops of flesh and burning them before his face; and into the wounds they poured scalding oil, rosin, pitch and brimstone, yet nothing would he reveal but that he did it by the instigation of the Devil, and the reason was because the King tolerated two Religions in his Kingdom.

Next they put upon his navel a rundle of clay, very hard, with a hole in the midst into which was poured molten lead till it was filled; yet still he revealed nothing but cried out with most horrible roars. At last they brought four strong horses to tear his body into pieces and to separate his limbs into four quarters, where being ready to pay his last punishment, he was questioned again to make known the truth; but he would not, and so died without speaking one word of God or remembering the danger of his soul.

So strongly was his flesh and joints knit together that for a long time these four horses could not dismember him, so that one of the horses fainted; which a merchant of Paris perceiving put to one of his own, a horse of exceeding strength. Notwithstanding for all this they were constrained to cut the flesh under his arms and thighs with a sharp razor by which means his body was the easier torn to pieces; which being done, the rage of the people grew so violent that they snatched the dismembered carcass out of the executioners' hands. Some beat it in sunder against the ground, others cut it with knives so that there was nothing left but the bones which were there burnt to cinders, and the ashes scattered to the wind as being unworthy of the earth's burial.

30th. About noon today Prince Henry accompanied, besides the ordinary train of his household, with divers young Lords and Gentlemen of special mark departed from his house of S. James's towards Richmond, where being come towards evening, he supped and reposed himself for the night.

Following upon the murder of the late King of France certain decrees have been ordained by the advice of the French Parliament. The new King Lewis XIII being still a minor is put under the guardianship of his Mother. The Edict of Nantes is affirmed; and toleration granted to those of the Reformed Religion. As for Ravilliac, his goods are forfeited to the King's use, his house in Angoulesme utterly ruinated and converted into a common laystall, his father banished the Realm, and all his kindred commanded to abandon the name of Ravilliac and to take upon themselves some other name.

31st. About 9 of the clock Prince Henry took water at Richmond, attended only with some four barges of his own followers, and passing softly down the stream, he was encountered by divers Lords who came to meet him. The Thames soon began to float with boats and barges, and the shores on either side swarmed with multitudes of people who stood to behold his triumphant passage. About 11, understanding that the tide was fallen so low that there would not be room for all the barges to go orderly down, notwithstanding that his first appointment was to come to London about noon when dinner was prepared for him at Whitehall, he made stay at Barn Elms, and there refreshed himself at an arbour by the waterside upon such things as could be provided of a sudden.

Meanwhile by 8 o'clock the Worshipful Companies of the City, to the number of 54, had made themselves ready in their barges, with streamers and ensigns displayed, and drums, trumpets, fifes and other music attending on Sir Thomas Campbell the L. Mayor. As soon as the L. Mayor had taken barge, they rowed upstream with a cheerful noise of harmony as far as Chelsea to await the Prince's coming. At 2 o'clock upon his near approach, a way was made for the Prince's barge, which was much impeached by the multitude of boats, but at length the Prince's barge accosted the L. Mayor's when the entertainment began, which was two artificial sea monsters, one in fashion of a whale and the other of a dolphin. From the whale's back, Corinea, a fair and beautiful nymph (representing the Genius of old Corineus' Queen and the Principality of Cornwall, and played by John Rice, the King's player), suited in a watery habit, yet rich and costly, saluted the Prince with a short oration.

Approaching near to Whitehall, the King, the Queen, with the young Duke of York and Princess Elizabeth, stood in the Privy Gallery to see the show, which for their better view passed along on the London side. At Whitehall Stairs the barges made a passage for the Prince to land, and here Amphion on his dolphin (personating the Genius of Wales and enacted by Richard Burbage) saluted him with a loyal speech concluding, 'Home again fair Fleet, you have brought a royal freight to landing, such a burden as hath made the river not meanly proud to bear. And since we must needs part, in our loudest voice of drums, trumpets and ordnance, be this one last accent: Long live our Prince of Wales, the Royal Henry?'

At this instant as the L. Mayor took his leave, off went the chambers and a triumphal noise of drums and trumpets; which done they returned again to London. This pageant was devised for the City by Anthony Munday.

Upon his landing the Prince passed through a guard of his servants and was received by the Officers of the King's household in several places according to their offices and so passed through to the Hall, where he was entertained by L. Knollys and L. Wotton, the Treasurer and Controller of the Household; likewise in the Great Chamber by the Viscount Fenton, Capt. of the Guard; in the Presence Chamber by the Earl of Suffolk, L. Chamberlain; and lastly by the King and Queen in the Privy Chamber.

2nd June. Today the House of Commons debated upon the matters of the prerogative offered by the L. Treasurer and of the support to be offered to the King. Upon this Sir John Saville said that £100,000 per annum already offered will be as much as the subjects can well yield. He wished also that the name of 'support' or 'supportation' had never been known, for though it be now unusual with us, yet he doubted hereafter it would become too familiar; for if they bargained for the things offered, which are all either straining of the prerogative royal or abuses of inferior officers, every Parliament there will be something or other found wherein the subject is grieved and will be forced to give further support for its discharge. He gave instance that thirty years ago, when Sir Walter Mildmay was Chancellor and two subsidies were demanded, he said that never before had two subsidies been given but only one; yet the House did yield to give two subsidies upon promise made to the House that the like should be never more heard of. 'But how this promise hath been kept' (saith he) 'you all know as well as I.'

3rd. The Lords and others (to the number of 24) who are to receive the honourable Order of the Bath repaired yesterday afternoon to Durham House in the Strand and there heard evening prayer, observing no ceremony but passing through the Hall, the Heralds going before them into the Chapel, whence, after service ended, they returned into the chamber for supper, which was prepared at one table, all sitting at one side of it and each having an escutcheon of his arms placed over his head. Having taken their repast, the tables were removed, and beds were made ready for their lodging in the same place, all one side. These beds were pallets with coverings, testers and canopies of red saye, but without curtains.

The Knights in the meantime withdrew into the Bathing Chamber where for each is provided a bathing tub, lined within and without with white linen and covered with red saye, and a ticket of every man's name set upon his tub. After the bath they betook themselves to their rest.

Early this morning they are wakened with music, and at their uprising invested in hermits' habits, which is a gown of grey cloth girded close and a hood of the same with a linen coif underneath, with a russet silk girdle and a handkercher hanging at this girdle, cloth stockings soled with white leather, but no shoes. Thus apparelled, with their esquires, the Heralds and sundry sorts of wind music going before them, they proceed from their lodging through the Hall, till they come to the Chapel where they take their seats, with the accustomed reverences; and after service ended, their oath is administered to them by the Earl of Worcester and the Earl of Suffolk, alternately, in a solemn and ceremonious manner, each standing before his stall, and at their coming out making a low reverence towards the altar.

The words of their oath are these: 'Right dear Brother, great worship be this Order unto you, and the Almighty God give you the praising of all knighthood. You shall honour God above all things. You shall be steadfast in the faith of Christ, and the same maintain and defend to your power. You shall love your Sovereign above all earthly creatures; and for your Sovereign's right and dignity live and die. You shall defend widows, maidens, and orphans in their rights. You shall suffer no extortion as far forth as you may, nor sit in any place where any wrongful judgement shall be given to your knowledge. And as great honour be this noble Order unto you, as ever it was to any of your progenitors.'

The oath being taken, while they are yet in the Chapel, wine and sweetmeats are brought them; and then they depart to their chamber to be disrobed of their hermits' weeds and revested in their robes of crimson taffeta lined with white sarcenet, having white hats on their heads with white feathers, white boots on their legs, and white gloves tied to the strings of their mantles. All which performed, they mount on horseback, their saddles being of black leather, with crosses on their breasts and the cruppers of their horses. Each Knight goes between two esquires, his footmen attending, and his page riding before him, carrying his sword with the hilt upward and his spurs hanging thereon. Being alighted at the Court gates they are conducted by the Heralds into the Hall where being placed in a semicircle the King soon after came down, accompanied with the Nobility, but no Bishops.

The King, sitting under a cloth of estate, then gave them their knighthoods. The principal Lord to receive his knighthood, which is the Earl of Oxford, then comes forward led by his two esquires, and his page before him bearing his sword and spurs and kneeleth down before his Majesty. The L. Chamberlain takes the sword of the page and delivers it to the King who puts the belt over the neck of the Knight aslope his breast, placing the sword under his left arm. Then two Noblemen put on his spurs, but the Earl of Northampton in putting on his spurs mistook the left spur for the right, at which the King, as though it were ominous, was offended and would hasten to the sermon, so that for the rest they put on only the right spur, and their pages when they came down put on the other.

When all had been thus knighted, they returned to Durham House where their dinner was ready for them in the same fashion as their supper yesterday, but being set at the table they did not taste anything but with modest carriage and graceful abstinence they refrained, and after a convenient time of sitting they arise and withdraw themselves leaving the furnished table to their esquires and pages.

About 6 of the clock they rode again to the Court to hear evening service in the King's Chapel which was very solemnly celebrated with singing of anthems and playing on the organs; and when the time of the offertory was come, after the Second Lesson, they are summoned two by two by the Heralds and brought up to the altar where they offer their swords and the Dean receives them, of whom they straightway redeem them with an angel in gold offered into a basin held by a minister in a cope. At the redelivery of their swords the Dean said: 'By the oath that you received this day, remember to use your swords to the glory of God, the defence of His Word, of your Sovereign and Country, and the maintenance of justice.'

The service being ended, at the Chapel door as they came forth they were encountered by the King's Master-Cook, who stood there with his white apron and sleeves, a chopping knife gilded about the edge in his hand, and challenged their spurs which they likewise redeemed with a noble, threatening them that if they proved not true and loyal to the King his Lord and Master, it must be his office to hew them from their heels.

And so they marched into the courtyard and taking their horses returned to Durham House, where each Knight alighted and put off his robes. Then every Knight went privately to his own lodging.

4th. The Lords and Peers of the Realm being all assembled in Parliament, the King accompanied with the Prince took water about half an hour after 10 at the privy stairs at Whitehall, and landing together at Westminster Bridge, his Majesty passed quietly to the Parliament House, and the Prince to the Court of Wards where he and such Earls as attended him apparelled themselves. Thence they proceeded in this order:

First went the Heralds and officers at arms in their coats; the

Knights of the Bath, in long robes of purple satin lined with white taffeta; then Garter Principal King of Arms bearing the letters patent; the Earl of Sussex the purple robes; the train borne by the Earl of Huntingdon; the Earl of Cumberland the sword; the Earl of Rutland the ring; the Earl of Derby the rod; and the Earl of Shrewsbury the cap and coronet. The Prince, supported by the Earls of Nottingham and Northampton, came bareheaded in his surcoat of purple velvet, and so entered the Parliament chamber, where the King was set in his throne and the whole State of the Realm in order, as well as divers Foreign Ambassadors. The Prince made low obeisance to his Majesty three times and after the third time when he was come near to the King, Master Garter kissed the letters patent and gave them to the L. Chamberlain who presented them to the King and the King to the Earl of Salisbury, Principal Secretary, who read them aloud, the Prince the while kneeling.

Then the King with two assistants at the reading of the words of investure put the robes on him and girded on the sword, invested him with the rod and ring, and set the cap and coronet on his head, with which ceremony the Creation being accomplished, the Prince arose and was by the Earls of Worcester and Suffolk brought and seated in his place on the King's left hand. Thereupon the King being advertised that he should kiss him, rose, and after reaching his hand to be kissed, and afterwards kissed him. Then the Deputy for the Clerk of the Crown read the *Testes*, beginning with the L. Chancellor (L. Ellesmere), the Archbishop of York, and the names of all the Lords present. Which done the L. Chancellor prorogued the Parliament till Thursday; the trumpets sounded, and the Lower House arose.

The ceremonies thus ended, the King and the whole Court of Parliament arose and descended into the Hall, and so passed forth in solemn and stately manner. The King and the Prince took water together, the trumpets sounding in the barge all the way. At Whitehall stairs they landed, where the Knights of the Bath and the Noblemen being already landed, stood ready to receive them and conduct them to the Great Chamber.

The King dined above in his privy chamber; but the Prince in the Hall, and was served with great state and magnificence. There were two tables set longways down the Hall; one of them stood in the middle where the Prince himself sat at the upper end. He was accompanied at his table with the Duke of York on the left hand, and some three yards lower divers great Lords as the Earls of Nottingham, Salisbury, Worcester and Derby. At another table sat the Knights of the Bath, all on one side.

About the midst of the dinner, Garter Principal King at Arms, with the rest of the Heralds approached the Prince's table and with a loud and audible voice proclaimed the King's style in Latin, French, and English thrice, and the Prince's in like manner twice.

The device of the fireworks on the Thames is put off till Wednesday. The rest of the ceremony that belongs to the Prince is to be performed in as private a manner as may be for the King in this time of necessity when he is so pressed to the Parliament is not willing to undergo any needless expense. There was otherwise intended a solemn entry and passage through the City of London, which is contracted to a passage by water from Whitehall to Westminster. The Court of Requests is dressed up and furnished for the place of the solemnity, with scaffolds for the Lower House.

All priests, Jesuits and seminaries are by proclamation commanded to depart the Realm by the 4th day of July and not to return upon pain of the Law; and all recusants to return home to their dwellings and not to remain in London nor to come within 10 miles of the Court.

5th. This night was graced with Daniel's *Masque of Tethys' Festival or the Queen's Wake*, which was double. In the first came in the young Duke of York, between two great sea slaves, the chiefest of Neptune's servants, attended by twelve little Ladies, all of them daughters of Earls or Barons. By one of these a speech was made expressing the conceit of the Masque which was that Tethys, Queen of Nymphs and Rivers, is come with her nymphs to greet the great Monarch of Oceans and the Prince of the Isles; and by the other a very rich cross sword all set with diamonds with the chape richly set was put into the Duke's hands who presented it to the Prince his brother. This done the Duke returned to his place in the midst of the stage and the little Ladies performed their dance to the delight of the beholders for it was full of many and intricate changes. These light skirmishers having done their devoir, in came the Princesses: first the Queen, next the Lady Elizabeth, the Lady Arbella, the Countesses of Arundel, Derby, Essex, Dorset and Montgomery, and the Ladies Haddington, Elizabeth Grey, Windsor, Katherine Petre, Elizabeth Guildford and Mary Windsor. By the time these had done, it was time to go to bed, for it was within an hour of the sun's rising. Howbeit a farther time was spent in view and scrambling at a most magnificent banquet. The Ambassadors of Spain, Venice and the Low Countries were present at all these sights, but the French Ambassador excused himself upon his mourning for his Master, whereby was taken away all contention with the Spaniard.

6th. This afternoon in the Tiltyard divers Earls and Barons, in rich and glowing armour, with costly caparisons, curiously embroidered with pearls, gold and silver, presented their devices and trophies before the King and the Prince, and then ran at tilt where there was a world of people to see them. At night there were naval triumphs and pastimes on the water over against the Court with ships of war and galleys fighting one against another, and against a great castle builded upon the water. After these battles for an hour's space many strange variable fireworks in the castle and the ships. It is said these sights were seen by almost half a million of people. These festivities are now ended.

8th. The Lords today sent a message to the Lower House wishing them to go roundly about their business and to use no more delays than of necessity they must. To this message great exception was taken, but no answer returned. The King is resolved to send another 600 men to Sweden out of Ireland under Capt. Richard Bingley. They shall be mere Irish and especially active Irish; and if they cannot be found in Ulster then from the other Provinces. They take their course round the north of Scotland.

13th. My L. of Northampton who is reputed a Catholic was asked by the King if he had any Catholic servants in his household. He replied that he knew only of one, called Penny. At which the King answered, 'Well, you have had so much from me that surely you can spare me a *penny*'. My L. has now dismissed this man and three or four more.

Two days ago a committee of the House of Commons met certain of the Lords in the Painted Chamber when the L. Treasurer, speaking from the King, would persuade them to supply the King's wants by subsidies and to suspend the matter of the support and grievances until the next meeting in October. He spoke especially of the cost of the Prince's creation, which hath been performed with greatness and magnificence; and of the consequences of the French King's death which doth threaten a general alteration in Christendom. This accident hath already drawn a present increase of the King's charge, for last Saturday £6,000 was delivered out of the Receipt towards the war of Cleves, and order given for £30,000 more. And therefore he wished that as that day was the longest day in the year, when the sun returns and alters his course, so that they might alter their course, having now spent almost five months in matters impertinent and extravagant discourses, whereof some square, some long, some short but all circular, for they were about where they first began. In conclusion he said, 'What will be the fruit of my speech I know not. But if any sow tares to hinder the fruit of it, I can be but sorry, but I hope you will take such a course as his Majesty will live no longer in anxiety and yourselves in danger.'

This speech being reported to the House, divers opinions were offered. Sir Thomas Beaumont moved that it was more for the King's safety and honour, for their reputation and for the satisfaction of the country to defer the supply till they had answer of their grievances, and had concluded the contracts for the tenures. Then M. Tay said that having sat so long, if they should now return into their counties with nothing done for the good of the commonweal, they would be said to have been all this while like children in catching butterflies. The debate is deferred till the morning.

20th. In Venice when he heard of the death of the French King, Signor Molin (who was Ambassador here five years ago) said to Sir Henry Wotton, 'Sir, we must put our fingers to our lips and contemplate the great works of God in veneration and silence'. It is said also that Fr. Coton the Jesuit and the late King's confessor, on receiving the King's heart to be enshrined in the College that he had built, said on kissing it that he would as willingly kiss the King of England's——.

26th. The funerals of the French King were celebrated for 3 days with great pomp in Paris on the 19th, 20th and 21st. On the first day the body was carried from the Louvre to Our Lady's Church; on the second to S. Lazarus' Church without the town; and on the third to his last lodging in S. Denis' Church. The number of assistants was such that the company was 3 or 4 hours passing the street. At the head went 500 or 600 poor people in mourning apparel with torches in their hands; then the archers and guards of Paris with the points of their halberds downwards; then the Orders of convents and parishes, 2,000 or 3,000 religious; then the University, and after those the officers of the Household and many other officers; then the King's Guard of French Swissers and Scots, with their pieces under their arms in very good order. Then came the body in a great hearse drawn with 6 horses, hearse and horses covered with black velvet to the ground, with a great white cross of satin; and before it 12 trumpeters and 12 drummers beating very mournfully with their drums all in black; and behind it 12 pages on horseback, the one after the other clothed all in black velvet. After them followed some of the greatest officers on horseback carrying the King's spurs, his gauntlets, his headpiece, his banner, etc. After them followed a great company of Abbots, Bishops, Archbishops and Cardinals; the Abbots and

Bishops were on foot but the 4 Cardinals and the 7 Archbishops upon mules, all in their habits. Between the Cardinals and the Bishops marched the Ambassadors of Spain, Venice and the Savoy. Then came the King's horse, with a great cover of blue velvet strewed all over with golden flowers de lys, led by 4 men, and accompanied with high heralds. M. le Grand followed next on horseback carrying the King's sword; and then the Court of Parliament in scarlet, and in the midst of them the King's effigies lying upon a bed of justice very richly dressed, and compassed about with Presidents and Councillors, representing the living authority of the Kingdom. After them followed certain of the chief of the nobility, Princes, Dukes and Counts, all on horseback, with long and broad trains, supported by gentlemen. After them came the Knights of the Holy Ghost on foot; then 12 pages of the King's Chamber in black velvet; and last of all a company of archers which shut in the convoy.

Several of the Princes and the Ambassadors did not assist the solemnity by reason of competition of places or of religion; and on the first 2 days there was like to follow great disorders by the competition which fell out between the Court of Parliament and the Bishop of Paris for the place nearest the effigy; which grew to such great heat by the strong partakings of both sides that the Court was ready to have departed the ceremony, if their respect to the late King's. memory had not tempered their choler. Yet the Queen's authority yielded the place to the Bishop, who took it immediately before the effigy; for the which the Court is so much stomached that they are about to make a decree against it.

This is the beginning of dissention in the State by the ambition of the Princes who emboldening themselves under the weakness and facility of a woman now seek by all means and open partialities to usurp the authority of government one upon the other.

30th. The ancient use of the Artillery Garden, fallen into disuse since 1588, has been revived this present year through the exertions of divers citizens and gentlemen of the City of London; and here is held a weekly exercise of arms and military discipline after the modern and best instruction. Further they have erected a strong and well-furnished armoury with arms of several sorts and excellent goodness.

2nd July. For four whole days during this fortnight past the House of Commons hath debated whether the King hath power to set impositions upon merchandises without assent of Parliament. After much quoting and noting of laws, precedents, taxes, customs, limitations, petitions, statutes, restraints, powers regal and legal, grievances, the Scriptures and the Fathers, Plato, Livy, Plutarch, Pliny, customs of their countries as Portugal, Spain, Germany, the Low Countries, Florence and Holland, the ancient Britons and the Romans, Saxons, Danegeld, Edward the Confessor, Magna Charta, and the rest, M. Nicholas Hyde proposed that they might prefer a Petition of Right, but the right must first be decided by question. So a sub-committee is chosen to frame a petition, without making a question of the right.

3rd. The famous Jesuit Baldwin has lately been taken passing through the Palatinate by officers of the Elector of the Rhine. He has now been handed over to Sir Ralph Winwood the King's Ambassador in the Low Countries, who has delivered him into the hands of two English captains, Sir John Burlacy and Capt. Dewhurst to be conducted into England under strong and safe convoy. Baldwin had disguised his habit and named himself Alessandra Prawn. Passing through the Palatinate he was examined but slightly and so entered into his inn, but in the stable he read certain letters which he had about him, amongst others certain letters of my Lady Lovell's which the ostler perceiving made known to the Magistrate, whereby he was discovered to be Baldwin, not Prawn.

6th. The pirates upon the coast of Ireland are so many and grow so bold that they are now come into S. George's Channel and have lately robbed divers barks, both English and Scottish, and killed some that made resistance. They lay for the Londoners' money sent for the works at Coleraine but missed it. They have bred a great terror to all passengers and will not spare the King's treasure if they light upon it. The pirates Coward and Barrett have been taken by Dutchmen that lay fishing upon the coast of Connaught.

7th. Today the Solicitor, accompanied by twenty of the Lower House, presented to the King their petition of grievances all drawn up into a great scroll of parchment, which the King said would serve for a piece of tapestry.

A few days ago the Lady Arbella was secretly married to M. William Seymour, in spite of the King's prohibition. Both were summoned before the Council. M. Seymour was brought in first and denied it, but the Lady Arbella freely confessed it and excused the denial of her husband as due to fear, saying he did no more than Abraham and Isaac had done, who disclaimed their wives for a time; and she laboured to show that neither by divine nor human law could she be prevented. But the King is offended, and she has been sent a close prisoner to Sir Thomas Parry's house at Lambeth, and her husband to the Tower. The law forbidding (under pain of treason and rebellion) descendants of the blood royal to intermarry without leave first had, is a great impediment to her. If she should be found to be with child, she might perhaps have greater fortune. When M. Seymour entered the Tower, Andrew Melville the Scottish minister who is still a prisoner there on account of his satirical verses welcomed him with this distich:

Communis tecum mihi causa est carceris; Ara
Bella tibi causa est, araque sacra mihi.

8th. Being again examined before the Council, M. William Seymour has confessed that upon Friday was fortnight (22nd June) he was married unto the Lady Arbella at Greenwich, in her chamber there. There was present one Blagew, son to the Dean of Rochester who was the minister that married them; also M. Edward Rodney, M. Crompton her gentleman usher, M. Edward Kyrton and M. Edward Reeves, and two women servants of the Lady. The marriage was between 4 and 5 of the clock in the morning, but without any licence. He came to Greenwich on the Thursday night about midnight, with Rodney and Kyrton, and sat up all night in the Lady Arbella's chamber until they were married.

9th. By command of the LL. of the Council the Lady Arbella is now to be restrained of her liberty. She is committed to the custody of Sir Thomas Parry, the Chancellor of the Duchy of Lancaster, in his house at Lambeth, where she shall have one or two of her women to attend her, without access of any other person.

15th. The English army for Juliers was mustered on the 6th and marched on the 8th from the Hague in excellent order.

16th. Sir Henry Wotton is returning from Venice and the new ambassador is Dudley Carleton. He sets forth with his wife in about a month.

17th. The King through the L. Treasurer has returned an answer to the latest demands of the Commons. He is pleased to grant that in cases of outlawry and attainder the debts of the delinquent shall first be paid; but to the 3rd and 4th (that it might be lawful to arrest the King's servants without leave and that no man should be enforced to lend money to the King nor give a reason why he would not) the King answered that he would not allow the precedents which they alleged, for these were brought from times of decaying or usurping Princes or of people too bold and wanton; that he desired not to govern in a Commonwealth where subjects should be assured of all things and hope for nothing. He therefore rejected them, but with the mitigation that would refuse no reasonable excuse in matters of loans, nor deny the arresting of any of his servants if just cause were shown. The 5th was that in cases criminal the party accused might bring in witnesses to clear himself. This was denied by the King because it would be often an occasion of perjury; for, said he, if men will forswear themselves for an ox or a sheep, how much more to save the life of a friend? It was a matter of conscience, and he would not part with it for money. The 6th he granted; which was the repealing a clause in a statute of Henry VIII whereby the King had power to make arbitrary laws over the Welshmen.

Thence the L. Treasurer came to the price; and here he said that the King would no more rise and fall like a merchant; and that he would not have the flower of his Crown (meaning the Court of Wards) so much tossed. So he delivered a pleasant conceit of the King: as concerning the number of 9 score thousand pounds which was the sum proposed by the Commons, he could not affect it because 9 was the number of the poets, who were always beggars though they served so many Muses; and 11 was the number of the Apostles when Judas was away, and therefore might best be affected by his Majesty; but there was a mean number which might accord us both, which was 10 score thousand. After further speeches, the L. Treasurer concluded that he had delivered the King's final and peremptory resolution; the distance was little and the bargain advantageous; if they now refused, the King would instantly dissolve Parliament and would never make the like offer.

So the members returned to their House and yielded to give the King a perpetual revenue of £200,000 a year upon conditions. Now remains to be resolved upon the assurance, and with what cords (as they say) they will bind Samson's hands, that is the King's prerogative; and also the manner of the levy. But at this time the King and Commons part in loving terms.

18th. When the late proclamation against the Catholics was published, the Spanish Ambassador said to the Earl of Salisbury that it was not to the King's interest to drive the Catholics to despair. My L. took some time to reply, and soon after when the Archbishop of Canterbury was complaining to the King that the chief Councillors never came to communion, my L. spoke of the matter and urged that greater leniency should be shown to the Catholics. Then my L. told the Spanish Ambassador that he would be informed of what passed with the King and this would serve for an answer; for my L. knows well that the Spanish have excellent means of discovering what happens in the Councils of Kings.

20th. The Catholic priests in England to the number of 180 (which is three parts of the whole clergy) have sent to Birkhead the Archpriest that he will petition the Pope to appoint Bishops for England.

23rd. The Parliament is prorogued till 16th October, and the Great Contract between the King and the Commons to be concluded at a price of £200,000 of annual revenue is put off till the next meeting.

The chief Statutes enacted in the late session are:

An Act for the better execution of justice in the north parts of the Kingdom of England, whereby anyone who shall commit felonious acts in Scotland and shall flee to England may, upon pregnant proofs, be sent back into Scotland for his trial; provided that an Act shall likewise be made by the Parliament of Scotland for the like remanding of persons to England.

An Act that all such as are naturalized or restored in blood shall first receive the Sacrament of the Lord's Supper and take the Oaths of Allegiance and Supremacy.

An Act concerning Rogues and Vagabonds, supplementing former Acts concerning vagabonds, whereby Houses of Correction shall be erected in every county. And because of the great charge arising by reason of bastardy, every lewd woman who shall have a bastard which may be chargeable to the parish shall be committed to the House of Correction for one year. And if anyone shall run away leaving his children chargeable to the parish, he shall be deemed an incorrigible rogue and endure the pains of such.

An Act for administering the Oath of Allegiance, and for the reformation of married women recusants, which shall be committed to prison without bail until she do conform herself, unless her husband shall pay for the offences of his wife for every month £10 or the third part of all his lands and tenements.

An Act to prevent the spoil of corn and grain by untimely hawking, and for the better preservation of pheasants and partridges; whereby it is made lawful for those who hold lands of the value of £40 or more yearly to take pheasants and partridges between the Feast of S. Michael and the Birthday of Our Lord. Persons of bad and mean condition who shall unlawfully take pheasants or partridges shall be committed for three months without bail and fined 20*s.* for every bird taken; and further the constables and officers shall have power to search the houses of persons suspected of having dogs or nets for the taking of birds, and to destroy the same.

An Act to avoid the double payment of debts. Certain men of trades do demand of their customers debts upon their shop-books long after they are due and when they suppose the particulars and certainty of the wares to be forgotten; or insert into their books other wares supposed to have been delivered and thus increase the debt; or leave their books uncrossed when the debt has been paid so that debtors or their executors are enforced to pay the debt twice. To meet these abuses it is enacted that no tradesman shall give his shop-book as evidence in any action for money due above one year before the action be brought.

The customary Act for the King's free pardon of such offences as are not excepted in the General Pardon is again enacted, but to the end thereof is added 'excepted out of this general and free pardon, Sir Stephen Proctor, Knight'.

25th. The King has gone on progress towards Northamptonshire. The L. Treasurer stays behind to marry his daughter to the L. Clifford with a dowry of £40,000. The young L. of Cranborne begins to look sour on his wife; so hath my L. of Essex cause, for they say plots have been laid by her to poison him. Many scandals are being whispered about the Court concerning the young Countess of Essex. Some say that by her father's uncle, my L. of Northampton, she was set on to catch the eye of the Prince, and that he had her virginity and enjoyed her. Others that she is in secret the mistress of the favourite Robert Carr. On a time at a masque, the Lady having dropped her glove, a courtier thinking to please the Prince picked it up and presented it to him, who replied that he scorned it since it had been stretched by another. It is notorious that there is little love between the Prince and Carr, whom once he threatened to have stricken with his racket when they were playing at tennis.

3rd August. The King and the Queen begin the Progress, which is for 6 weeks. With them goeth the Prince, who now that he has taken his seat in the Council desireth to have to do with some of the more weighty affairs, and he is so strict in his dealings that he pushes aside many difficulties, for all are afraid of falling into his displeasure. It is said that in the recent disagreements in the Parliament he effected much by restraining the ardour of some.

12th. The army is before Juliers which they besiege. There is a report that Spinola will come against them with 15,000 men. The town is not strong but by reason of the stony ground the approaches will be long in making. In a night sally from the town 4 officers were hurt and many soldiers, and some slain; and the Prince of Anhalt had his horse killed under him. Many of our young gallants are gone into Cleves, as Sir Thomas Somerset, Sir Thomas Howard, and Sir Edward

Sheffield; and my L. of Walden goes also and there is a speech of my L. of Cranborne.

13th. Because of the many slanders declaring that Ravilliac murdered the French King by the instructions of the Jesuits, Fr. Peter Coton of that Society addressed a letter to the Queen Regent declaring that they are much maligned, for their doctrine is clean contrary. They hold that obedience is due to Kings not because they are virtuous or endowed with commendable qualities but because they are Kings, established by God; and it is not lawful to revolt against them although they were vicious, hard to endure and froward. To attempt their persons is an execrable parricide and a detestable sacrilege. This letter is now printed in English, with another denying it, and proclaiming that the Jesuits have a secret and hidden mystery and sundry ceremonies and conjurations whereby they sanctify murderers.

14th. A certain Josippus Barbartus who was born at Memphis in Egypt is on his way to Oxford recommended to the Vice-Chancellor by my L. of Canterbury to the end that he may read the Arabian tongue there, which is natural to him. He speaks French and Italian readily and Latin well enough to explicate his mind, and is likewise reported of a kind and honest disposition. He takes with him also a letter from Sir Thomas Bodley asking that he may be provided of a competent entertainment to keep him in Oxford lest Cambridge should endeavour to draw him away.

17th. Sir Thomas Dutton who is one of the captains at Juliers hath a quarrel with Sir Hatton Cheke, Colonel of the English, having as it seems called the General's commission in question. He is come to Court with news of the siege and to excuse himself; but by the King's command he is arrested and to be punished according to a maxim of his in *Basilicon Doron* 'that faults in war are of all others straightest to be looked into'.

23rd. Sir Thomas Gates is alive and returned to England, with Capt. Newport, and good news of Virginia, for the L. De la Warr has arrived there, and all the people safely landed. They have come in two small ships which were built in the Bermudas.

When the Virginia fleet was scattered by the great tempest on S. James's Day last year, the *Sea Adventure* (with Sir Thomas Gates the new Governor, Sir George Somers and Capt. Newport) was separated from the company and sprang a great leak, the ship in almost every joint having spewed out her oakum, so that in a short time the water was five feet above the ballast. Three days and four nights they manned the pumps, every man, even the Admiral, taking the pump or bucket for an hour and resting an hour. One huge sea broke right over the ship like a vast cloud, so violent that it wrested the whipstaff from the helmsman, and when he would have seized it again, so tossed him from starboard to larboard that it was God's mercy it had not split him. During all this time the heavens were so black that they never had sight of the Pole or the sun, only one night there was an apparition of a little round light, like a faint star, trembling and streaming upon the mainmast and shooting sometimes from shroud to shroud. So from Tuesday to Friday they shifted every hour out of the ship 1,200 barricos of water, besides three deep pumps which quitted 100 tons of water every 4 hours. At length when all hope was gone, Sir George Somers descried land, and ordered the helmsman to bear up towards it; but since there was no hope of coming to anchor, the ship was run ashore within three quarters of a mile of land, and ere night all the men, women and children (to the number of 150) were brought safe to the Island, which they found to be the dreaded Isle, or Islands rather, of the Bermudas, which for tempests, thunder and other fearful objects are commonly called the Devil's Islands. These Bermudas be broken islands, 500 of them, in figure of a crescent.

So soon as they were settled a little, they made up the long boat in fashion of a pinnace, fitted with a little deck made of the hatches of the ruined ship, proposing to send her to Virginia, in which the Master's mate, Henry Ravens, set out with seven others. He carried instructions from the Governor appointing Capt. Peter Winn to be his Lieutenant Governor and adding sundry instructions for the well ordering of the colony, Ravens set forth on 1st September, promising to return with the Colony's pinnace the next new moon; but he never came back, and afterwards it appeared from the scoffing reports of the savages that they reached the coast but missed the river and were cut off.

Meanwhile Sir George Somers coasted the islands and made a plot of them. Also at this time Richard Frubbisher, a shipwright of Limehouse, was making a new pinnace to transport them all to Virginia, to which the Governor assigned 20 of the ablest to hew and square timber; moreover in that other island where Sir George had his company a second pinnace was in building. These labours were the cause of the first conspiracy; for sundry of them tried to delay the work, preferring to settle where they were to the wretchedness and labour to be expected in Virginia. These sought to draw to them the smith and one of the carpenters, with whom they purposed to leave the rest and possess an island by themselves. When their conspiracy was found out, they were condemned to what they would have chosen, and carried to an island far off and there left; but they soon missed the society of their acquaintances and humbly besought the Governor to readmit them; which he easily granted upon their earnest vows to redeem their offence.

There was a second mutiny in January, led by one Stephen Hopkins, a fellow who had much knowledge in the Scriptures and could reason in them, whom their minister had chosen to be his clerk to read the psalms and chapters on Sundays. This Hopkins brake with two others and declared that it was no breach in conscience or religion to refuse the Governor's authority which, said he, ceased at the wreck; but those two revealed it to the Governor who brought Hopkins to a public affront. At the tolling of a bell before the whole company who were assembled before a corps du gard, the prisoner was brought forth in manacles and sentence of death passed on him by court martial. But he made so much moan, alleging the ruin of his wife and children, that the better sort of the company went to the Governor and never left him till they had got his pardon.

Nevertheless some of them still plotted against the Governor and had a purpose to surprise the storehouse. This conspiracy came to no fruition for the confederates were divided, some in the island with the Governor, others with Sir George in his island. Moreover the sentinels and nightwatchers were doubled so that nothing was attempted until a gentleman named Henry Paine, when called to be upon guard, gave evil language to his captain, and struck at him, and went off guard, scoffing at this double diligence, and declaring that the Governor had no authority, and therefore let him (said he) kiss, etc. These words being common talk, next day were at length delivered to the Governor who called Paine before him and the whole company, where he was convicted by witness of many who were on the watch with him. The Governor having the eyes of the whole colony fixed upon him condemned Paine to be instantly hanged; who, after making many confessions, earnestly desired that being a gentleman he might be shot to death; and at sunset had his desire.

When they heard of Paine's death, certain of Sir George's company in fear betook themselves to the woods like outlaws, and thence sent the Governor a formal petition that they might stay there, importuning him to leave them two suits of apparel and their proportion of the meal. Hereupon the Governor wrote to Sir George to apprehend them, if he could, by some secret pretence, and to reconcile them; which was effected except for two men who were left behind. During the whole time of their stay upon these islands one marriage was celebrated, and two children were born and baptized, a girl called Bermuda, and a boy called Bermudas; but both died. Also four of the company were buried, one untimely, a sailor killed by his fellow Robert Waters (who was one of the two left behind) with a shovel; for which he was appointed to be hanged. He was tied to a tree with many ropes, and guarded by six sentinels; but his fellow sailors, taking advantage of the sentinels sleeping, and disdaining that justice should be shown upon a sailor, cut his bands and conveyed him into the woods, where they fed him nightly until he was pardoned by the mediation of Sir George Somers. Every Sunday they had two sermons preached by M. Buck their minister at the ringing of a bell, at which time the names of the whole company were called by a bill, and those wanting duly punished.

All this while the pinnaces were building; the greater was about 80 tons burden; 40 foot by the keel; 19 foot broad at the beam; 8 foot deep under the beam, with a forecastle. The most part of her timber was cedar, which was found bad for shipping, but her beams were of oak from the ruined ship. The Governor called her the *Deliverance*. The pinnace they built on Sir George's island was smaller, which he named the *Patience*.

These two ships set sail from the Bermudas on 10th May, the Governor having first set up a wooden cross from the ship's timber, with a silver shilling for the King's portrait, and an inscription graven in copper in Latin and English. They reached Chesipiack Bay on the 20th; and next day came to Point Comfort where the captain of that fort discharged a warning piece, at which they sent off the longboat to certify who they were, and there learnt of the miserable state of Jamestown, which they reached two days later. Here they saw the palisadoes torn down, the ports open, the gates taken off their hinges, and empty houses rent up and burnt rather than the dwellers would slip into the woods a stone's cast off to fetch other firewood; where it is true the Indians killed as fast without as famine and pestilence within.

Of 490 odd persons left there at the departure of Capt. John Smith not past 60 men, women and children were still alive, most miserable and starving. At the time of his departure Smith had left the colony with three ships, seven boats, commodities for trade, 24 pieces of ordnance, 300 muskets with shot and powder sufficient, curats, pikes, swords and morions more than men, 100 trained and expert soldiers who knew the savages' language; with tools of all sorts, 6 mares and a horse, 500 and more swine, hens, chickens, goats and sheep; and besides Jamestown strongly palisadoed, with 80 new houses, and other forts and plantations. But those sent out were for the most part poor gentlemen, tradesmen, serving men and libertines more fit to spoil a commonwealth than begin one.

As soon as the savages understood that Smith was gone, they revolted and murdered all they encountered. M. Percy the President was too sick to go or stand. Capt. Ratcliffe (alias Sicklemore) and Capt. West sought abroad for trade, but Ratcliffe trusting in Powhatan with about 30 others as careless as himself were all slain, and only one escaped, besides a boy called Henry Spelman who was saved by Pocahontas. Powhatan, as he found means, cut off their boats and denied them trade so that West sailed for England. In these extremities they consumed all their horses, hogs and whatever lived, traded everything with the savages until at last those who lived were preserved by roots, acorns, berries and now and then a little fish. So great was their famine that the poorer sort took up a dead savage they had slain and ate his body, and one man slew his wife and salted her, and had eaten part of her before it was discovered, for which he was executed. In this starving time, they all had perished within 4 days but for the coming of the pinnaces.

In the next 2 weeks the Governor consulted with Capt. Percy and the other gentlemen. Seeing no other remedy, and all the provision, even racked to the uttermost, good for no longer than 16 days, he concluded to abandon the country, and in the 4 pinnaces (the *Discovery* and the *Virginia* which had come from England and the two newly made in the Bermudas) with all speed to make for the Newfound Land where they might meet with English ships.

Upon 7th June everyone upon beat of the drum came aboard, but the Governor commanded that the town should be preserved, which some of the company threatened to burn. Next morning they reached Mulberry Island, and here lying at anchor they discovered a longboat coming toward them from Point Comfort, whence they learnt of the arrival of the L. De la Warr and his fleet. So next day Sir Thomas Gates bore up the helm and on the 10th relanded his men at Jamestown whither his Lordship likewise brought his ships; at whose disembarking caused his company with arms to make a guard.

Upon landing, the L. De la Warr fell on his knees in long and silent prayer, and after marched up into the town and passed into the chapel where he heard a sermon by M. Buck. Then he caused his commission to be read out, which entitled him to be L. Governor and Captain General during his life of the colony and plantation in Virginia. So Sir Thomas Gates rendered up his commission. The new Lord Governor said a few words to them all, blaming their many vanities and idleness, earnestly wishing that he might no more find it so, and heartening them that he had brought sufficient provision to serve 400 for a whole year. Next day he constituted the chief officers of the colony, and so advised with his Council for obtaining victual for the store. Sir George Somers proposed to go to the Bermudas and fetch thence six months' provision of flesh and fish and some live hogs; on which expedition he set out on the 15th in his own pinnace the *Patience* and Capt. Argall in the *Discovery*.

As for that savage King Powhatan, the L. De la Warr sent to say he could not suppose the outrages committed against our men were contrived by him, and requiring him to punish or send in such savages as had killed four of our men at the blockhouse since his coming, and return all English prisoners which he held. Powhatan replied that either all our people should depart his country or confine themselves to Jamestown, or he would command his men to kill them and do all the mischief they could; and further not to send any more messengers unless they brought him a coach and three horses, which he understood from those Indians who have been in England is the state of great Weroans among us. Soon after two of Powhatan's people were taken, men who had been especially venomous. These were convented before the Council, and one of them having had his right hand struck off was sent to Powhatan with the message that unless he returned the Englishmen and the arms which he had stolen, the other prisoner would die, and all other savages that shall be taken; and further the L. Governor will fire his corn, fields, towns and villages, and that suddenly. How this will work is yet to be seen.

The King is on progress and being hunting the other day the two Earls Essex and Montgomery were stealing a quarrel grounded upon a small matter as if the latter Lord had set the ground tree upon the other's head, but the matter for the present is appeased. The Prince is going to Oxford. The plague is rife at Cambridge.

25th. The L. Deputy now deals with Bishop the pirate to perform some acceptable service upon the rest of the pirates. Coward is being sent over as a prisoner; he says that the pirates intend next spring to fire the fleet of the fishermen upon the coast of Newfound Land, and advises that they be received into mercy, otherwise they are resolved to prey upon the subject as well as the stranger. Sackwell has been slain. He was carried aboard his ship sore wounded, and Easton one of his men threw him overboard, and now offers to submit himself.

Upon the coming of the L. De la Warr to Virginia those two Dutchmen who remained with Powhatan and formerly betrayed Capt. Smith asked leave to go to his Lordship promising to work wonders with him. But Powhatan replied, 'As you would formerly have be-

222

trayed Capt. Smith to me, so will you me to his Lordship, for you that would be false to him, cannot be true to me.' And with that he caused his own men to beat out their brains.

28th. From Juliers it is reported that three ravelins have been taken. In one the enemy quitted the work instantly, which made our men walk on the more warily suspecting a mine. An ensign with one or two soldiers ran up the rampart to view, but the mine sprung and took them. The town is full of good marksmen both for the small and great shot, and we have lost many men in the trenches by particular bullets, but few or none by sallies. One English captain and two lieutenants are lost, but very many sergeants which set out the perdus, and many gentlemen. The French army has now arrived, but not exceeding 5,000 foot and 1,000 horse, able in body but pitifully armed. When they arrived their commander flourished his sword, offered a thrust, kissed the handle of it, and presented it and himself to the service of the Count Maurice who is in command of the Dutch and English soldiers. The battery continues, with the building of a counterscarp and galleries.

31st. Capt. Poole is returned from a voyage set forth by Sir Thomas Smith and the Muscovy Company to Cherry Island and discovery towards the North Pole for likelihood of trade or a passage that way. He encountered extreme cold weather in the latitude of 73°, but in 78° the sun was hot and the water unfrozen which putteth him in hope of a mild summer in those parts so he is of opinion that a passage may as soon be attained by the Pole as by any other whatsoever.

The plague deaths these 4 weeks past again are more than 50 in each week, and this week past 99.

1st September. On the 19th the Duke of Anhalt summoned the town of Juliers to surrender and the Governor desired three days to give the answer, which was allowed. The time being expired, the Governor wrote to the French Marshal de la Chastre to entreat that the Romish Church might be continued in the town, and he would treat upon surrendering. For two days the Generals met together before noon and afternoon, and after some going to and fro from the town the articles were agreed in the evening of the 22nd. Next day the garrison came out to depart out of the territories of the Princes to whom both town and castle are delivered. The army is now being dissolved. The honour of the conduct of the siege belongs chiefly to the Count Maurice, who was the master workman, but he doth attribute it to the diligence and judgement of Sir Edward Cecil.

223

They both yielded the command to the good old French Marshal, who is 78 years old.

2nd. This day the L. Chief Justice Coke was sent for to attend the L. Chancellor, the L. Treasurer and others to give his opinion whether the King by his proclamation may prohibit new buildings in and about London, and also whether by proclamation he may prohibit the making of starch of wheat, for these were professed to the King as grievances and against the law and justice. To which the L. Chief Justice desired to have conference with his brethren the judges, but, said he, without precedent the King cannot without Parliament change any part of the Common Law, nor create any offence by his proclamation which was not an offence before, adding thereto that individual indictments conclude '*contra leges et statuta*' but he never heard any indictment conclude '*contra regiam proclamationem*'.

6th. It is expected that about Michaelmas the Prince will be established in his own household and many seek to be honourably employed in his service. There hath been no Prince of Wales since 1537 and Sir Robert Cotton is busied in discovering precedents in his style and status, as in what manner he ought to sign; whether the Queen or he ought to sign first; and the like.

9th. These past weeks many both noblemen, gentlemen and citizens continually resort to Woolwich to see the great ship. This evening divers London maids brought in their company a little boy of 12 years, the only child of a widow in Thames Street, who carelessly going up and down upon the main orlop, fell down into the hold, and was so broken and bruised that he died before midnight. This is the first mischance in the whole time of the ship's building.

20th. On the return of the King from his progress, the Lady Arbella persuaded the Lords of the Council to present to his Majesty a petition drawn up and written out by herself for greater freedom. At first they were unwilling, but they agreed to humour her. When the petition was presented to the King, he was annoyed that she should subscribe herself 'Seymour', but after reading it through, he gave it to the Earl of Salisbury, who declared that he did not blush to admit that his style, for all that he is Secretary, could not rival that of a woman, for he thought it would tax all Parliaments to draw up an answer as pithy and as eloquent. The King demanded whether it was well that a woman so closely allied to the blood royal should rule her life after her own humour; and said he would reserve his answer.

21st. The merchants of Marseilles have manned three of the galleons belonging to Dansecer, who sets forth against the pirates, but to make sure of him he is allowed only two or three of his old companions, and he leaves all his wealth at Marseilles. These galleons sail for Algiers and Tunis, and Dansecer promises that if the reinforcement is sent him, he will root out those pirates in a year.

24th. These past days there have been great preparations for the launching of the great ship at Woolwich, such as a rich standard of taffety with his Majesty's arms upon the poop, and a standing in the yard for the Queen and her children, and places for the Ladies and the Council, all railed and boarded. Yesterday came Sir Robert Mansel and others to see how everything was ordered; and very late at night a messenger to M. Pett from the Court at Theobalds to search the ship's hold for fear some treacherous persons might have bored holes privily in the ship to sink her when she was launched.

This morning the dock gates were opened, and all things made ready against the tide, but the wind blowing very hard at south west kept out the flood so that it proved little better than a neap. About 11 o'clock the King came from Theobalds, though he had been very ill at ease with a scouring taken of eating grapes; and with him Prince Henry and most of the Lords of the Council. The L. Admiral, attended by the principal Officers of the Navy received the King on land out of his barge and conducted him to the place appointed, where he had dinner. After dinner came the Queen, accompanied by the Duke of York and the Lady Elizabeth and divers great Lords and Ladies. The drums and trumpets were placed on the poop and fore-castle, and the wind instruments by them; so everything was done with great royalty.

When it grew to high water and all ready, and a great close lighter had been made fast at the stern, the L. Admiral gave order to taut the crabs and screws, whereupon the ship started and would have launched but the dock gates pent her in so strait that she stuck fast between them by reason that she was nothing lifted by the tide as was expected she should; and she settled so hard on the ground that there was no possibility of launching her that tide; and besides there was such a multitude of people got into the ship that one could scarcely stir by another. The Prince himself and the L. Admiral and other Lords were upon the poop with the great gilt standing-cup ready filled with wine to name the ship as soon as she was afloat.

The King was much grieved to be thus frustrate of his expectation; and about 5 o'clock the King and the Queen and all their train departed away to Greenwich. The Prince stayed a good while conferring with the L. Admiral and Pett on what was to be done; and leaving the L. Admiral to stay to see all things performed, he took horse and rode after the King to Greenwich, promising to return after midnight.

25th. Yesterday evening after the multitudes had gone, many scavelmen and labourers made all things ready before the return of the flood; while the L. Admiral sat up all night in a chair in his chamber till the tide was come about. The beginning of the night was very fair and bright moonshine, but after midnight the weather was overcast with a very sore gust of rain, thunder and lightning for about half an hour. Notwithstanding the Prince made little account of it but came through and calling for Sir Robert Mansel came aboard the ship about 2 of the clock in the morning, almost an hour before high tide; and no sooner was he entered than word was given to set all taut, whereat the ship went away without any straining on the screws and tackles till she came clear afloat into the midst of the channel to the great joy of the Prince and all the rest. The Prince then standing on the poop with a select company, and with the ceremony of drinking in the great standing-cup, threw all the wine forwards towards the half-deck, and solemnly called her by the name of the *Prince Royal*, the trumpets sounding the while. Then he gave the standing-cup to Pett; nor would he go from the ship till he saw her fast at her moorings. In heaving down to the moorings they found that all the hawsers laid on shore for land-fasts were treacherously cut. In the interim of warping to the moorings, the Prince went down to the platform of the cook room where the ship's beer stood for the ordinary company, and there finding an old can he drew it full of beer himself and drank it off to the L. Admiral, and caused him and all the rest to do the like.

At 9 o'clock the Prince took barge, accompanied with the L. Admiral and rowed against the tide to Greenwich where he made relation of all the circumstances to the King.

The King for some days past has been sick of a flux caused by a surfeit of grapes, in so much that he was today unable to stand godfather at Greenwich to my L. of Argyle's son, and was forced to his bed, and to send to London and Cambridge for doctors, which he has never before done. At the baptism the Prince took his father's place, together with my L. of Salisbury. When the Queen heard of the King's sickness she left Hampton Court and came to Greenwich; but the King will soon leave for Royston for his hunting, to which he attributes his health, and so impatient is he to be gone that he can hardly be persuaded first to recover his strength.

30th. These 4 weeks past 333 died of the plague in the City and the Liberties.

1st October. My L. of Montgomery hath made a great feast at his house at Sheppey, where for 4 days sports were provided as hawking, hunting, fishing, dancing, and the King's Players with comedies and tragedies each day. Sir John Grey and the Earl of Essex have quarrelled, which is taken so ill by the friends of both that he hath lost their loves.

3rd. The King's Men have a new play of Ben Jonson's writing called *The Alchemist*, whereof the scene is set in London. Herein one Face, servant to a gentleman who has quit his house for fear of the plague, entertaineth a cheat and his punk. The cheat pretendeth himself to be an alchemist and to them come divers gulls all seeking speedy wealth or fortune, as Dapper a clerk who would win at games, Drugger a tobacconist who would have luck in selling, Sir Epicure Mammon that would be young again and to enjoy all costly pleasures, together with two Puritan brethren of Amsterdam with the kitchen stuff of their congregation which they would have transmuted into pure gold. But in the end these juggling companions overreach themselves and the owner of the house returning, being pleased with the jest, forgives his man. 'Tis said that Jonson had his hint of the Alchemist from Dr. John Dee. The play is now to be printed.

5th. The Lady Arbella continueth to petition the King for freedom and to be restored to his favour, and to this end her letter was presented to the King by the Queen, which he received well enough but gave no other answer than that she had eaten of the forbidden tree.

8th. There is a new book by John Davies of Hereford called *The Scourge of Folly*, containing 292 epigrams, mostly upon persons with feigned names, but some by their own; and other short poems in honour of many noble and worthy persons, with a descant upon English proverbs.

11th. The King's sickness hath continued longer than was expected, but his strength is now returning though but slowly. Today he is come to London, but tomorrow purposeth to go to Theobalds and thence to Royston. Now that the Elector Frederick IV is dead, their Majesties are the more inclined to marry the Princess Elizabeth to the young Count Frederick. In Scotland, Bishop the pirate has been taken. He had gone to Scotland to lay in provisions and under cloak of friendship was entertained by a Scot who at a time when a part of Bishop's people were away to get water attacked his ship and carried him away prisoner to his own house. Tomkins, another notorious pirate, has been condemned to death. He pleaded his own case with such boldness that had not the judge been against him he would have been acquitted for lack of testimony. He shows no fear of death, and told his judges that he regretted only that he had not killed everyone on board the ship for which he is charged. This Tomkins about two months ago in his own person presented a petition to the King, begging for some favour, but the King instantly recalled him to mind that it was many years since he had any dealings with the man, and remembering that the Venetians had complained against his piracies, his Majesty caused him to be arrested forthwith.

Baldwin the Jesuit is now lodged in the Tower, where he is well treated. He hath been thrice examined by the Council, and questioned also concerning the death of the French King, but they have got nothing out of him, and he answers boldly and acutely. He was asked what he would do if the Pope should excommunicate the King and deprive him of his Kingdom, but he answered that he stands charged with complicity in the Powder Plot, and that he must give his mind to those charges. He hath declared that there is no evidence against him and they will never get from him what they seek. As yet he has not been tortured, and it is said that the King and the Council are in a mind to send him back for they think they would gain as much in the good opinion of Catholics as they would lose credit even with the Protestants if Baldwin should remain firm under torture and die.

15th. There are many complaints made by the recusants in Yorkshire of gross abuses by magistrates, ministers and officers, and even of the L. President and the Council, who have as their agents five lawyers, all strangers and men of base condition, gaping only after gain. They complain also of the Archbishop and the High Commission of which the chief doers are a company of hungry and malicious ministers. These keep every 3 weeks or month their court and have authority to send for any recusant to offer him the Oath and to use him as they will. They have their pursuivant also with an under agent. Their manner of proceeding is that they send out process to serve upon any Catholic whom they will have appear. If the party do appear, it is rare if he escape the tendering of the Oath; if he do not appear, they set a fine upon his head of £50 or £100. These fines are certified to the Exchequer from which a writ is granted upon the party's lands and goods to the value of the sum. Upon this are sent out officers to take what goods soever they find, not respecting whose they be, whether the gentleman's own or his tenants' or some other person's. Here they will take for the fine of £100, goods worth £200 and cause them to be prized and sold at the next town at half their worth. Neither does the gentleman appear either to rescue his goods or to make his complaint, and often all is done before any notice of it come to him.

16th. The Prince's Court will be established before Christmas, and today at Richmond he himself drew up certain ordinances which he will have observed. His gentlemen shall attend him and be present at times of prayers when he goes to his private chapel, in which service he will dispense no man. He will be properly attended at tennis play; and in his standing house where he is resident, a convenient store of munitions and arms for any sudden occasion shall be kept. A standing table to be ready for the entertainment of any nobleman or stranger of account that may visit him upon the sudden. He will have his officers choose his servants without partiality or bribes; and the men of his guard shall be of known honest conversation and well qualified in some activity, as wrestling, tossing the pike, shooting or suchlike skill, and more than able only to wait with a halberd; and those places of the guard shall not be trafficked or sold. Nor shall those his servants who shall adjudge themselves to be aggrieved revenge themselves by violence or with the sword. All his servants shall receive the communion four times in the year.

21st. This day in the chapel of the Bishop of London were consecrated Bishops according to the Church of England the Archbishop of Glasgow, and the Bishops of Galloway and Brecin by the L. Bishops of London, Ely, Worcester and Rochester.

25th. By the King's command the sentence of death on Tomkins the pirate has been suspended, for he is of good family and has powerful friends. Fr. Baldwin is still in the Tower and no resolution has yet been taken in his case. From France is come in the train of the L. Wotton, Isaac Casaubon, who was librarian to the late King. Our King begged for him very earnestly, and hath given him a canonry at Canterbury worth £200 a year for he would use him in many ways as he is very learned. This man was born in Geneva but is said to hold doctrines not far removed from the Catholic.

31st. Parliament came together again on the 16th, but little is accomplished; and today they were summoned before the King at Whitehall when he made a speech blaming them for their slackness and many delays in the great matter of the Contract, by means whereof his debts daily swell and his wants increase upon him. He therefore required them to review the memorial agreed upon at the end of the last session and thereupon to send him a resolute and speedy answer whether they will proceed with the Contract, yea or no. And therein, said he, he would be beholden to them, though they did deny to proceed, because he might then resolve to cut his coat according to his cloth, which he could not do till he knew what cloth he should to make it of.

These past 4 weeks 250 persons died of the plague.

1st November. Christian, Prince of Anhalt, arrived last week, pretending that at his departing out of Cleveland he had no further purpose than to visit Count Maurice, and that after a few days at the Hague he resolved to visit his Majesty only in a capricious humour, not having commission to treat. Upon the short notice that was given at Gravesend of his arrival, the Lords assigned him to lodge in Alderman Harvey's house, where the Alderman, unwilling to undergo any such charge or trouble immediately after his shrievalty, entertained him with such sour looks as made the Prince in a few hours remove to the Dutch ordinary in Lombard Street where he remains without any further provision. To expiate some of Harvey's currishness he was treated on Monday in the Guildhall at the L. Mayor's Feast.

The Great Contract sticks like the great ship in the launching. The sum is too great for the subject to pay, and too little for his Majesty to receive.

2nd. Last week M. Hall, cupbearer to the King, coming to Sir Everard Digby's house, quarrelled with the Steward about certain words spoken to the disgrace of one of the gentlewomen of the house. The Steward cut his guts out of his belly; but he being a strong-hearted man, his bowels not being pierced, he gathered them into his belly and put his hand into his body to make room for the stowage of the tripes and sewed up the wound with pack-thread, and may live. Last week there was a robbery upon London way out of Bedfordshire, and a trunk was taken in which was £1,200, for which fact sixteen of my L. Clifton's men are apprehended at a clap and imprisoned.

Dr. Richard Bancroft, the Archbishop of Canterbury, died today of the stone. He came to his see from London to which he was appointed by Queen Elizabeth. In former years he wrote against sectaries, who laid a false imputation of papistry against him, for which some were punished in the Star Chamber; for it was he that set the Secular priests against the Jesuits, Watson against Parsons.

6th. The Contract is still being debated in the Commons, and yesterday and today they are concerned with the King's late speech, and whether they shall meet with the Lords to confer about it; but at last they resolve against it.

8th. After two days' debate, it is resolved in the Lower House to

230

send the King a letter thanking him for giving leave to treat of the matter of tenures which was accounted a rare favour, and for making known his intentions to them so that they may the more speedily grow to a resolution; and to signify that upon great and mature resolution in their House they resolve that they cannot proceed with the Contract according to the King's last declaration. But their letter is worded with great caution lest it may be inferred that they impute any contrariety between the memorial and the King's last declaration.

The Council of Virginia have published *A True Relation of the Estate of the Colony* with a confutation of the scandalous reports. Declareth it not unlawful to possess part of the land because there is no other way to bring the savages to conversion but by daily conversation. As for that report that the famine was so bitter that a man ate his dead wife, Sir Thomas Gates reporteth that in truth this man mortally hated his wife and secretly killed her, cut her in pieces and hid her in divers parts of the house. When the woman was missed and the man suspected, his house was searched and divers parts of her mangled body were found. To excuse himself, he said that when his wife died he hid her to satisfy his hunger, and so fed daily upon her. Upon his house being again searched, they found a good quantity of meal, oatmeal, beans and pease. He was therefore arraigned, confessed the murder, and was burned for that horrible villainy. Admitteth the improvidence of the company and the greediness of the mariners; nevertheless the country is indeed very rich and fertile, with abundance of woods, hemp, furs, fish, soap ashes and the rest, and a few years' labour will furnish all the defects of Virginia.

The weekly return of deaths from the plague is now but 40.

15th. Yesterday a committee of the Commons met with the Lords, when the L. Treasurer said that the King had made known his wants more particularly than experience had found fit, for what is spoken in the Parliament cannot possibly be kept secret; but these are refused, not (as he was persuaded) for want of willingness in the King to perform what he had offered or of affection in his subjects, but because of diffidence and distrusts and fears and distractions in opinions. The King is now £50,000 worse than he was at the beginning of the Parliament. Further, he wished that both Houses would join in petition to the King for ease and good of his subjects. My L. of Northampton also spoke, giving reasons to persuade a supply and answering the objections.

16th. The King called 30 of the Commons before him at Whitehall, and then said that he had sent for them to ask four questions whereunto he desired a direct answer. The first was whether they thought he was in want? Sir Fr. Bacon began to answer in an extravagant style but the King cut him short and picked out Sir Henry Neville to answer according to his conscience. Sir Henry said that he thought the King was in want. 'Then' (said the King) 'tell me whether it belongeth to you that are my subjects to relieve me or not?' To this, quoth Sir Henry, 'I must answer with a distinction: where your Majesty's expense groweth by the Commonwealth, we are bound to maintain it; otherwise not'. And so he went on to say that the King had received four subsidies and seven-fifteenths which is more than ever was given by any Parliament at any time; and yet withal they had no relief of their grievances. It is commonly said that the Parliament could be content to replenish the royal cistern of the King's Treasury were they assured that the King's largess to the Scots' prodigality would not cause a continual and remediless leak therein. Also, that one in the Lower House lately promised to produce a bill of £100,000 of debts owing to the Crown by Scotsmen who bear their creditors in hand that they shall all be paid when the new taxes come into the Exchequer.

18th. The King hath sent a message by the Speaker that he finds no expectation to receive such proportion of help as he did ever expect before he would bind himself and his posterity to any absolute bargain to depart with so many ancient flowers of the Crown. He intendeth not to entertain any further speech about the Contract, which is now at an end, and so requires the House to forbear further speech about the supply of himself or his estate until they shall have heard something more from him.

20th. The L. Cranborne, who is now again on his travels with his brother-in-law, M. Henry Howard, has come to Venice where they lodge with the Ambassador. Both young men were entertained by the City and presented to the Doge.

22nd. Yesterday and today there is much complaint in the Commons that the King should have sent for divers members to confer with them as private men; and in the end it is agreed that an order be drawn to prevent the like hereafter.

23rd. The Commons again debated impositions and among them M. Thomas Wentworth would have them signify to the King the causes of their doubts, and willingness to give supply rather than put it suddenly to the question. He would have his Majesty reminded of that saying of Constantine that it is better to have his treasure in his subjects' purses than in his treasury; and he quoted Ezechiel 'Let it suffice you, ye Kings, and take away exactions'. And, said he, how glad would we be to hear of Spain that the King there spent all upon his favourites.

24th. The Speaker declared that he had received a letter from the King signifying that he had offered divers things of grace to give them contentment for the good of his subjects; but the more he was desirous to give them contentment, he did perceive the less it was regarded, and that new grievances and complaints were raised to his dishonour. He hath commanded the House to be adjourned till the 29th.

27th. The King hath written to my L. of Salisbury by Sir Thomas Lake that he will not again meet with the Parliament which he would have dissolved with fairest show; for if they meet again, they will be in the same humour. The King saith that he hath now had patience with this assembly these 7 years, and from them received more disgraces, censures and ignominies than ever Prince did endure. He followed my Lord's advice to have patience; but he cannot have *asinine* patience, he is not made of that metal. He is now resolved that though at their next meeting they would give him supply, were it never so large, and sauce it with such taunts and disgraces as have been uttered of him and those that appertain to him (which by consequence redound to himself), nay, though it were another Kingdom, he will not accept it.

28th. A bill of extraordinaries for Sir Ralph Winwood being presented to the L. Treasurer, he replied that the King was now disfurnished of money. Request was then made that he would at least rate it and give it over for a privy seal that when the money should come in Sir Ralph might have the speedier despatch. At which my L. said, 'Sir Ralph Winwood is no poor man; he can wait well enough'; and so fell into a great passion of the penury of the Exchequer.

29th. On Sunday last Dr. Abbot, the Bishop of London, preached the funeral sermon in Lambeth for the late Archbishop who was buried there a fortnight before. There is a general speech that he will be placed in that see of Canterbury; yet some affirm that the Archbishop of York will be translated hither, and others Dr. Andrewes from Ely. Upon Saturday, late at night, 3 seminaries broke through a piece of wall at Newgate and are not yet apprehended.

1st December. The L. Deputy reports that those sent from England for the plantation in Ulster are for the most part plain country gentlemen who promise much but give little assurance of performing. If they have money, they keep it close; and the least trouble or alteration of the times will scare them away. The Scottish come with more port and better assurance, but less money. Some of them at their first entrance bargained with the natives to supply their wants, promising to get them license that the natives may stop upon their own lands as tenants, which is greatly pleasing to the natives who will strain themselves to stay the uttermost not to be removed from the places of their birth, hoping at some time to find an opportunity to cut their landlords' throats. They hate the Scottish deadly, and out of their malice towards them they even begin to affect the English better than before.

2nd. The King was so greatly angered at the report of certain speeches of Wentworth and others in the Parliament that he wrote to the Council to have them punished; to which the Lords replied there was no evidence but hearsay which is no evidence; they would be partial Judges (unless his Majesty would give the censure in his own person) and so not fitted to be accusers; and the speeches were so delivered that the party would easily evade any ill sense that he might be charged withal. To this the King has answered that the Lords are trying to cast the burden upon him, and he would not have any Councillor of his afraid to do him service. He requires them to certify what evidence Queen Elizabeth had or used in like cases when she punished this Wentworth's father and many others by commitment, and whether she proceeded on a legal formality or by authority. There were in the Lower House three Privy Councillors who would give them sufficient information and would not be afraid to deliver the truth. He therefore expected an answer as to what words were spoken and by whom, and why he should be tied to other formalities than Queen Elizabeth was.

7th. The King hath again written very bitterly to the Council, complaining of Wentworth's speech about Jotham, and wishing that Councillors in the Lower House had taken heed to a speech that concerned his honour more than the refusal of a subsidy. As to their fear lest they might have moved more bitterness in the House, he wonders what more unjust complaints they could have found than they have already, since no House but the House of Hell could have found so many as they have done. Lamenteth his ill fortune in this country to which he came with an unstained reputation. Saith he: 'Our fame and actions have been tossed like tennis balls among them, and all that spite and malice durst do to disgrace and defame us hath been used. To be short, this Lower House by their behaviour have perilled and annoyed our health, wounded our reputation, emboldened all ill-natured people, encroached upon many of our privileges, and plagued our purse with their delays.'

8th. The King is nothing pleased at the answer of the Council to his late letter but Sir Thomas Lake persuaded him that the worst punishment for the insolent speeches could be but commitment, which would raise much malice against the Scots; and it seems that the King will refrain from further action.

10th. Two priests were this day executed at Tyburn, by name Thomas Somers a secular and John Roberts a Benedictine; Roberts because he had been five times banished and last year was one of those handed over to the French Ambassador, and by him taken out of the Kingdom; Somers because being interrogated by the Bishop of London, he replied with close arguments whereby his Lordship was put down. Both might have saved themselves if they would have taken the Oath. They were accompanied to the place of execution by a crowd of about 3,000, and among them many great Ladies and Gentlemen. Many of the crowd insisted on drawing the little cart on which they were laid; many fell down on their knees to receive their blessing and kissed their feet; nor was anyone hindered except that after the quartering those who tried to gather their blood were driven back. Roberts before his death declared to the people that whoso findeth himself not in the Catholic Faith at the time of his death cannot reach salvation. He urged them to pray for the King and the Council, blaming their innocent deaths on the heresy of the Kingdom, and even the Protestants applauded him. Notwithstanding they were buried under the bodies of sixteen thieves who were also hanged, yet their bodies were carried off for relics.

Sir Hatton Cheke and Sir Thomas Dutton have fought in Flanders; Cheke is slain and Dutton sore hurt.

12th. Twelve new granaries, sufficient to hold 6,000 quarters of corn, and two store houses for 4,000 loads of coal for the poor, have now been completed in Bridewell.

15th. A few days since the best moneyed men of the City to whom the King is in debt were sent for to Whitehall, where the L. Treasurer told them their interest would be readily paid them, and prayed them to forbear their principal for a while longer and withall to lend what more they could upon very good security; but they could not be induced to any further loan nor very willingly to forbear that which is already out of their hands. Since then, the Exchequer Officers have been dealing with divers citizens in particular to lend upon private security, but their motions had very small effects, so the Treasurer will be in some pain even to furnish the expense of the approaching feast; yet doth the Prince make but one masque and the Queen two which doth cost her £600. It is expected that Marshal Laverdin will bring with him of the French King's debt 100,000 ducats at the least which makes us attend his coming with the better devotion. Lambeth House remains in readiness to lodge him, and the revenues of that archbishopric may serve to entertain him, for there appears no haste to the election of another Archbishop now that special commission is granted to the Archbishop of York and the Dean and Chapter of Canterbury to despatch the affairs of that see.

20th. The Prince hath now established his household, whereof the principal officers are Sir Thomas Challoner, Chamberlain; Sir Charles Cornwallis, Treasurer; Sir John Holles, Controller; Sir David Foulis, Groom of the Stool; Sir Robert Douglas, Master of the Horse; Sir Edward Philips, Master of the Rolls; M. Adam Newton, Secretary; Sir George More, Surveyor-General; and M. Augustin Nichols, Sergeant. Very strict orders have been made to be observed by all gentlemen and officers. The prices to be paid for flesh in the Household are: £9 10s. for an ox of 600 lbs. the four quarters; 2s. 3d. for a stone of 8 lbs. for a mutton, which should weigh 46 or 44 lbs.; veals to be by goodness only, and the price commonly 17s.; lambs at 6s. 8d. the piece.

23rd. Sir Dudley Carleton is now in Venice where he was received in public audience as the new Ambassador with Sir Henry Wotton who presented him to the Doge. Many speeches of compliment passed on both sides, the Doge praising Sir Henry for his 6 years' service in that State; who in reply spoke somewhat of the way our King's name had been mishandled; but (quoth he) the King is of profound judgement and knows how to distinguish between the government of a State and religion. As is customary the Senate bestowed a gold chain worth 1,000 crowns upon the late Ambassador. Sir Dudley brought with him 4 carriages, and 19 or 20 persons, including the women, and was freely received in every place, except that when he came to Crema from Milan the Mayor would not allow him into the city because of the laws concerning health; but by order of the Senate of Venice he and his train were allowed to proceed without further impediment, only the baggage was left behind for to be aired.

31st. The King hath dissolved the Parliament by proclamation.

Cassaubon, who since his coming to England has shown a resolve to return to France, has now accepted a living of £400 a year; but he aims higher for he would serve the King in matters of study, especially at this time when so many books are put forth.

Other Books and Plays Printed in 1610

i, ii. *A Variety of Lute Lessons* by Robert Dowland, namely: fantasies, pavins, galliards, almains, corantos and volts, selected from the best approved authors; with certain observations belonging to lute playing by John Baptisto Besardo of Visconti, and a short treatise by John Dowland. Also, *The Muses' Garden* by Robert Jones, a fifth book of 21 airs for the lute, base viol and the voice.

iii. From Cambridge by Giles Fletcher, *Christ's Victory and Triumph*, a poem in two parts.

iv. *Two Centuries of Epigrams* by John Heath, Fellow of New College in Oxford.

v. *The Catalogue of Honour*, or a treasury of true nobility, dedicated to the Earl of Salisbury by Thomas Milles, which is a collection historical of all free Monarchs as well Kings of England as Scotland, with the Princes of Wales, Dukes, Marquises, and Earls, their wives, children, alliances, families, descents and achievements of honour.

vi. Our Catholics at the English College of Douay have now brought out the Old Testament Scriptures in English, translated out of the authentical Latin, and diligently conferred with the Hebrew, Greek and other editions.

vii. This year these plays were entered for printing: Ben Jonson's *Epicoene* and *The Alchemist*, *Histriomastix* and *Ram Ally*.

ABBREVIATIONS

The following abbreviations have been used for works frequently cited:

Aubrey. *Aubrey's Brief Lives.* Edited by Oliver Lawson Dick, 1949.

Birch's *James I. The Court and Times of James the First.* Edited from the collections of T. Birch by the Author of *Memoirs of Sophia Dorothea* [R. E. Williams], 2 vols., 1848.

Birch's *Pr. Henry. The Life of Henry, Prince of Wales. . . .* By Thomas Birch, 1760.

Bodley. *Letters of Sir Thomas Bodley to Thomas James, First Keeper of the Bodleian Library.* Edited by G. W. Wheeler, 1926.

Brodrick. *The Life and Work of Blessed Robert Francis Cardinal Bellarmine, S.J., 1542-1621.* By James Brodrick, S.J., 2 vols., 1928.

Buccleuch. *Report on the Manuscripts of the Duke of Buccleuch and Queensberry, preserved at Montagu House, Whitehall.* Historical Manuscripts Commission.

Chamberlain. *The Letters of John Chamberlain.* Edited by N. E. McClure, 2 vols., 1939.

Chapel. *The Old Cheque-book of the Chapel Royal.* Edited by E. F. Rimbault, Camden Society, 1872.

CJ. The Journals of the House of Commons from November the 8th 1547 to March the 2nd 1628, 1803. [vol. i.]

CSPIre. Calendar of the State Papers relating to Ireland. . . . Edited by Rev. C. W. Russell and John P. Prendergast, vols. i, ii, iii, 1874.

CSPVen. Calendar of State Papers and Manuscripts, relating to English Affairs . . . in the archives of Venice and other Libraries of Northern Italy. Edited by Horatio F. Brown, vols. x, xi, xii, 1905.

De Fonblanque. *Annals of the House of Percy.* By E. B. De Fonblanque, 2 vols., 1887.

De L'Isle. *Report on the Manuscripts of Lord De L'Isle and Dudley, preserved at Penshurst Place.* Historical Manuscripts Commission.

Devereux. *Lives and Letters of the Devereux, Earls of Essex . . . 1540-1646.* By the Hon. W. B. Devereux, 2 vols., 1853.

DNB. Dictionary of National Biography.

Downshire. *Manuscripts of the Marquis of Downshire preserved at Easthampstead Park, Berks.* Vol. ii. *Papers of William Trumbull the Elder, 1605-1610.* Edited by W. K. Purnell and A. B. Hinds.

Edwards. *The Life of Sir Walter Ralegh.* By Edward Edwards, 2 vols., 1868.

III Eliz. J. A Last Elizabethan Journal . . . 1599-1603. By G. B. Harrison, 1933. (Three vols. in one 1938.)

Eliz. Stage. The Elizabethan Stage. By E. K. Chambers, 4 vols., 1923.

238

Gardiner. *History of England . . . 1603-1642.* By S. R. Gardiner, 10 vols., 1893.

Gosse. *The Life and Letters of John Donne.* By Edmund Gosse, 2 vols., 1899.

Grimestone. *A General History of the Netherlands.* By Edward Grimestone, 1608.

Hawarde. *Les Reportes del Cases in Camera Stellata, 1593-1609.* By William Hawarde. Edited by W. P. Baildon, 1894.

Howell. *Cobbett's Complete Collection of State Trials,* vol. 2, 1603-27. Compiled by T. B. Howell, 1809.

Howes. *Annales, or a General Chronicle of England. Begun by John Stowe . . . Continued . . . until 1631.* By Edmund Howes. The pagination is so wild that I have omitted it.

I Jac. J. A Jacobean Journal . . . 1603-1606. By G. B. Harrison, 1941.

Jonson. *Ben Jonson.* Edited by C. H. Herford, Percy and Evelyn Simpson, Oxford, 11 vols., 1925-52. The relevant volume of the Commentary should also be consulted.

Lancaster. *The voyages of Sir John Lancaster to the East Indies . . . with abstracts of the Journals of voyages to the East Indies.* Edited by C. R. Markham, Hakluyt Society, 1877.

Lodge. *Illustrations of British History. . . .* By E. Lodge, 3 vols., 1838.

Loseley. *The Loseley Manuscripts.* Edited by A. J. Kempe, 1836.

Mathew. *The Life of Sir Tobie Mathew.* By A. H. Mathew, 1907.

Nugae. Nugae Antiquae: being a miscellaneous collection of original papers. . . . By Sir John Harington, etc. Edited by T. Park, 2 vols., 1804.

Parl. Deb. Parliamentary Debates in 1610. Edited from the notes of a member of the House of Commons. By S. R. Gardiner, Camden Society, 1862.

PC. MS. Additional 11,402. A manuscript Abstract of the Registers of the Privy Council 1556-1610, in the British Museum.

Pett. *The Autobiography of Phineas Pett.* Edited by W. G. Perrin. Navy Records Society, 1918.

Plague. The weekly lists of plague deaths were recorded in John Bell's *London Remembrancia,* 1665-6; reprinted in *English Dramatic Companies,* by J. Tucker Murray, 1910, 2 : 186-7, 174-5. The weekly list was issued in London each Thursday. Bell's accuracy can often be checked from the letter writers.

Progresses. The Progresses, processions and magnificent festivities of King James the First. . . . By J. Nichols, 4 vols., 1828.

Purchas. *Hakluytas Posthumus or Purchas His Pilgrims.* By Samuel Purchas, 1625. References are to the Maclehose Edition, 20 vols., 1906.

Rutland. *The Manuscripts of the Duke of Rutland preserved at Belvoir Castle.* Historical Manuscripts Commission.

Salisbury. *Manuscripts of the Marquis of Salisbury, preserved at Hatfield House.* References to 'xix' are to the Calendar; otherwise to the original volumes.

Sanderson. *The Travels of John Sanderson in the Levant, 1584–1602.* . . . Edited by Sir William Foster, Hakluyt Society, 1931.

Scott. *Secret History of the Court of James the First:* containing, I. Francis Osborne's *Traditional Memoirs.* II. Sir Anthony Weldon's *Court and Character of King James.* III. *Aulicus Coquinariae* [an answer to Weldon]. IV. Sir Edward Peyton's *Divine Catastrophe of the House of Stuarts.* Edited by Sir Walter Scott, 2 vols., 1811.

Shirley. *Discourse of the Turks.* By Sir Thomas Shirley. Edited by E. Denison Ross, Camden Miscellany, vol. 16, 1936.

Smith. See Virginia below.

SP 14. State Papers Domestic for the reign of King James I, preserved in the Public Record Office in London. These are briefly summarized in the *Calendars of State Papers Domestic.* Edited by Mary Anne Everett Green, 1857.

Spedding. *The Life and Letters of Francis Bacon.* By James Spedding, 7 vols., 1861 [vols. viii–xiv in the Spedding-Ellis edition of Bacon's Works].

SR. A Transcript of the Register of the Company of Stationers of London, 1554–1640. Edited by E. Arber, 5 vols., 1875–94.

STC. A Short Title catalogue of books printed in England, Scotland and Ireland . . . and abroad, 1475–1640. Compiled by A. W. Pollard and G. R. Redgrave, 1926.

Tierney's Dodd. *Dodd's Church History of England.* . . . With notes, additions and a continuation by the Rev. M. A. Tierney, 5 vols., 1843.

Virginia. The longer accounts of events in Virginia are taken from George Percy's *Observations* (in Purchas, 18 : 403–540), and the various records and pamphlets printed in *Travels and Works of Captain John Smith.* Edited by Edward Arber and A. G. Bradley, 2 vols., 1910. These are *A True Relation . . . Virginia,* 1608; *The Proceedings of the English Colony in Virginia . . . 1603–1612*; *The General History of Virginia,* 1624. Where two or more accounts have been combined the reference is to 'Virginia'.

Wilbraham. *The Journal of Sir Roger Wilbraham . . . 1593–1616.* Edited by H. S. Scott, Camden Society, 1902.

Wilson. *The History of Great Britain, being the Life and Reign of King James the First.* . . . By Arthur Wilson, Esq., 1653.

Winwood. *Memorials of Affairs of State . . . from the original papers of . . . Sir Ralph Winwood.* By Edmund Sawyer, 3 vols., 1725.

Wotton. *The Life and Letters of Sir Henry Wotton.* By Logan Pearsall Smith, 2 vols., 1907.

Yonge. *Diary of Walter Yonge, Esq.* . . . *1604 to 1628.* Edited by George Roberts, Camden Society, 1848.

NOTES

1607

January:
1st. *CSPVen* 10:739; from a long and very well-informed report on England, by the retiring Venetian Ambassador, Nicolo Molin.
3rd. *STC* 12918.
6th. *Progresses*, 2:103–21.
7th. *SR* 3:334; *STC* 24719.
8th. *CSPVen* 10:666.
10th. Tierney, 4:74; *CSPVen* 10:666.
12th. Shirley.
15th. Purchas, 18:403.
18th. SP 14/28:5; *STC* 23138—a sensible little book.
21st. *STC* 7261.
23rd. Howes; *STC* 10011.
28th. *CSPIre* 2:123.
30th. Salisbury, xix:15–16.

February:
2nd. SP 14/26:41.
6th. Chamberlain, 90.
13th. *CJ* 1:333–4. The Parliament first assembled on 19th March 1604. The third session opened on 18th November 1606, and was adjourned on 17th December.
14th. Birch's *Pr. Henry*, pp. 81–3. *CJ* 1:334–5.
16th. *CJ* 1:335–6.
17th. *CSPVen* 10:691; Spedding, 3:307–25.
20th. *STC* 7261; 3434.
21st. *SR* 3:347; *STC* 3434.
22nd. Howell, 2:559–69.
24th. *STC* 7261.

25th. *CJ* 1:340–2.
26th. Howell, 2:567–75; *STC* 7261.
27th. *STC* 7261; *CJ* 1:343–4.
28th. *CJ* 1:344: Salisbury, xix:59.

March:
1st. Winwood, 2:277, 285.
3rd. *CJ* 1:346.
5th. *CJ* 1:348.
6th. *SR* 3:343; *STC* 3671.
7th. SP 14/26:79.
8th. *The Autobiography and Diary of James Melville*, edited by Robert Pitcairn, Woodrow Society, 1842, pp. 653–709.
9th. Salisbury, xix:163.
14th. *CJ* 1:352.
17th. Lodge, 3:195. See *I Jac. J.*, p. 314.
20th. Bradley, 2:215–21.
21st. *SR* 3:344; *STC* 20340.
23rd. *CJ* 1:353–54.
24th. *CJ* 1:354; Wilson, p. 54; Weldon (in Scott, 1:374–5). Warrants for liveries and payments for Carr's first employment for 30th August and 31st October 1604 are preserved in SP 14/9:27, 91.
26th. *CSPVen* 10:716.
28th. *CJ* 1:356.
30th. *Nugae*, 2:48–50; *DNB*.
31st. *CJ* 1:357–63. The King's speech, which was long and sensible, is fully reported in *CJ*.

April:
1st. Purchas, 2:502.

April:
2nd. Salisbury, xix:61, 63.
3rd. *Chapel*, p. 171.
5th. *Chapel*, p. 171-2.
7th. Salisbury, 124:152.
12th. Winwood, 2:302-3; *CSPVen* 10:720-22.
15th. SP 14/27:7.
17th. Purchas, 13:294.
19th. *An Elizabethan Recusant House*, edited by A. C. Southern, 1954, p. 54.
20th. *SR* 3:347; *STC* 6532. The play was presumably acted at the Fortune, as the prologue (imitated from *Henry V*) begins, 'The charms of silence through this square be thrown'. The Fortune, unlike the Globe, was square. Howes; *STC* 3434.
21st. *CJ* 1:364.
25th. *CSPVen* 10:731.
29th. *CSPVen* 10:730.

May:
1st. Wilson, p. 54; Weldon (Scott, 1:375).
2nd. *CJ* 1:366-68. *SR* 3:348; *STC* 15540—a poor poem, but interesting as one of several attempts to beatify Queen Elizabeth I.
4th. *CJ* 1:368.
6th. *CJ* 1:370.
7th. *CJ* 1:370-1.
10th. As for 8th March, p. 709. *CSPIre* 2:179, 186, 195.
12th. Winwood, 2:300. For Garnet's Straw see *I Jac. J.*, p. 337.
15th. Howes; Yonge, p. 14.
16th. *SR* 3:349; *STC* 18336. An obviously topical and personal poem in the vein of *A Lover's Complaint*.

18th. *CJ* 1:375.
22nd. *Progresses*, 2:127; Jonson, 7:151-8.
24th. Bodley, p. 167.
25th. Shirley, pp. 28-9; Wotton 1:384-91.
27th. *CJ* 1:376.
28th. Grimestone, p. 1368; *SR* 3:350; *STC* 21507; *CSPVen* 11:1.
29th. SP 14/27:12

June:
2nd. Lodge 3:197.
3rd. Rawdon Hastings MSS 4:192; *CSPIre* 2:236, 273.
4th. *CJ* 1:378-9.
8th. *SR* 3:352; *STC* 18592.
9th. *CJ* 1:381.
10th. Hawarde, pp. 322-3, 326-7. Wilbraham, pp. 98-9. Sir Walter Ralegh was a notable amateur of medicine. There was some poetic justice in Popham's end, for he had presided at Ralegh's trial in 1603. Winwood 2:308.
11th. *SR* 3:353; *STC* 14690. Full of odd and interesting details.
12th. Howes. Rawdon Hastings MSS 4:192-94. Reynolds and some others were hanged.
14th. Yonge, p. 14.
15th. Grimstone, p. 1370.
16th. *CJ* 1:384; *CSPVen* 11:14.
17th. Spedding, 3:346-61.
18th. *CJ* 1:384-5.
20th. *CJ* 1:388-9.
25th. Howell, 2:534-59.
29th. *STC* 6417. Though a poor play, it is interesting for its many topicalities, and as one of the few plays surviving which deal with contemporary persons and events.

June:
30th. Gosse, 1:156–61. *Biathanatos* was posthumously printed in 1648.

July:
1st. *CSPVen* 11:24.
3rd. *Progresses*, 2:135.
4th. *CJ* 1:391; Statutes, *Anno IV Jacobi Regis.*
5th. Howes.
7th. Tierney's Dodd iv, App. xxix; SP 14/28:5; Mathew, pp. 100–1.
9th. Salisbury, 19:177.
10th. *CSPIre* 2:279, 281.
13th. Salisbury, 19:179–80.
16th. *Progresses*, 2:136–43; Howes; Jonson, 11:586.
21st. *CSPVen* 11:36.
24th. Buccleuch, 3:117–18; *STC* 8402.
28th. *SR* 3:357; *STC* 16622. This doggerel effusion is remarkable for the number of classical and biblical allusions.
29th. *CSPVen* 11:43. *Original Letters . . .*, edited by Henry Ellis, 3rd Series, 1825, 2:85–8.
31st. Grimestone, pp. 1374–8. *SR* 3:357; *STC* 25635. The dialogue is lively, and—as a social document—the play stresses the fact that betrothal was regarded as legal marriage. Scarborrow repeatedly insists that by his enforced marriage he was compelled to commit adultery.

August:
2nd. Birch's *Pr. Henry*, pp. 87–9.
5th. *CSPVen* 11:45.

8th. Salisbury, 19:210.
12th. *CSPVen* 11:50. For further information on Stephen Bogdan, see Sanderson, pp. xxxv–xxxvii. If not actually an impostor, he was at least an optimist.
14th. *CSPIre* 2:313, 315, 316.
15th. *CSPVen* 11:35.
18th. SP 14/28:34.
19th. *CSPVen* 11:52–3. The Grand Duke was Ferdinand de Medici.
20th. Smith, lxx, 385–90; Purchas, 18:403–16.
25th. Salisbury, 19:235–6.
27th. SP 14/28:37; Buccleuch, 3:118–19.
31st. Plague. The deaths from plague exceeded 30 a week from 9th July to 19th November in this year.

September:
2nd. *CSPVen* 11:59.
6th. Salisbury, 19:242.
7th. Grimestone, pp. 1374–5.
9th. *CSPVen* 11:71.
12th. SP 14/28:51; *CSPVen* 11:74.
15th. Purchas, 13:294–313.
16th. Lodge, 3:201, 203–4; SP 14/28:51.
17th. Lodge, 3:200–2.
21st. Wotton, 1:397–8.
27th. Winwood, 2:340–2. For the previous effort of the Spaniards in Ireland see *III Eliz. J.* under 'Kinsale'.
28th. *CSPIre* 2:343, 354, 358.
29th. *CSPIre* 2:380.
30th. Plague; *CJ* 1:391.

October:
2nd. Buccleuch, 3:118.
7th. *Nugae*, 2:390–7; Wilson, pp. 54–5.
10th. Salisbury, 19:241.

October:
12th. Howes; *Progresses*, 2:155. Howes.
13th. Lodge, 3:205.
14th. *CSPVen* 11:93; *SR* 3:362; *STC* 21514. The play caused a great sensation and was recorded in two pamphlets and a ballad. It is possible that this account was the remote source for Donne's famous sonnet 'At the four corners of the imagined world . . .'
15th. Tierney's Dodd, iv, 24.
16th. Hawarde, pp. 328–30.
20th. *Nugae*, 2:390–7.
21st. *DNB; John Gerard: the autobiography of an Elizabethan*, translated and ed. by Philip Caraman, S.J., 1951, pp. 35–6.
24th. *SR* 3:362; *STC* 21366.
27th. *CSPIre* 2:419.
31st. Lodge, 3:206; Plague.

November:
1st. Tierney's Dodd (in Latin), iv. App. xxv, xxviii, xxx: in English in *STC* 14344, 14400–2.
2nd. Wotton, 1:404–6.
3rd. *SR* 3:363; *STC* 6496; *John Stow's Survey of London*, ed. by C. L. Kingsford, 1908. 2:118.
5th. *CSPIre* 2:434, 412.
7th. Lodge, 2:206–7.

10th. *STC* 5900; preface dated 3rd November. For the later troubles of the author, see pp. 183–8.
12th. Pett, pp. 31–2.
13th. Tierney's Dodd, iv, App. xxx.
15th. *STC* 8409; *CSPVen* 11:123.
17th. Grimestone, pp. 1383–6; Lodge, 3:208–9.
18th. *CSPVen* 11:122.
19th. Hawarde, pp. 341–3.
20th. Winwood, 2:348–9.
25th. *CSPVen* 11:126.
27th. Hawarde, pp. 343–6.
28th. Winwood, 2:358.
29th. Lodge, 3:212–13.
30th. Plague.

December:
1st. Salisbury, 228/14.
6th. SP 14/28:100.
9th. *CSPVen* 11:131.
10th. Howes.
24th. *Progresses*, 2:161; Chamberlain, 94; Osborne (in Scott, 1:274–6).
28th. Howes.
31st. Bodley, pp. 170, 173.

Books and Plays Printed 1607:
i. *STC* 19403.
ii. *STC* 24967; a useful account of contemporary psychosomatic notions.
iii. *STC* 20778.
iv. *SR* 3:340–66; *Eliz. Stage*, 4:389–91.

1608

January:
4th. Chamberlain, 93, 94, 95, 96.
5th. Chamberlain, 95.
7th. Chamberlain, 96; *Eliz. Stage*, 3:382; *CSPVen* 11:148, 149; De Fonblanque, 2:292.
11th. *CJ* 1:391.
14th. *Progresses*, 2:164–74; Jonson, 7:181–94; *Eliz. Stage*, 4:379; *CSPVen* 11:154.
15th. Howes; Chamberlain, 96; *STC* 11403.
17th. *STC* 11403.
19th. Grimestone, p. 1391.
20th. Wotton, 1:399, 407–8.
21st. *CSPVen* 11:160.
22nd. Lodge, 3:224.
26th. Lodge, 3:224–5. PC.
28th. *CSPIre* 2:517, 756.

February:
2nd. Howes.
7th. Chamberlain, 97; PC; Salisbury, 120/66.
9th. *STC* 14400–8; Brodrick, 2:186. The book first appeared without any author's name but there was no secret about the authorship. It includes full reprints of the Papal Briefs (the first of which reprints the Oath of Allegiance in full), as well as Bellarmine's letter to Blackwell; *CSPVen* 11:177.
10th. Chamberlain, 97; *Progresses*, 2:176–89; Jonson, 7:243–63. For the bridegroom's part in the Gowry affair, see *III Eliz. J.*, pp. 104–9.
11th. Chamberlain, 97.

13th. SP 14/31:66. The original reads '700 or 8000 yards'.
14th. *CSPVen* 11:151, 153, 156, 181, 210. As usual in such affairs there are contradictory accounts. The case gave Wotton and the Venetian Senate much trouble.
15th. SR 3:370; *STC* 21625; Wotton,1:415; the apron was such a sensation that it was reported to the Pope, and is mentioned by Bacon in *Novum Organum*.
16th. Grimestone, pp. 1392–5; Salisbury, 120/52, 76.
17th. *DNB*.
23rd. Salisbury, 120/19.
26th. Grimestone, pp. 1396–1400.
27th. Downshire, 2:41.
28th. PC.

March:
7th. *Eliz. Stage*, 3:257.
10th. Howes.
11th. SP 14/31:73; *Eliz. Stage*, 2:53; 3:257.
12th. Wotton, 1:414.
14th. SR 3:372; *STC* 6480. By Dekker who claimed authorship in *Lanthorn and Candlelight*.
24th. *CSPVen* 11:215, 216.
25th. Grimestone, p. 1409.
29th. *Eliz. Stage*, 3:258.
31st. Wotton, 1:415; Gardiner, 3:66; Tierney's Dodd, iv, App. xxxi.

April:
1st. Pett, pp. lxi–lxiii.

April:
4th. *STC* 19067; preface dated 4th April.
8th. Devereux, 2:232–3.
9th. Grimestone, pp. 1406–8.
10th. Lodge, 3:232–5; Tierney's Dodd, iv, App. xxxii; PC.
11th. PC.
12th. Howes.
13th. Tierney's Dodd, iv, App. xxxii.
19th. Wilbraham, pp. 98–9; *DNB.*
21st. *SR* 3:375; *STC* 25262.
25th. Osborne (Scott, 1:280).
28th. *CSPIre* 2:686, 687, 689.
29th. Howes.

May:
6th. Wilbraham, pp. 99–100.
10th. Purchas, 6:367–406.
14th. *STC* 5808; PC (18th April).
24th. Virginia; PC.
26th. PC.
28th. Downshire, 2:59–60.
29th. *CSPIre* 2:718.

June:
1st. Loseley, pp. 264–5.
4th. Salisbury, 195/11.
5th. Tierney's Dodd, iv, App. iii.
7th. SP 14/34:10, 11; Howell, 2:659–95; *STC* 7540.
8th. PC; *Eliz. Stage*, 3:428. Presumably Marston was the author of one of the satirical plays.
12th. *CSPIre* 2:737.
18th. MSS. Addit. 15,476—Memoirs of Sir Nicholas Overbury; Weldon (in Scott, 1:375–7).
20th. Salisbury, 125/164.
23rd. Howes, 892.
25th. Wilbraham, pp. 99, 100
30th. Salisbury, 195/25.

July:
5th. *Eliz. Stage*, 3:222–3; Aubrey, p. 21; see *II Eliz. J.*, pp.106–7.
6th. SP 14/35:6.
7th. Chamberlain, 98; Purchas, 18:478; Smith, p. xciii.
10th. Salisbury, 195/30; Chamberlain, 98.
13th. *CSPVen* 11:268, 197.
14th. SP 14/35:17. The Latin words are thus translated in Cooper's *Thesaurus*, 1578: *cantus, cantio:* a song, an incantation. *cantilena:* a bragging report. *balatrones:* rascals, babblers (with a pun on ballad-makers). *spina:* a thorn. *dolium:* a tun. The comment is Dudley Carleton's.
15th. Chamberlain, 99. The Dean was Dr. John Overall whose lady was notorious for her beauty and frailty. Aubrey (p. 226) records a ballad of this scandal.
16th. *CSPIre* 2:817, 818.
20th. *CSPVen* 11:291.
21st. *CSPIre* 2:843.
29th. SP 14/35:31.
31st. Smith, p. 445.

August:
1st. Spedding, 4:96–104.
7th. SP 14/35:76, 77.
9th. *Eliz. Stage*, 3:214, 55–8, 508–10.
10th. *CSPVen* 11:270.
12th. *CSPIre* 3:7.
13th. *SR* 3:388; *STC* 1980. Pleasantly nostalgic in its old-world flavour of *Rosalynd* and *Menaphon.* Pett, pp. 34–6; *SR* 3:388; *STC* 22795.
18th. Grimestone, pp. 1409–10.

August:

19th. Howell, 2:675–707.
28th. Purchas, 13:313–32: the *mermaid* is at p. 318.
29th. Purchas, 13:275–6. A *morse* is a walrus. Cherry Island lies south of Greenland.
30th. *CSPVen* 11:323.
31st. *CSPVen* 11:324; Plague.

September:

3rd. Salisbury, 126/32.
4th. *CJ* 1:391–2.
5th. Salisbury, 195/45.
14th. Salisbury, 126/51. The mine proved a failure.
15th. Grimestone, p. 1412.
17th. Salisbury, 195/48; Lodge, 3:242–5. See 8th November 1608.
19th. *CSPIre* 3:40.
20th. SP 14/36:23; *Liber Famelicus*, by Sir James Whitelocke, ed. J. Bruce. Camden Soc., 1858, pp. 7–11; Donne's Letters, 1654, pp. 52–3 (Gosse, 1:192–3). See *III Eliz. J.*, pp. 274–5. Whitelock was a Parolles in real life (perhaps even the living original), whose doings excited much contemptuous interest.
21st. *SR* 3:390; *STC* 744.
24th. Wotton, 1:435–5.
27th. Chamberlain, 100.
29th. *CSPVen* 11:340; *Responsio Matthaei Torti . . . 1608*; summarized in Brodrick, 2:191–6; Pett, p. 37.
30th. Plague.

October:

3rd. *STC* 5808; *SR* 3:391; *STC* 20985.
10th. Gosse, 1:208.

12th. *Progresses*, 2:210–11.
14th. Chamberlain, 103; Downshire, 2:76.
16th. *CSPVen* 11:354; Gardiner, 2:31.
17th. Grimestone, p.1412; *CSPVen* 11:346; *SR* 3:392, 375; *STC* 24395–6.
18th. Salisbury, 134/123.
20th. Salisbury, 134/104.
21st. Salisbury, 126/67; Wotton, 1:473; Gosse, 1:199; Chamberlain, 101. Mole (or Molle) remained a prisoner of the Inquisition for nearly thirty years until his death at the age of 80, steadfastly resisting all efforts to convert him, to the deserved admiration of his friends.
22nd. Salisbury, 134/98. Since this letter was to be shown to the Council, doubtless it was well publicized.
24th. Salisbury, 126/68; *CSPIre* 3:100.
25th. *SR* 3:392; *STC* 6485.
28th. Chamberlain, 102; Plague.

November:

1st. De L'Isle, 4:60–1; *CSPVen* 11:376,391; Chamberlain, 103.
2nd. *Chapel*, pp. 140, 132.
10th. Chamberlain, 104; according to the scandalmongers, the Scots in general did not believe the official version of the Gowry story; *SR* 3:393; (see *III Eliz. J.*, pp. 104–9); *STC* 12894.
11th. Chamberlain, 104.
20th. *STC* 25771; printed at St. Omer. Preface dated 1st October.
27th. SP 14/37:98.

November:

28th. De L'Isle, 4:75. In accounts of the murder of Sir Thomas Overbury it is usually stated that Essex returned to England 'about Christmas 1609'.

30th. Salisbury, 126/75; Osborne (in Scott, 1:233-4)—not dated, but 'before Somerset had either wife or beard'. Plague.

December:

1st. Chamberlain, 105.

2nd. Salisbury, 126/77.

5th. *SR* 3:397. The printer was William Jaggard, and the *Register* notes 'Provided that yf any question or trouble growe hereof. Then he shall answere and discharge yt at his owne losse and costes.' *STC* 13366.

9th. Chamberlain, 105.

12th. Purchas, 14:358-400.

15th. Pett, pp. lxvi-lxix.

16th. Chamberlain, 106.

17th. *CSPVen* 11:393.

20th. De L'Isle, 4:91.

23rd. Chamberlain, 107.

28th. *DNB.*

Other Books and Plays printed in 1608:

i. *STC* 19697: Perkins was a famous preacher and a popular writer. His book gives the full Puritan belief in witchcraft in all its fundamentalist horror.

ii. *STC* 12374: Grimestone's book was entered on 4th June 1607, but the narrative is continued to September 1608.

iii. *STC* 1445. The preface to Sir Edward Coke is dated 10th February 1608: the book may belong to 1608-9.

iv. *STC* 17927: no printer's name. A reader who can surmount the symbolic and pietistic obscurities of this book will ultimately find some acute economic reasoning.

v. *SR* 3:372-96; *Eliz. Stage*, 4:391. *A Yorkshire Tragedy*, though rightly omitted from the Canon, is inscribed ' by William Shakespeare'. No copy of a quarto of *Antony and Cleopatra* is known.

1609

June:

2nd. *SR* 3:411; *STC* 25022. The book was entered on 2nd June 'provided that yt is not to be printed without further Aucthoritie'. To the entry was added the note 'Aucthorised to be printed by master Richard Etkins 12 Junij 1609 And yet he is forbidden to prynt it in Court this day.' Probably the book had already been printed by the 2nd.

3rd. Howes.

5th. Purchas, 19:1–2.

8th. Birch's *James I*, 1:99–100; Winwood, 3:51.

10th. Pett, pp. 69–70.

15th. *CSPVen* 11:539.

19th. Pett, p. 77; Chambers' *William Shakespeare*, 1:555; *SR* 3:410 (20th May); *STC* 22353; Edward Alleyn bought a copy of the *Sonnets* on 19th June for which he paid 5*d.*

20th. *SR* 3:414; *STC* 12032.

23rd. Howes.

July:

3rd. *CSPIre* 3:410.

5th. *CSPVen* 11:555, 592; *STC* 626; Howes.

11th. *STC* 4192. Preface dated 11th July. A sensible book, obviously the result of intelligent observation and practical experience—unlike most contemporary pronouncements on bees.

12th. Wotton, 1:457. This pleasing custom of setting up the *impresas* of distinguished students was also followed at the University of Padua, where many still remain in the court and great hall.

14th. *CSPVen* 11:554.

20th. Gosse, 1:230–1. The episode seems almost incredible, but it is recorded by Donne in a letter (undated) in the 1651 collection which can be dated by internal evidence.

24th. Lodge, 3:266–7.

27th. *CSPVen* 11:576, 579, 580.

31st. Lodge, 3:268–73.

August:

3rd. Birch's *James I*, 1:100. J. Tucker Murray notes (in *English Dramatic Companies, 1558–1642*, 1910, p. 2:175) that in 1609 or thereabouts playing was allowed until the weekly plague deaths rose to 40; previously the figure had been 30. These were lean months for the players, for plague deaths exceeded 40 a week from 28th July 1608 to 30th November 1609 with the exceptions only of the weeks ending 29th December 1608 (39 deaths), 2nd and 16th March 1609 (32, 33) and 15th June (36). From 7th December 1609 to 5th July 1610, the rate fell below 40, but it rose again from 12th July to 8th November 1610.

4th. *CSPIre* 3:454.

7th. Birch's *Pr. Henry*, pp. 161–5.

10th. *STC* 22331–2; *SR* 3:400.

16th. De L'Isle, 4:145.

20th. *Advice to His Son*, by Henry Percy, 8th Earl of Northumberland, ed. by G. B. Harrison, 1930; Wood's *Athenæ Oxonienses*.

26th. Sanderson, pp. 240, xxxiii–v.

August:
29th. *DNB.*
30th. Purchas, 13:277-91.
31st. Downshire, 2:121; *CSPVen* 11:599.

September:
2nd. Purchas, 13:281.
4th. Wotton, 1:465-7.
8th. *CSPVen* 11:578.
10th. De L'Isle, 4:151-2, 154.
16th. *CJ* 1:392.
17th. Wotton, 1:106; *CSPVen* 11:635; *Sydney Papers*, 2:325.
27th. Downshire, 2:147.
29th. *CSPVen* 11:562, 606, 614, 615, 618, 625; Wotton, 1:463-5, 471-4.
30th. Plague.

October:
4th. Downshire, 2:154.
5th. SP 14/48:81.
16th. *SR* 3:419; *STC* 24148.
19th. *CSPVen* 11:685.
20th. Winwood, 3:66-8.
23rd. *CSPIre* 3:502.
26th. Plague.
29th. *CSPIre* 3:504, 511.

November:
2nd. *CSPVen* 11:643; Downshire, 2:191.
3rd. *CSPVen* 11:495, 610, 648.
7th. Winwood, 3:73.
9th. *CSPVen* 11:714, 564.
10th. Downshire, 2:182, 184, 185; Rutland, 1:419; *CSPVen* 11:719.
15th. SP 14/47:109; dated '? August' in Calendar, 'November' in the original MS.
22nd. Purchas, 13:333-74.
23rd. Downshire, 2:187, 191.

25th. Downshire, 2:179-80.
28th. Rutland, 1:420-1.
30th. Downshire, 2:195-6; *CSPVen* 11:575, 663, 687. Dansecer is variously spelled Dantziger, Dancicker, Dansker, Danzer, Dancer, *alias* Capt. Simon Simonson. Purchas, 18:577; Plague.

December:
1st. Downshire, 2:195; Virginia.
6th. *CSPVen* 11:724, 730, 736.
7th. *Apologia S.R.E. Cardinalis Bellarmini . . . in qua Apologia refellitur Praefatio Monitoria Regis eiusdem*, 1609. Summarized in Brodrick, 2:217-24; *CSPVen* 11:738; Plague.
10th. SP 14/50:34.
11th. SP 14/50:44.
12th. De L'Isle, 4:170; *CSPVen* 11:728; Wotton, 1:476-7.
14th. Downshire, 2:199, 201; *SR* 3:425; *STC* 11564.
16th. *CSPIre* 3:528, 537.
21st. Downshire, 2:204.
22nd. *STC* 12805.
29th. *CSPVen* 11:752; *STC* 12805.
30th. Pett, pp. 75-6; *CSPVen* 11:778; Chamberlain, 116.
31st. *Progresses*, 2:266-7.

Other Books and Plays printed in 1609:
i. *STC* 6500.
ii. *STC* 13014; argued quite seriously; for the 'act', see 14th July 1608.
iii. *STC* 10652.
iv. *STC* 19936.
v. *STC* 20607.
vi. *SR* 3:400-3; *Eliz. Stage*, 4:391-2.

1610

January:
3rd. Winwood, 3:95–6, 99–100.
5th. *CSPVen* 11:763.
6th. *Progresses*, 2:269–82; Howes; Chamberlain, 117.
7th. As for 6th January.
12th. Downshire, 2:216–17; *CSPIre* 3:571, 574.
13th. Chamberlain, 117
18th. Downshire, 2:219, 221; *CSPVen* 11:774, 609.
25th. Winwood, 3:98, 104. There is a good engraving of the famous turban in *Progresses*, 2:430–1.
26th. PC; Downshire, 2:xix.
28th. *CSPIre* 3:588.
31st. *CSPVen* 11:783.

February:
1st. *CSPVen* 11:786; *SR* 3:425 (2nd December 1609); *STC* 7048. *Pseudo-Martyr* was much discussed; it is very long and very dull, with hardly a good paragraph throughout, for Donne never perceived the principles at issue. However, the book achieved its immediate purpose and Donne won royal patronage.
2nd. *CSPVen* 11:792. Little Charles at this time was aged 10, and, as the Ambassadors note in this report, and elsewhere, 'his father's and his mother's joy'.
5th. *CSPVen* 11:761. Those who have had to do with the double calendar will sympathize with the Doge.
6th. Howes.
8th. *CSPVen* 11:794, 795.
10th. *CJ* 1:392.
11th. *CSPVen* 11:801, 802, 803.
14th. *CJ* 1:392–3.
15th. *CSPVen* 11:803; *Parl. Deb.*, pp. 1–9 (where further details are given).
17th. Winwood, 3:103.
19th. *Parl. Deb.*, pp. 9–13. *CSPVen* 10:739, from Molin's report on England (for January 1607).
20th. Bradley, 2:237–40; Winwood, 3:117.
21st. *SR* 3:429; *STC* 6029. The preacher was the father of Richard Crashaw, the poet.
23rd. Downshire, 2:247.
24th. *Parl. Deb.*, pp. 13–16.
25th. *CSPVen* 11:813.

March:
2nd. *Parl. Deb.*, pp. 19–23; *STC* 5900.
3rd. Downshire, 2:253; Chamberlain, 31, 67, 73, 124; *Queen Elizabeth's Maids of Honour*, by Violet A. Wilson, 1922, pp. 223–5.
4th. Downshire, 2:253.
8th. *Parl. Deb.*, pp. 22–7; *CJ* 1:399, 407, 426.
11th. SP 14/53:12.
12th. *Parl. Deb.*, pp. 27–8.
15th. De L'Isle, 4:189.
18th. Winwood, 3:136.
22nd. Downshire, 2:267; Buccleuch, 1:98 (misdated 1611).

March:
24th. *CJ* 1:414.
26th. Howes.
29th. Winwood, 3:145–6.
31st. *SR* 3:430; *STC* 21400; by Samuel Rowlands.

April:
1st. Wotton, 1:486–7. Wotton's own comment; he bought and read the book on 3rd March—the day of its publication.
4th. Edwards, 1:481.
5th. Buccleuch, 1:98; Downshire, 2:269, 272.
7th. Lancaster, p. 145.
9th. Downshire, 2:276.
11th. Downshire, 2:275.
17th. Purchas, 13:374. He did not come back.
19th. Downshire, 2:279, 280; Chamberlain, 119.
20th. Howes.
22nd. Wilbraham, p. 107. *The Court of King James I*, by Godfrey Goodman, edited by J. S. Brewer, 1839, 2:127–32.
27th. *SR* 3:436; *STC* 5118.
30th. *SR* 3:432; *STC* 20992.

May:
2nd. Downshire, 2:486; Chamberlain, 119.
5th. De L'Isle, 4:198.
7th. Downshire, 2:293.
8th. Howes; SP 14/54:29; *SR* 3:432; *STC* 11123; full of a vast variety of miscellaneous information of great use for lexicographers and commentators.
9th. Howes; Winwood, 3:160, 158, 160–1.
11th. *Parl. Deb.*, p. 32.
12th. Purchas, 2:507–49; Lancaster, p. lx; Downshire, 2:296.

14th. *Parl. Deb.*, p. 33; *STC* 19565.
15th. *Parl. Deb.*, pp. 124–5; *CJ* 1:426.
16th. Downshire, 2:296.
19th. *Parl. Deb.*, p. 34.
21st. *Parl. Deb.*, pp. 35–6; Chamberlain, 120—whose comment is unusually bitter for one normally so placid. *CSPIre* 3:750.
22nd. *Parl. Deb.*, pp. 36–41. The petition is given in full in *CJ* 1:431.
24th. *Progresses*, 2:317–8; Chamberlain, 120.
25th. *Parl. Deb.*, pp. 41–3. *Dell' Istoria Della Compagnia de Giesu L'Inglilterra*, by Bartoli, p. 611—through the kindness of the Rev. Leo Hicks, S.J.
29th. *STC* 20755.
30th. *Progresses*, 2:325; *SR* 3:434; *STC* 20755.
31st. *Progresses*, 2:315–27; *Eliz. Stage*, 4:72.

June:
2nd. *Parl. Deb.*, pp. 46–7.
3rd. *Progresses*, 2:355–41.
4th. *Progresses*, 2:327–31; Birch's *James I*, 1:112; Howes.
5th. Winwood, 3:179; *Progresses*, 2:346–62.
6th. *Progresses*, 2:361–2; Howes.
8th. *Parl. Deb.*, p. 50; *CSPIre* 3:776.
13th. *CSPVen* 11:955; *Parl. Deb.*, pp. 50–6.
20th. Wotton, 1:498, 492.
26th. Winwood, 3:188–9.
30th. Howes.

July:
2nd. *Parl. Deb.*, pp. 58–121. Modern legislators might

July:
well study the account of this lengthy debate, noting the level of education of the members of this Parliament and their jealousy to protect the subject against unjust impositions.

3rd. Winwood, 3:210, 211, 212. See *I Jac. J.*, pp. 269, 273. Baldwin was accused of being an active though distant participant in the Gunpowder Plot, and many attempts were unsuccessfully made to persuade the Archduke to have him arrested and sent to England.

6th. *CSPIre* 3:798.

7th. Birch's *James I*, 1:122; Winwood, 3:201; Birch's *James I*, 126; *CSPVen* 12:24.

8th. Bradley, 2:282.

9th. Bradley, 2:241.

15th. De L'Isle, 4:208.

16th. *CSPVen* 12:30, 34.

17th. Winwood, 3:193-4.

18th. *CSPVen* 12:23.

20th. Tierney's Dodd, v, 49-51.

23rd. Winwood, 3:200. Statutes of the Realm; *Anno VII Jacobi Regis*.

25th. Downshire, 2:328. Aulicus Coquinarius (in Scott, ii, 239); Wilson, p. 56.

August:
3rd. *CSPVen* 12:30.

12th. De L'Isle, 4:210-16.

13th. *SR* 3:441; *STC* 5861: violent anti-Jesuit propaganda.

14th. Bodley, pp. 193-4.

17th. De L'Isle, 4:216; SP 14/57:8.

24th. *CSPVen* 12:41; Downshire, 2:353-4; Smith, pp. 456-500; Purchas, 19:1-66.

25th. *CSPIre* 3:818, 817; Purchas, 18:529.

28th. Downshire, 2:345; De L'Isle, 4:218-20.

31st. Purchas, 14:1-23; Plague.

September:
1st. De L'Isle, 4:227; Winwood, 3:210-11.

2nd. Howell, 2:723-6.

6th. Birch's *Pr. Henry*, pp. 154-5.

9th. Pett, pp. 78-9.

20th. *CSPVen* 12:64.

21st. *CSPVen* 12:59.

24th. Pett, pp. 79-82. The 'dock' was not an affair of wooden or iron gates, but an earthwork to keep out the water, which was dug down to enable the ship to float over. 'Crabs' were small capstans used to give a first haul on the ship.

25th. Pett, pp. 82-4; *CSPVen* 12:68. When the Venetian Ambassador sent to ask after the King's health, 'he sent back an answer which I cannot repeat without blushing'.

30th. Plague.

October:
1st. Downshire, 2:370.

3rd. *SR* 3:445; *STC* 14755; Jonson, 5:273-408; *Eliz. Stage*, 3:371; Aubrey, p. 90. Jonson, in his Folio of 1616, noted the names of the principal comedians, which include Richard Burbage, Heminge, Condell and Armin.

5th. Bradley, 2:251.

8th. *SR* 3:446; *STC* 6341. The title page has a cut of Wit scourging Folly (with bared

October:
buttocks) hoisted on Time's back. A useful work for editors, with poems on most notable persons, from Carr to Shakespeare.

11th. *CSPVen* 12:79, 81.
15th. Tierney's Dodd, iv, 160–79.
16th. *Archaeologia*, 14:249–61.
21st. Howes.
25th. *CSPVen* 12:91, 92.
31st. *Parl. Deb.*, p. 126; Plague.

November:
1st. Downshire, 2:388.
2nd. *DNB; Nugae*, 2:25–30; for Bancroft's career, see previous *Journals*, indexes. Downshire, 2:391.
6th. *Parl. Deb.*, pp. 128–31.
8th. *Parl. Deb.*, p. 131; *SR* 3:448; *STC* 24833; Plague.
15th. *Parl. Deb.*, pp. 132–3.
16th. Winwood, 3:235–6.
18th. *Parl. Deb.*, pp. 136–7.
20th. *CSPVen* 12:90.
22nd. *Parl. Deb.*, pp. 137–40.
23rd. *Parl. Deb.*, pp. 140–4.
24th. *Parl. Deb.*, p. 145.
27th. SP 14/58:35.
28th. Winwood, 3:235.
29th. Sanderson, p. 87.

December:
1st. *CSPIre* 3:915.
2nd. SP 14/58:52.
7th. *Progresses*, 2:370–1.
8th. SP 14/58:62.

10th. *CSPVen* 12:151; Downshire, 2:407; Rutland, 1:426.
12th. Howes.
15th. Winwood, 3:239.
20th. Birch's *Pr. Henry*, pp. 467–8; App. xvii. The orders are too long to digest, but they give an exact and interesting picture of the organization and economy of the household.
23rd. *CSPVen* 12:129, 86, 103.
31st. Howes; *CSPVen* 12:153.

Other Books and Plays printed in 1610:
i, ii. *STC* 7100, 14736. The number of books of music published at this time is remarkable.
iii. *STC* 11058.
iv. *STC* 13018. The epigrams are poor, but cleaner than most, and reveal the topics which interested a young Oxford don. There is an interesting comment on the latinism of the new Catholic translation of the Bible.
v. *STC* 17926. A magnificent and portly volume of 1130 large folio pages, sumptuously set out, with many coats of arms: an early specimen of *Complete Peerage*.
vi. *STC* 2207. The New Testament had been published at Rheims in 1582.
vii. *SR* 3:444–8; *Eliz. Stage*, 4:392.

INDEX

INDEX

269

For Product Safety Concerns and Information please contact our EU
representative GPSR@taylorandfrancis.com
Taylor & Francis Verlag GmbH, Kaufingerstraße 24, 80331 München, Germany